THE SUBVERSIVE
HARRY POTTER

THE SUBVERSIVE HARRY POTTER

Adolescent Rebellion and Containment in the J.K. Rowling Novels

Vandana Saxena

McFarland & Company, Inc., Publishers

Jefferson, North Carolina, and London

Library of Congress Cataloguing-in-Publication Data

Saxena, Vandana, 1977–
    The subversive Harry Potter : adolescent rebellion and
containment in the J.K. Rowling novels / Vandana Saxena.
        p.   cm.
    Includes bibliographical references and index.

    ISBN 978-0-7864-6674-0
    softcover : acid free paper ∞

    1. Rowling, J. K.— Criticism and interpretation.
2. Potter, Harry (Ficticious character)   3. Adolescence
in literature.   4. Fantasy fiction, English — History and
criticism.   I. Title.
PR6068.O93Z853 2012
823'.914 — dc23   2012010088

British Library cataloguing data are available

Front cover images © 2012 Shutterstock

Manufactured in the United States of America

McFarland & Company, Inc., Publishers
  Box 611, Jefferson, North Carolina 28640
  www.mcfarlandpub.com

Contents

Acknowledgments

I am grateful to the Indian Institute of Technology, Delhi, for enabling me to pursue this study. A major part of this work comes from my doctoral dissertation at IIT Delhi. Many people have offered advice and encouragement in different forms. I would like to thank Angelie Multani for her invaluable supervision. Thanks go to V. Sanil, Ravinder Kaur, Suman, Kamayani Kumar, Roberta Trites and Simi Malhotra. I am particularly grateful to G.S Srivastava, Malini Srivastava, Madhur Saxena, Kalpna Saxena and Kuldeep Saxena for their personal support and encouragement. But the deepest thanks go to Vrinda, who has grown up with this project, and Gaurav, who has always stood by me.

List of Abbreviations

References to the *Potter* books are abbreviated as below; publication details of the books appear in the Bibliography. This study uses the British editions unless otherwise indicated.

PS—Harry Potter and the Philosopher's Stone

CoS—Harry Potter and the Chamber of Secrets

PoA—Harry Potter and the Prisoner of Azkaban

GoF—Harry Potter and the Goblet of Fire

OotP—Harry Potter and the Order of the Phoenix

HBP—Harry Potter and the Half-Blood Prince

DH—Harry Potter and the Deathly Hallows

Preface

This book focuses on the dynamics of subversion and containment in young adult fantasy literature through a detailed study of J.K. Rowling's *Harry Potter* series. It is an exploration of the limits of the formulaic structure of fantasy literature and the impulse of subversion and resistance contained within the formula as it resonates with the experience of adolescence. Further, the work explores fantastic narratives as an amalgam of various cultural models of growth, especially for young boys, and the extent to which a fantastic text like Rowling's series problematize the notions of "growth," "adolescence," "real," and "normal," highlighting the incoherencies and gaps that mark the narratives of growth and development even as they follow the teleology on an overt level.

The texts chosen for the study — the seven books of J.K. Rowling's *Harry Potter* series — have been phenomenally popular for over a decade. The text offers a suitable case for young adult fantasy fiction. The formulaic structure and accompanying marketing blitzkrieg are integral strategies of the genre often dubbed "remedial" literature designed to lure reluctant adolescent readers. The seven-book series itself follows the pattern of growth where, with the growth of the protagonist and the reader, each book also grows in complexity. The series also brings together a variety of popular aspects of young adult fiction including the hero myth, fantasy, school setting, adventure and revenge. Through a detailed analysis of the series, the study juxtaposes adolescent subversion with the attempts of cultural containment.

This book builds on several essays and books that have approached the *Potter* series from a variety of perspectives. Some longer studies have also explored the series from partial perspectives. Philip Nel's *J.K Rowling's Harry Potter Novels: A Reader's Guide* provides an overview of the novels and the Potter phenomenon. Andrew Blake's *Irresistible Rise of Harry Potter* underscores the political prejudices of Rowling's story. Another important reader of the *Potter* series is John Granger, who has approached the series from an extremely detailed Christian perspective and also provides material for the final chapter. This study attempts to approach the *Potter* series as an integrated text. I have attempted to locate the series in the Western literary tradition, tracing its Greco-Roman elements alongside the religious narrative of Christianity. It has also been located in a specifically English context not only through Anglo-Saxon mythology but also through the themes of citizenship and nation-building which have been central to English children's fiction. At the same time, the study also reflects on the contemporary aspects of the series — its existence in the postcolonial context and its stance on issues like terrorism, capitalism, gender equality and multiculturalism. The most important part of this study is an attempt to locate the series in the field of contemporary young adult literature and explore the way the abovementioned literary canons interact with the themes and concerns of adolescence.

Since the literary genre officially came into existence barely 50 years ago,[1] literary commentary exclusively on YA fiction is still in its early stages. Most commentary on adolescent fiction can still be found in critical works dedicated to children's literature. However, there are some specific studies focusing on the literary representations of adolescents and young adults. Patricia Meyer Spacks' *The Adolescent Idea* outlines the social myth-making centered on the idea of adolescence in the novel over the last two centuries. Spacks takes into account canonical authors from Henry Fielding to Doris Lessing. More recently, scholarly interest in the young adult literature has concentrated on books and genres popular among the young readers. The complexities and ambiguities in the books at social, political and moral levels reflect the sophistication of young adult literature and thereby the reader. Alice Trupe's *Thematic Guide to Young Adult Literature* and Sarah Herz and David Gallo's *From Hinton to Hamlet* outline the thematic peculiarities of young adult literature. Herz and Gallo deal with thematic continuities between YA literature and the classics, especially in the context of the classroom where YA fiction becomes a means to approach the canonical literature in a more student-friendly manner. Roberta S. Trites' *Disturbing the Universe* concentrates on the dynamics of power and repression operational in the themes like authority, selfhood, otherness, sexuality and death. Robyn McCallum's *Ideologies of Identity in Adolescent Fiction* is a Bakhtinian approach to ideas of selfhood, subjectivity and agency. Both books have been immensely valuable to the arguments in this study.

Coming to the subgenre of fantasy within YA fiction, it is difficult to find a book-length study (though Trites and McCallum touch on generic fantasy). Alison Waller's *Constructing Adolescence through Fantastic Realism* is one book that I came across during the course of my research. Waller studies generic fantasy through the lens of "fantastic realism"—a concept used by Bakhtin for Dostoevsky's method of heightened realism produced through an unrealistic access to the protagonist's inner psyche. Waller, referring to the combination of fantastic and realism in fantasy fiction, stresses on the experience of the "fantastic as it is embedded into a recognizable world" (22). Waller's study indicates that fantasy adolescents emerge as "images of youth that adults desire and fear: as mirrors showing contemporary teenage life 'as it really is' according to the dominant discourse" (187). Within this reading of generic fiction, she also indicates "the anxieties that are generated when adolescents threaten to appear on their own terms, rather than as a progression towards unified adulthood" (187). It is these moments of fantasy that are central to the present work — the moments of possibilities of adolescence even when constrained by structures, hierarchies or genres. The three cultural icons — the hero, the schoolboy and the savior — as well as their antithesis, the monster, together symbolize the conception of adolescence as the promise of hope and regeneration as well as a threat to be mastered.

Introduction

Each new generation of children has to be told: "This is the world, this is what one does, one lives like this." Maybe our constant fear is that a generation of children will come along and say: "This is not a world, this is nothing, there's no way to live at all." — Hoban 114

The present study is an attempt to explore the dynamics of adolescent or young adult fiction, especially the subgenre of adolescent fantasy fiction, through a detailed study of J.K Rowling's Harry Potter series. It explores the limits of the formulaic structure of fantasy fiction like that of Rowling's and also examines the impulses of exploration, subversion and resistance contained within the formula. The three models of boyhood in the series — the hero, the schoolboy and the savior — are cultural patterns of growth envisaged for young boys. The study is also concerned with the deconstruction of these interrelated templates of growth in the *Potter* series. It examines these stereotypical performances as attempts to fix and contain the processes of growth and the elements that resist this process of containment. Within the co-existing networks of subversion and containment in the narrative, young adult fantasy becomes an embodiment of the experience of adolescence — its angst, its rebellion and also its journey of personal maturation.

The subgenre of adolescent fantasy can be characterized as a mix of illusion, escape, entertainment, formula and also instruction and guidance. Fantasy and adolescence, as we shall see in a detailed discussion of the two concepts, reinforce each other. An adolescent can be seen as an "other," an outsider to the categories of child and adult, embodying the gap between the two states of being in the chronology of growth. Many critics agree that young adult literature expresses the trials of adolescence, the process of individual coming-of-age set against a specific social and cultural background. Sarah Herz and Donald Gallo point out the situational archetypes and themes in YA fiction, which include coming-of-age rituals, quest and search for self (12). The literature centers on the youthful protagonist as much as it centers on the cultural background that frames his/her growth.[1] Robyn McCallum defines adolescent fiction in relation to the essential humanist ideology that traditionally underscored the idea of child and children's literature: "*preoccupation* with personal maturation ... is commonly articulated in conjunction with a perceived need for children to overcome solipsism and develop intersubjective concepts of personal identity within this world and in relation to others" (7). This feature of YA literature derives from the unique position that an adolescent occupies in society. On the one hand, an adolescent is an outsider to the social and political frameworks of the society. At the same time, s/he occupies an important position in the collective psyche — preparing adolescents to become responsible members of the community is a major cultural preoccupation. It is important to contain adolescence through the discourses of growth, development and maturity since an adolescent, by the virtue of his/her position on the cultural periphery, has the potential to question and subvert these very discourses. According to Roberta Trites, "the distinction between a children's and an adolescent novel lies not so much in how the protagonist grows — even though the gradations of growth do help us better understand the nature of the genre — but with the very determined way that YA novels tend to interrogate social constructions, foregrounding the relationship between the society and the individual" (*Disturbing* 20). Rowling's series portrays this two-way relationship that characterizes adolescence. Adolescence, as we shall see in a detailed discussion, emerges not as a stage of life, but as a state of being — an existence on the margins and in a constant dialogue with the center, always challenging and negotiating with the attempts at containment. Thus, young adult literature emerges as a volatile field of engagement with institutional politics and dominant social constructions.

Fantasy also shares a similar complex relationship with the idea of reality. Like the ambiguous position that an adolescent occupies with respect to the surrounding order, the relationship between fantasy and reality rests on a paradox. On the one hand, fantasy has been conventionally seen as the literature of escape — a detachment and defamiliarization from the rules, orders and hierarchies that govern our everyday life. However, this defamiliarization also has the potential to critique the orders of reality. Fantasy has been characterized as the narrative of interstices existing between cultural categories, of events "which cannot be explained by the laws of this same familiar world" (Todorov 25). Linked to fantasy, adolescent fiction emerges as a potent dialogue with otherness and difference. Playful subversions, deviance, magic and the supernatural make the world of fantasy a place of escape; at the same time, the world of illusions offers new perspectives to understand the actual world. The zone of experimentation and adventure hence emerges as a powerful critique of "reality." The structural constraints of the fantasy formula simultaneously embody the impulse of defiance and subversion that characterize adolescence.

J.K. Rowling's Harry Potter series, as a mix of subgenres of young adult literature, becomes an ideal text to study; the heroic quest, the boarding-school fiction, fantasy, magic and adventure — the series brings together all these narratives of boyhood, portraying youthful subversion as well as cultural containment and an adolescent's negotiations through these conflicting forces. Secondly, the charges leveled against the series — that it is formulaic, that its popularity rests on aggressive marketing strategies rather than the content, and that, in guise of its engagements with difference, it foregrounds conventionality and conformity — rather than working against the series, as we shall see, make it a suitable representative text of postmodern children's literature.[2]

Prominent literary critic Jack Zipes, discussing the institutionalization of children's literature, cites the case of Harry Potter:

> For anything to become a phenomenon in the Western society it must become conventional; it must be recognized and categorized as unusual, extraordinary, remarkable and outstanding. In other words, it must be popularly accepted, praised or condemned, worthy of everyone's attention; it must conform to the standards of exception set by the media and promoted by the culture industry [*Sticks* 175].

Zipes' summation of the "phenomenality" of the Potter books rests on their ability to conform to the tastes of the hegemonic groups driven by "institutional corporate conglomerates" (*Sticks* 172).

To an extent the charges ring true. Harry Potter is after all a conventional hero of a late capitalist world. He is an orphan but belongs to an ancient powerful family of wizards. His Cinderella-like transformation from rags to riches is an oft-repeated fairy tale. Surrounded by aides and by virtue of owning some unique magical objects, the White English boy overcomes all evil to save the world. As a school story, Harry's relationship with his friends and teachers eventually reassert the boundaries of gender and race that are inherent to the culture from which the text emerges. His "girl trouble" has been pointed out by critics such as Jack Zipes (*Sticks*), Nicolas Tucker ("The Rise and Rise"), and Christine Schoefer ("Harry Potter's Girl Trouble"). So the Harry Potter series is a particular kind of discursive narrative, contained within the privileged value system of the culture in which it is produced and received, and which it upholds. For some critics like Andrew Blake, Rowling's story is even "reassuring" because in the garb of contemporary narrative it provides security derived from the return to older patriarchal and colonial value systems.

Linked with these are the charges of aggressive marketing and promotion of the series. Like Zipes, critics and thinkers like Harold Bloom, A. S. Byatt and John Pennington deem the series to be a product of marketing and publishing strategies, responsible for "dumbing down" its young readers. Adolescent readers of such fantasy have been characterized as "cultural dupes" taking a delusional escape route that ends in the reproduction of given ideologies. The critics laying the charge of commodification also have some justification. The Harry Potter brand is worth about 15 million dollars. Movies, computer games, a Harry Potter theme park — all are part of the phenomenon now termed Pottermania.

To an extent, sales and statistics are valid since popular could be defined as that which people enjoy, buy and consume.[3] As of 2011, the series had sold more than 450 million copies and has been translated into 70 languages. Also in circulation are unauthorized translations of true *Harry Potter* books and published pastiches or fanfictions that have attempted to pass themselves off as real books. One such book, *Harry Potter and Leopard Walk Up-to-Dragon*, was published in China in 2002 — a market that had remained resistant to earlier phenomena of Western popular culture like the Star Wars series (Henderson, "Globalization, Consumerism"). A text in such blatant association with materiality can easily be seen as a tool in the hands of the power block.[4] Nevertheless, theorists of popular culture insist that a popular text (especially something as popular as the Harry Potter series) exists in a complex dialogic relation to the surrounding social context. John Fiske underlines the element of creativity that lies behind every act of consumption, especially of the "unaesthetic" and "vulgar" texts of popular culture. According to him, though popular culture encodes the ideology of the powerful, it simultaneously traces the forces of subversion within the system. The texts of the dominant culture are invaded by "guerilla tactics" of the "lower" cultural forms (*Understanding* 33). For Fiske, this constitutes the progressive core of pleasure arising from popular culture. Its progressiveness is concerned with redistributing power within these structures towards the disempowered; it attempts to enlarge the space within which "bottom-up" power has to operate. Several critics have found the Potter series worth serious academic scrutiny precisely due to its popularity. Anthologies of critical essays problematize the simplistic equation of the popularity of the series with market strategies (Anatol, *Reading Harry Potter*; Whited, *The Ivory Tower*; Hielman, *Critical Perspectives*). Critics like Alison Lurie have embraced the idea of commercial success as a part of the series, an indispensable element of the Harry Potter phenomenon ("Pottery").

The question that arises then is whether the Potter series ends up simply reasserting the dominant discourses of growth and boyhood that culminate in "the planned production of commonality" (*Sticks* 175), or if the presence of fantasy, magic and elements of adolescence succeeds in queering the narrative. An oft-cited fact about Rowling's series is that it has succeeded in bringing children back to books and reading in droves. Bloom hardly sees merit in the fact, pointing out the disjunction between "reading" and "good reading"—an attitude that most YA fiction faces.[5] Herz and Gallo also point out the traditional status of YA fiction as remedial reading for unmotivated readers (though they are concerned with the mistaken nature of such perception). Marketing, sensational covers and advertising to lure the reluctant reader are an integral part of the YA genre.[6] Therefore, the case of Harry Potter offers suitable material due to its "conventionality" as well as the mass-mediated nature of the Potter phenomenon that impinges on any discussion of the series.

The intrusion of market forces is seen as inevitable in the postmodern condition of late capitalism. Trites marks this as a defining feature of the postmodern narratives of growth: "the popularity of the traditional *Bildungsroman* with its emphasis on self-determination gives way to the market dominance of the young adult novel, which is less concerned with depicting growth reverently than it is with investigating how the individual exists within society" (*Disturbing* 19). The representation of growth and adolescence in postmodern fiction often emerges as an institutional project (bound by capital). In the Potter series, apart from the aggressive promotion, the depiction of money and capitalism within the story has also been taken as an evidence of its complicity with capitalism (Pennington, "From Elfland to Hogwarts"; Hensher, "A Crowd Pleaser"; Blake, *The Irresistible Rise*).

At the same time it is important to analyze the way in which the series succeeds in de-naturalizing the conventions of growth and its cultural forms. The juxtaposition of Harry's rags-to-riches story alongside the acquisitiveness of his surrogate family interrogates any simplistic reading of the series as a fairy tale of late capitalism. The Potter series does not shy away from locating its youthful protagonists in socio-cultural networks of power, knowledge, sexuality, race and so on. The series also problematizes the cultural equation between adolescent and adult. By associating Harry's surrogate family, the Dursleys, with the "normal," the series, right from the beginning, problematizes the notions of normality and abnormality. Unlike the older school stories, Harry's world is, at least overtly, more open to cross-cultural encounters. And, unlike most other children's fantasy, there is no journey into an ideal never-never land; the series presents no relief in a utopia. The world of Harry Potter exists in close relation to the material world of today, the world of flux, a globalized world where the power equations of the imperial setup have been challenged if not completely over-turned. It draws on a variety of cultural narratives surrounding the figure of an adolescent, to explore the threads of continuity as well as points of tension and fragility. This study is an attempt to see the extent to which the *Potter* series resists the definition of popular culture that is totally encapsulated by the dominant narratives surrounding adolescence and growth. The subsequent chapters analyze various models of growth, especially of boyhood, as foregrounded in the narratives of young adult fantasy and unravel the strands of defiance and difference within these cultural templates. The last chapter deals with the micro-narratives of growth that surrounds the central narrative — the story of fantastical monstrous creatures that challenge, question and supplement the story of the boy hero. Though Harry (as well his story) seems conventional and conservative, a part of the condition of late capitalism, it effects a "strange kind of critique, one bound up too with its own *complicity* with power and domination, one that acknowledges that it cannot escape implication with that which it nevertheless still wants to analyze and maybe undermine" (Hutcheon, *The Politics* 4). Hence there is critique embedded in its complicity, which, according to Linda Hutcheon, is a feature of postmodern representation. Though the fantasy formula of coming-of-age may not be revolutionary, several potential forms of subversion can be traced within the raw material, like the cultural activity of a *bricolage* where particular ritualistic spaces are adopted and used to negotiate difference (Hall, *Resistance* 45); in the ritualistic process of boyhood and growth — the hero, the schoolboy, the savior — there can be seen moments of subversion and re-vision. Such ritualized resistance is a process of ongoing negotiation rather than a solution.

Another unique point that makes Rowling's text appropriate material for this kind of study is the way in which the series itself enacts the process of psychical and moral growth of the protagonists (Westman, "Perspective" 146). As the protagonist and the reader grow, the books grow in complexity — what seemed like a straightforward struggle between good and evil in the early books becomes a means to reflect on institutional politics, terrorism, changing power equations and moral relativism. Together, they form a complicated backdrop to the traditional theme of YA fiction — construction of identity and the place of the self vis-à-vis the external world. The ten-year-long adolescence of Harry and his friends is also a part of the process of initiation of a generation that has grown up with Harry[7]; a critic reflecting on the end of the series says that the real children of Harry would be the people who have grown up and would now encounter the world armed with what they learned along with Harry Potter (Rollason, "Harry Potter, The Last Spell Cast").

Therefore, though organized for adolescents by adults, an important aspect of adolescent literature, especially popular YA fantasy, is its deep and influential roots in the culture and experience of the adolescent. It has the power to represent adolescents in the traditional forms, and simultaneously, since it is a text about adolescent subculture, it has power to rework those forms. In other words, the narrative of popular fantasy becomes a place where adolescence is constructed and deconstructed. Stuart Hall reads culture as a continuous battlefield where "there is a continuous and necessarily uneven and unequal struggle, by the dominant culture, constantly to disorganize and reorganize popular culture; to enclose and confine its definitions and forms within a more inclusive range of dominant forms. There are points of resistance; there are also moments of suppression" ("Notes" 67). Rather than a revolution, then, it is a symbolic struggle articulating the experience of the subordinated — a subordinate marked not in terms of age but in the state of being an outsider. Fantasy, adolescence and magic reinforce this idea of a battlefield where structures and hierarchies of "reality" are constantly challenged.

The two terms to which I repeatedly turn — adolescence and fantasy — are complex concepts. Fantasy, in the study, carries with it the complex networks of desire and suppression, and adolescence means more than simply an age-defined category. (In telling someone not to be an adolescent, we often use the term as a signifier that has more to it than simply age.) In a broad sense the two terms can be interlinked by creative and imaginative activity, playing, challenging boundaries, dreaming and aspiring. These associations link the phenomena and process of adolescence and fantasy intricately. Therefore, it is important to discuss the two terms in detail.

Fantasy

Adolescent fantasy is commonly understood to be about adolescents and their fantasies, populated with superheroes, subverting and challenging the dominant authorities and then saving the world by returning to those very stereotypes. Peter Hunt and Millicent Lenz sum up the charges against fantasy succinctly — it is childish, formulaic and escapist (2). Such fantastic narratives can also be seen as cultural fantasies about adolescence. They speak of adult fantasy, at times, more often than they speak of the adolescent's — it is a world where adults rule, formulate norms and articulate their concerns about children; the narrative traces the way adolescent protagonists and, thereby, the young readers enter and become a part of this order, ensuring its survival. Therefore, as discussed earlier, the common charge leveled against such fantasy is its manipulative tendencies in favor of the dominant ideologies. Harry Potter, as critics like Maria Nikolajeva point out, emerges as a stereotypical protagonist of a romantic heroic fantasy ("Harry Potter — A Return"). Such fiction dictates and is dictated by the common perceptions about the promise of adolescence, its angst and its ultimate integration.

According to Rosemary Jackson, such ideological complicity is a prominent characteristic of *fantastic-marvelous*— a genre to which she relegates fairy tales, folklore and popular fantasy (154). Her analysis builds on Tzvetan Todorov's classification of the fantastic, in which he characterizes *marvelous* as the genre where the incomprehensible fantastic events are explained in terms of the supernatural. *Fantastic*, according to Todorov as well as Jackson, begins in the zone of hesitation when the reader is not sure whether to believe an event or not. It is the experience of impossibility and ambiguity beneath the words of a text. In most of the texts, it appears as the breakdown of order, the incoherence in the absence of any rational explanation. Fantasy, which, in Jackson's cultural critique, begins at the gaps in the structures of knowledge and rationality, progresses to deliberate on the interstices of the cultural networks through which one can glimpse the disorder or chaos beneath the structures of the actual world. According to Jackson, while the *fantastic* arouses anxiety and unease by its confrontations with chaos and, therefore, becomes a means of interrogating the "naturalness" or "giveness" of reality, the *marvelous*, by its magical references, renders this unease ineffective. *Marvelous*, thus, according to Jackson, turns the reader into a passive consumer. Critics like Catherine Belsey have criticized *marvelous* for adopting the paradigms of classic realism since it creates "the illusion while we read that what is narrated is 'really' and intelligibly happening" (*Critical Practice* 51–52). The attitude of characters, the narrator, and the modes of narration in fantasy produce a suspension of disbelief and hence render the split, the initial condition of the fantastic, ineffective.

To analyze the cultural aspects of fantasy, especially that which features an adolescent protagonist, it is important to understand what a *fantastic-marvelous* narrative implies for the culture from which it emerges and in which it is disseminated. The *marvelous*, which begins in the fantastic zone of hesitation, veils the split of the fantastic by imaginary devices, the supernatural *deus-ex-machina*. In psychoanalytic terms, a culturally conditioned *marvelous* text, to which Jackson refers, reflects the desire of the *Other*, the superego bolstered by symbolic agencies like the family, state, church and so on. A child, when s/he is initiated into language and subsequently into social and cultural networks, becomes a part of the symbolic order. The imaginary flights of *fantastic-marvelous* are meant to suture the split in the subject that comes into being with his/her entry into the symbolic order of the *Other*. Fantasy, therefore, narrativizes Jacques Lacan's conception of the desire of the split subject ($) to heal the split, for the lost object (a), and for the lost wholeness ($<>a). This desire always comes from and is framed by the symbolic *Other*. Thus, *fantastic-marvelous* seems to become a narrative that reinforces the symbolic, the ideological fantasies of the cultural order. An adolescent is sought and fixed as a symbol of hope and continuity, someone who overcomes the threats to the cultural order and hence preserves it for the posterity.

However, at the center of fantasy are the children who do not fit — orphans and abandoned misfits who arouse discomfort and unease. Their adventures begin in the symbolic order of "reality." In some texts like *Peter Pan* or the Potter series or *Groosham Grange*, the story begins with heavily caricaturized "reality." Some like C.S Lewis' *The Chronicles of Narnia* begin on a rainy day during vacations when children cannot amuse themselves outdoors. Vacation signifies a break, a time off from the routine of everyday life. It is the time to play and fantasize. Susan Cooper's *The Dark Is Rising* series also begin during vacations when the children come across mysteries hidden from the adult world. Texts like Lewis' *The Chronicles of Narnia* and Phillip Pullman's *His Dark Materials* undermine the idea of "reality" in a complex manner by positing multiple worlds co-existing simultaneously. In Phillip Pullman's *Northern Lights*, Lyra Belacqua, an eleven-year-old orphan at Oxford (in a parallel world), sets the plot in motion by secretly entering the forbidden "retiring room" of the college and chancing on a plot to poison Lord Asriel, her uncle (later revealed to be her father). Lord Asriel's research in experimental theology in Lyra's world has far-reaching consequences that resound in the other worlds of the universe. Thus, fantasy often is preceded by the world of "reality" but textual strategies, from the beginning, render it as only a surface reality.

Such beginnings point to the poststructuralist engagements with the nature of "real" and "reality." After all, the Dursleys could surely not be the only, the practical or the "normal" way to be. Dursley's obsession with appearing "normal" is a superficial façade of normalcy — something one can pretend to, rather than something that is. Their representation is the first step towards the rupture with the cultural "reality" and its signifiers in the text. The "realistic" beginning of these texts hints that the given order of things could be only an illusion on the surface. The universal reality therefore turns out to be "reality" which is consensual and constructed rather than natural. Pullman's series *His Dark Materials* begins in Lyra's Oxford, a fantastic world. The reader accepts the alternate world as he/she gives into the generic tradition of the *marvelous* only to be surprised later by the description of Will Parry's world which is a fictional representation of the reader's own familiar world. Pullman's strategy defamilarizes the reader from his/her own familiar or "real" world, which turns out to be only one of several alternate and simultaneously existing realities. This complex relation of "reality" with fantasy in the *marvelous* can be explored through a two-way analysis:

1. By deconstructing the reading of "reality" as universal.
2. By narrating that which lies outside "reality" and hence highlighting the moments of "unreality" (that which is pushed into the realms of "non-reality" and "non-sense" by constituting the boundaries of "reality" and "sense").

Therefore, after the destabilization of reality, the succeeding narrative of a fantasy can be seen as a zone of interface between the "reality," which gradually emerges to be only a masquerade, and the "unreal" which *seems* to hold and simultaneously withhold the answers. Thus, poststructuralist analysis throws light on the complexities that lie behind the supposedly simplistic formula fantasy, its ideological complicity and its relation with "reality."

One of the most ambiguous critiques of popular fantasy, and also of the Potter series, is its complete reliance on the formulaic pattern. The series predictably follows the narrative pattern of fantasy and romance outlined by critics like Vladimir Propp and Northrop Frye. Formula is an integral feature of the three symbolic narratives of boyhood and growth — the hero, the schoolboy and the savior; it also encodes the story of the monsters, the others whose stories are set up as an antithesis to the hero's story. A set pattern of moves and countermoves, of plot and action, of beginning and end dictate them. Frye sums up the complete form of romance and heroic tale by the threefold structure of the quest — the perilous journey and preliminary minor adventures, the struggle or the battle in which the hero or his/her foe or both die, and finally the exaltation of the hero. All these stages are easily discernible in Harry's story. A similar notion of quest characterizes the narrative of Christianity and redemption. Christian, Bunyan's pilgrim, undertakes a similar perilous journey as he reaches out for the Kingdom of Heaven. This tripartite structure can be read in terms of the three stages of the initiation rites that mark an adolescent's entry into adulthood — separation, transition and integration. In their varied disguises, these stages dictate the fantasy *Bildungsroman*.

Poststructuralism destabilizes this totalizing nature of the fantasy formula. In the detailed analysis in subsequent chapters, the formula of fantasy *Bildungsroman* emerges as a pattern of growth full of alterity and explorations outside the linear model of development. The formulaic pattern of the *marvelous* holds within it the moment of the *fantastic*. The narrative of fantasy becomes a site of play, of alterity; it includes the element of invention along with convention. John Cawelti insists that the formula in genres of popular fiction ensures continuity; it responds to the specificity of its historical moment. The formula represents a synthesis of several important cultural functions that have been taken over by popular arts; they are important socio-cultural rituals, a form of the communal entertainment, a collective expression and wishful resolution of the intrinsic conflicts that a culture faces. Thus a generic formula is closely connected to time and place. Cawelti insists on the dialogic interaction between the genre and the social in the popular narrative.[8] Though the narrative remains within the formulaic constraints, the story itself spills beyond the totalizing hold of the structure.

Poststructural analysis also problematizes the simplistic equation of the *marvelous* with hegemonic narratives. According to Todorov, the moment of hesitation which entails the experience of the *fantastic* cannot be sustained once the reader gives or is given an explanation of the events, and the hesitation is overcome. "At the story's end, the reader makes a decision even if the character does not; he opts for one solution or the other, and thereby emerges from the fantastic" (41). If the reader decides that the events are to be explained in a rational manner, despite the bizarre nature of the explanations, then the work moves to the adjacent genre — the *"fantastic-uncanny."* If, on the other hand, the explanation is supernatural, the work becomes a *"fantastic-marvelous"* or simply the *"marvelous."*

Jackson, who reads Todorov's definitions through a socio-cultural lens, insists that the presence of the supernatural in the *marvelous* glosses over the serious cultural confrontations inherent in the fantastic. The supernatural explanations of the marvelous veil the deep unease aroused by the fantastic confrontations with the "unreal." While the fantastic leaves the reader uneasy, *marvelous* dulls the sense of discomfort and makes the reader a "passive receiver of events" (Jackson 154). The hero of *fantastic-marvelous* therefore comes to be seen as a powerful point of identification because s/he is an amalgam of all the qualities privileged in the dominant social constructions and hence desirable. An adolescent hero, as mentioned earlier, is instated within the cultural symbolic as a symbol of regeneration. The hero is placed within the networks of school, family, religion and other such institutions that circumscribe his/her world and which s/he is expected to uphold. Heroism like that of Harry Potter's becomes a performance that reiterates the cultural constructions of adolescence, the "correct" pattern of adolescent growth and boyhood; in other words, the hero reflects the "the imaginary relationship of individuals to their conditions of existence" (Althusser 162).

Yet, while Jackson contends that the *marvelous* simply reflects the ideological fictions of its era, genres of *marvelous*, like marvelous realism, have become synonymous to the narratives of resistance, subversions and negotiation. Cristopher Nash, for instance, insists that the characterization of the explanations given for the *marvelous* as "unnatural" or the "supernatural" is in itself problematic. Nash insists that when it is proposed and

> a given event remains unexplainable, the tacit or explicit assumptions on which this is based is that the text itself first calls to mind (in order to put them into question) natural explanatory canons. Yet in fact, when looked at closely, these "canons" turn out to be "natural" only within the frame-

work of *a certain kind of narrative*: specifically and virtually exclusively Realist narrative. If in considering those works which theorists have earnestly sought to find "imaginative" on "purely internal, textual" grounds, we were to set aside the textual expectations of Realism, the inexplicability of the "inexplicable" event would itself become questionable [114].

Nash is questioning the assumption that certain events are unexplainable for they are unexplainable only if the criteria of realism continue to be the fundamental basis of explaining everything. It is similar to the prohibition of the word "magic" in the Dursley household. For "normal" people like the Dursleys, magic is unreal because it is inexplicable. It belongs to the order of reason or sense that is deemed to be irrational. Behind the complete prohibition of magic and its use lies their fear of it. They do not possess or understand it but it is accessible and empowers the underdog of the household. The impossible antagonisms of the Dursley household show the complex nature of contemporary fantasy pointed out by postmodern critic Brian McHale:

The shared reality between the members constitutes the common ground of interaction among the members of society, these same members also experience a multiplicity of private or peripheral realities: dreaming, play, fiction and so on. But these other realities are felt to be marginal; it is the shared reality that is paramount [37].

The dismissal of *marvelous* seems to hint at an attitude to reality that echoes the structures of hierarchy; the explanatory canons of "shared reality" hold sway dismissing the implications behind the marginal experience of magic.

In its focus on the supernatural, alterity, and the non-normative, then, the *marvelous* highlights the partial or rather the constitutive nature of "reality" or the symbolic order. What is seen as "reality" and its explanatory canons are revealed to be cultural constructs, discursive formations of ideological frameworks that are assumed to be natural. The first effect of the *fantastic*, including *marvelous*, therefore, is that it throws us in a deeper engagement with the nature of "reality"; it necessitates a revised look at the established order and appearances. The moment of hesitation described by Todorov is a revisit to the moment when the symbolic order came into being through a split in the subject. Jackson cites Guy de Maupassant's story "The Horla" as an example of pure *fantastic* where a shadowy presence infringes on the rational mind of the narrator; the "reality" of its existence is ambiguous; however, what constitutes its reality is not the materiality but the experience of total breakdown or rupture that its presence causes in the consciousness of the narrator. It is the Lacanian *real*, that which is outside the symbolic denominator, outside the language and verbal description, resisting symbolization absolutely. It is "the impossible" because it is impossible to imagine; it is impossibly attainable since it can be glimpsed only through a breakdown of the existing order. It is "the essential object which is not an object any longer, but this something faced with which all words cease and all categories fail, the object of anxiety par excellence" (Lacan, *Seminar II* 164). In this sense, the *real* is the inversion of the category of "reality" as assumed in everyday usage.

In the *marvelous* and its narrative of the supernatural, the Lacanian *real* is pushed away further by the magical devices and fantastical narrative which seem to support the structures of the symbolic. However, the very force of this repression reveals the contours of the *real* as it presses against the reinforced boundaries of the symbolic order. Freud's reading of the uncanny throws some light on the *real* and the counterforce that resists it in the symbolic order. Freudian Uncanny has been read at two levels[9]: as the uncanny that is estranged, and also as the discovery of that estrangement. On the one hand, the uncanny is that which is alienated or lost in our structures of "reality" which are naturalized by the cultural constructions and reinforced by the mythologies, fairy tales and other such fictions. On the other hand, the uncanny is also the discovery of the estrangement, the revelation of the "unreality," of the fictional nature of cultural constructions. Though the *marvelous* is accused of reinforcing the ideological symbolic denominator, the presence of magic and other supernatural devices underline the unconventionality of the narrative. The *deus-ex-machina* of the *marvelous* reveals the fictional nature of this reinforcement. The *marvelous* works by ritually and ceaselessly trying to push away ever-returning repressed, impinging on its narratives through magic, adolescence and fantasy. These elements of the *marvelous* act as points of force and counterforce, as the interface between the symbolic and the *real*; the very devices through which the *marvelous* seeks to normalize, conventionalize and hence contain the *real* outside its boundaries become points of negotiation.

The first point of emphasis then, is that the basic premise of popular fantasy texts, rather than their existence as "conventional vehicles for social and instinctual repression" (Jackson 155), is their break from order. Popular fantasy begins with the assumption that things as they are are not the only way to be; it presents us with other orders of reality and, in general, erodes the rigid fixities of our consciousness. The devices of the so-called "instinctual repression," that is magic and supernatural, become points of maximum awareness of "unreality" or the fictional nature of the socio-cultural constructs. According to Nash, both the *fantastic* and the *marvelous* are modes of anti-Realist fiction. They are based on the creation of alternative orders; while the *fantastic* is close to the anticosmic way of thinking, the *marvelous* is neocosmic (Nash 174).

Marvelous, with its tussle with the *real*, therefore, can be seen to embody elements of protest and resistance. Put in other words, as it stands in a complex relation to "reality," it is an embodiment of the symbolic matrices of a culture; at the same time, it expresses the desire that is not allowed in social life, a longing forbidden by the orders of "reality." The world-creation in formulaic narrative turns around the "uncustomary" fantastical elements: it not only refers to their unfamiliarity of but also the constructed nature of "reality" evident in the root word "custom." Uncustomary prefigures a break with the customary. The literary genre of the *fantastic-marvelous* is located at such peripheries of experience. Cultural categories cognate with this notion of uncustomary are the adolescents, the queers, the miscegenates; these are categories of ambiguous signification. Zipes notes that "the first step toward resisting the debilitating effects of the culture industry and guarding fantasy from instrumentalization must lead toward a counter public sphere which could lend force and expression to groups opposed to the systematic alienation that results from commodity production" (*Breaking* 144). Adolescence can be seen as one such zone. Before examining the way popular fantasy reinforces or undoes the cultural narratives of adolescence, it is important to analyze the cultural constructions of adolescence.

Adolescence and Its Fictions: A History

Adolescence, as theorists of childhood like Phillippe Aries point out, is a relatively recent cultural construct. According to Aries, childhood itself is an eighteenth-century invention.[10] Adolescence came later with the extension of childhood, accompanied with developments in elementary education, the progressive aging of student populations in the eighteenth and nineteenth centuries and requirements of specialization in the post-industrialized world — all of which delayed the entry of an individual into the productive workforce. The period beyond the basic schooling, of specialization and apprenticeship, roughly from twelve years onwards to later teens, can be defined as adolescence.

But these points cannot be taken too literally. If one goes by literary history, books aimed specifically at children and adolescents were written before the previous two centuries wherein Aries' childhood and adolescence came into being. The texts range from didactic literature to the development of a genre like the novel, which, as Felicity Hughes points out, was especially meant for women and children. This seems to be an enormous cultural preoccupation, going by the privileged position that adolescence occupies in the classical canon. Shakespeare, Goethe, Austen, Twain, Joyce and Lawrence: all have dealt with "strum und drang" of adolescence in narratives that vary across cultures and epochs. This implies a perception of the child and adolescent as individuals different from the adult self. A young adult is perceived to be somebody in the process of being initiated into the ways of the world and adulthood.

On the other hand, adolescent narratives also carry the pejorative connotations of genres that are in poor taste. Comic books, science fiction, fantasy, detective stories and lately video games: all belong to the "lower" forms associated with adolescent narratives. The dual trend hints at a complex cultural attitude towards adolescents, who are at once the hopes of a community and also juveniles often bordering on irresponsibility if not downright delinquency. Such attitudes can be traced back right to the conception of an adolescent at the beginning of the last century by its "discoverer." Granville Stanley Hall was the first to study adolescence in 1904 as a separate category of age. The traits foregrounded by Hall continue to define adolescence today: "development is less gradual and more salutatory, suggestive of some ancient period of storm and stress when old moorings were broken and a higher level attained." Under suitable guidance, a successful resolution of the crisis of adolescence rings in hope of communal continuity and improvement. Patricia Meyer Spacks, studying the enormous amount of literature surrounding the figure of adolescence in the last three centuries, comments on how consistently

> in our culture notions of imaginative vitality about the young, in whom novelists — like the rest of us — perceive meaningful conflict internal and external ... they have evoked adolescents who oppose the existent social order, enjoy more vital passional involvements than their elders, face in their lives crucial and compelling decisions — the stuff of drama [15].

Etymologically, the words *adolescent* and *adult* come from forms of the same Latin word, *adolescere,* meaning "to grow up." The present participle of the word, *adolescenc*, means "growing up," while the past participle, *adultus,* is the source of *adult*, which means "grown up." As a present form of *adultus*, adolescence signifies a liminal time between the past and the future. Adolescence is constructed with respect to both child and adult through constant interactions between the two, as new roles and responsibilities are assumed. Therefore, the two things that primarily characterize an adolescent are, firstly, its state of being in-between, that is, its liminal position; secondly, adolescence can be defined in terms of constant movement, in terms of growth, of becoming that is supposed to be unidirectional, always oriented towards adulthood.[11] Movement towards adulthood — which is more mature, more responsible, and hence, a qualitatively "better" state of being — has also been used to conceptualize growth in terms of evolutionary recapitulation theory where stages of human growth are said to re-capture the evolution of humankind. The adult therefore represents *homo sapien sapien* while the children at various stages of growth capture the aspects of primitive races. The reflections of the recapitulation theory can be seen in literary classics like Charles Kingsley's *The Waterbabies* where the infants and children are closer to the "lower" forms of life like fishes and water animals.

Thus, in the process of growth, adolescence itself becomes something that needs to be done away with. The movement envisaged for a young adult towards the center, towards integration, dictates the complicated "stories" of adolescence. In terms of Freud's psychosexual stages of development, this movement takes the form of a series of repressions and sublimations that, in a way, "resolve" various crises, mainly sexual in nature, associated with a particular age. Later, psychologist Erik H. Erikson modified Freud's psychosexual study to a wider psychosocial study of individual development, which includes environmental and social factors. The psychosocial stage of adolescence is characterized by the crisis of identity versus role confusion. Identity crisis is, therefore, a proper psychological aspect of adolescence, an abnormality that defines its "normal" state. Thus, the narratives of coming-of-age are characterized by the emphasis on the pathological state of raging hormones, on socialization and peer orientations, and on movement outside the household. A grading model of development maps every aspect of life to measure and evaluate the individual development as per the psychosocial standard.[12] This time frame compels the parents, the educators and society at large to attend towards the precocity of the adolescence. Therefore, Nancy Lesko, in a recent book *Act Your Age!*, calls adolescence a panoptical time; its temporal movement emphasizes "the endings toward which youth are to progress and places individual adolescents into a temporal narrative that demands a moratorium of responsibility yet expects them at the same time to act as if each moment of the present is consequential" (107). Underlying is the promise of individual and collective regeneration posited in the process of growing up. The young are meant to save the world, the human species, the adult community by becoming a part of it. This has endless cultural repercussions: "the modern scientific adolescent became a multifaceted social site for talk about the productive use of time, the glorious future, and sometimes the inglorious past. Slow, careful development-in-time was identified as the safest path" (Lesko 111).

The obvious literary genre providing the framework for the coming-of-age narratives is the *Bildungsroman*. As a prototype of adolescent fictions, the *Bildungsroman* genre can be seen as an accretion of coming-of-age narratives like the adventure and school stories and also fantasy stories. It can be studied as a trans-literary genre ranging from cultural rites to comics, films and video games. For Mikhail Bakhtin, the genre, unlike its predecessor the picaresque, portrays the development of a hero rather then presenting the reader with a fixed character type. Hence, the framework itself is cognate with the process of adolescence. As the plot evolves, time in *Bildungsroman* is "introduced into man": the hero "grows," beginning from the peripheries and moving towards the center of his/her world. Adolescent growth therefore emerged as a familiar trope for the stress on individualism and intense preoccupation with selfhood that marked the novel of the eighteenth century. Hence the historical complicity between adolescent and children's literature and the humanist projects of growth that were based on the romantic conception of an "innocent" child in need of guidance and protection against cultural degeneracy, the project underlies canonical texts like Rousseau's *Emile* which

> typically assume and valorize humanistic concepts of individual agency, that is the capacity to act independently of social restraint. However, the image of empowered individuals capable of acting independently in the world and of making choices about their lives offers young readers a worldview which for many is simply idealistic and unattainable [McCallum 6].

Yet this cultural conception continues to underwrite most literature written for children and young adults. Hence Jacqueline Rose underlines the fundamental impossibility of children's fiction, insisting that it is the adult fantasy about the child that holds center stage in children's literature:

the idea which they (genres of children's fiction) share of a primitive or lost state to which the child has special access. The child is, if you like, something of a pioneer, who restores these worlds to us, and gives them back to us with a facility or directness which ensures that our own relationship to them is, finally, safe [9].

Going by the criterion of coming-of-age, since most young adults novels deal with growth, it would seem that most fit into the category of *Bildungsroman*; Alice grows, Max, the king of wild things grows, Hodgson Burnett's Sara Carew and Mary Lennox grow, Kipling's Stalky and Hughes' Tom Brown grow from schoolboys to important members of British society, Burroughs' Tarzan grows among the apes and Phillip Pullman's Lyra and Will grow in the worlds of fantasy and so do Rowling's Harry, Ron and Hermione. However, it would be an enormous generalization to lump such diversity together. A closer look at these literary instances shows the tremendous cultural and racial implications behind the cultural conceptualization of adolescence and growth. In the juxtaposition of the coming-of-age narrative of a white English male wizard with that of girls, witches, non-wizards and non-English protagonists, the process of growth emerges as inherently sexualized and racialized. In terms of recapitulation theory, women, non-whites and the racial others seem to be strictly limited or stunted with respect to the central male protagonist, as creatures left at the lower rung of the evolutionary ladder. The growth of boys becomes a special cultural and national concern. Kenneth Kidd reflects on the inherently gendered, racialized and constitutive nature of "boyology" — an enterprise that links biology with the cultural concerns, literary and social practices and numerous other discourses surrounding the figure of a boy.[13] Narratives of boyhood, as we shall see in the following chapters, are a complex codification of growth and development in terms of nation, class, religion and sexuality. The trend of "boyology" can be traced to the social institutions like schools and to cultural and national movements like the Boy Scouts and the YMCA in the last century.[14]

The *Bildungsroman* concerned with boyhood like adventure fiction, school stories or feral tales encodes the masculine ideal; the narrative projects, portrays, and, by providing a role model for the young reader to emulate, sustains the cultural ideal. Jerome Buckley and Roberta Trites therefore insist that the growth of the hero into adulthood in a *Bildungsroman* is self-conscious; the so-called rebellion is a process towards a greater understanding as one works out a place for the self in the larger scheme of things. A *Bildungsroman* ends with the protagonist self-consciously coming to terms with the communal ideals and social roles, and thereby emerging as an adult member of a community.

An important element of any account of children's and young adult literature, therefore, is the cultural context in which it comes into being. In the exclusive focus on the adolescent as a transitional figure, one is often in danger of assuming that the surrounding contexts are unchanging, finished products. What thinkers like Aries point out is not so much that childhood did not "exist" prior to eighteenth century but that constructs like childhood and adolescence are cultural categories that have varied over the centuries. The "storm and stress," the role confusion and the identity crisis that the above scholars have defined as fundamental traits, rather than being a study of pathological state of adolescence, need to be located in a socio-historical landscape in which the process of adolescence occurs. The process of growth is driven by cultural impetus, or in a Freudian paradigm, the superego, which, Karen Coats insists, is multivocal, bolstered by symbolic constructs like religion, nation and family into which an adolescent is initiated and also by peer pressure, dictates of current fashion and style, and discourses of sexuality which flood most aspects of adolescent experience (*Looking Glasses* 141).

Conflict presupposes the presence of at least two players. Adolescent crisis too implies the presence of a rival — the rivalry could be between the generations, in which case the parents become the opposition; it could be against the institutional authorities, which implicates teachers, families and other authorities; or it could be ideological, which could then implicate social, cultural or political systems of the world around. The aberrant state of adolescence is permeated with multiple discourses from both sides of the divide — of childhood and adulthood. Since in itself it is a polysemic, unorganized space of experimentation, rebellion and transgression do not apply; these are charges leveled top down.[15] Coats defines adolescence in terms of its abject state of being; the process of adolescent growth is defined in terms of the construction of selfhood by distancing the self from the abject.

> It is an in-between time, a time where that we know and believe about children is challenged, and where what we hope and value about maturity is also challenged. Adolescents are both more and less sophisticated and knowing than we want them to be. They challenge the borders of identity, trying to become adult without becoming adulterated. Striving for social recognition but not wanting to stand out, locating with specificity their status as sexual subjects and objects, seeking the terms of individuation within affiliative groupings, adolescents are intensely involved in the con-

struction of social boundaries and in reaffirming their distance from the socially abject ["Adolescence" 292–293].

The point, then, is that any study concerning adolescence involves not just the adolescent; it needs to take into account the cultural perceptions of adolescence as well. For the purpose of this study, adolescence, rather than a mere category defined in terms of age, implies a state of being, like Julia Kristeva's "'open systems' of which biology speaks, concerning living organisms that live only by maintaining a renewable identity through interaction with another, the adolescent structure opens itself to the repressed at the same time that it initiates a psychic reorganization of the individual" ("Adolescent Novel" 9). It is a state of being that is alienated from networks of domination; it resists complete subservience; it is a state of being during transition from child to adult, that is, from the margins to the center. It evokes anxiety since, in wider perceptions about adolescence, the dichotomy between the stages go beyond child and adult; there are other blurred distinctions during the transition — between asexual and sexual (sexual "perversion") is one of the prime worries about adolescence), rational and emotional (since adolescents, it is believed, can think more rationally than children and yet remain subject to emotions and mood swings), civilized and savage (boyhood and savagery are assumed to be closely associated).

The negotiation between subversion and containment is the main concern of most adolescent novels which deal with institutional networks of power to which adolescents do not have access because of their "not children and not yet adult" condition. The tension between subjectivity, "a conglomeration of provisional subject positions" (McCallum 4) that an adolescent occupies in the systems and the discursive constructs s/he inhabits, and agency, the power to resist or choose, occupies center stage as the protagonist negotiates his/her place in the networks of domination and repression. These issues have been the main concerns of the adolescent fiction in the West. Trites cites the difference between American adolescent literature that is replete with adolescent rebellion linked to social critique and European adolescent literature, which "grew out of a romantic emphasis on the maturation of the individual's creative spirit" (*Twain* ix). The present study is concerned with tracing the possibilities of social commentary in the genre of adolescent fantasy specifically from Britain and located in the context of the twentieth century. The elements of social critique, as we shall see, arise from the conflation of fantasy and adolescence in Rowling's Harry Potter series even though the overt narrative seems to be grounded on the humanist notions of childhood. The conditions of *Bildungsroman* in fantasy *de-doxify* the normative pattern of growth revealing the cultural stakes in it, and at the same time, embody subversion in its form and content.[16]

Adolescent Fantasy

This study is concerned with the course of adolescent growth that deconstructs the heroism embodied by the figure of an adult who stands at the end of the formulaic narrative of young adult fantasy fiction. It is concerned with the elements that queer the naturalized cultural assumptions regarding growth, bringing to the fore the troubled relations of adolescence and fantasy with the structures of the familiar world. As pointed out by critics like Trites, adolescent narrative works by propelling the subject out of his/her subject position; thus adolescence becomes a series of obstacles which the young adult protagonist overcomes on his/her way to adulthood. The construction of adulthood therefore works by abjecting adolescence and its troubled world; the narratives of adolescence embody this "othering" of the adolescence as the narratives seek to understand, to know and to fix its protagonists.

This seems to make the adolescent narratives as well as the *fantastic-marvelous* complicit in the cultural project of growth. The narrative of adolescent fantasy like the *Potter* series positions an outsider, an orphan adolescent wizard, at the center of the narrative — a young man who becomes one of us by saving the world for us. The story of the rite of passage is combined with the idea of redemption of a community through the means of a child-hero. The overlap of genres in Harry's narrative is significant. Fantasy shares space with the school story and with the narrative of the savior; one that is said to explore the interstices of culture and society, the other that deals so obviously with discipline, training and preparation to become a part of the same socio-political networks, and the third that is meant to guard and save the socio-symbolic denominator as a divinely instituted order. The quest romance featuring adolescent protagonists expresses the hope posited in the youth — the desire to be saved by a child and his/her innocence. Northrop Frye highlights this element of desire that is central to the hero myth and romance. The "perennially childlike quality" of romance is related to the "extraordinarily persistent nostalgia" manifested in the form of the quest, "the search for some kind of imaginative golden age" (*Anatomy* 186). Hence, as Rose insists above, the child emerges as a pioneer who would restore the lost world to us. At the end of the narrative is an adult; in the *Potter* series it is the father, husband and a mature and responsible member of a community. The adult that an adolescent is supposed to grow into embodies the normative ideal in terms of race, sexuality and gender.

Yet the narratives of adolescence as well as fantasy work at multiple levels. Fantasy and the *marvelous*, as discussed above, give the narrative a potential to de-naturalize the cultural assumptions that accompany growth. Organized around the principle of lack and wish-fulfillment, fantasy seeks to fill the void in the symbolic "reality" with imaginary or mythic narratives. The elements of fantasy, magic and the supernatural therefore signal a lack, the point of suture, cementing the hierarchies of "reality" and at the same time, by their very presence, deconstructing those very hierarchies, revealing their strangeness. Imaginary narratives of the *fantastic-marvelous* offer support to the orders of "reality" and, at the same time, reveal the points of fragility. In these imaginary stories, heroism emerges as an imitative gesture, a performance of the cultural project of ideal growth that allays the anxieties aroused by adolescent angst and deviance. The growth patterned on the heroic ideal emerges as a culturally encoded performance.

This performative aspect of identity formation in adolescent fantasy can be approached through queer theory — a paradigm that underlines the essentially constitutive and imitative nature of gender and sexual identity. The imitative aspect of gender performance highlighted in the figure of a "queer" is echoed in the figure of a hero of adolescent fantasy who performs the process of growth in a magical, fantastic or larger-than-life manner. Linked to this, as pointed out earlier, are the aspects of race and gender which are upheld in a narrative through the supernatural devices. Growth of a hero in fantasy is essentially a masculine performance.[17] Queering the normative conceptions of gender identity, Judith Butler links the masculine performance of the hero with homosexual melancholia: "the disavowed homosexual love is preserved through the cultivation of an oppositionally defined gendered identity. In other words, the disavowed male homosexuality culminates in a heightened or consolidated masculinity" (*Gender Trouble* 89). Butler insists that the more masculine the performance of the hero, the stronger is the homosexual melancholia which becomes "the never-never [that] supports the naturalized surface of heterosexual life as well as its pervasive melancholia" (*Psychic* 138).[18] Similarly, the more conventional the performance of the hero, the stronger is the cultural anxiety that lies beneath the performance — anxiety that underlies the concept of magic, the "abnormality" of the wizard heroes. It adds another dimension to Jackson's argument of cultural complicity of the *marvelous*, making it imperative to review the theory. Though the story of Harry Potter seems to re-confirm the myths of growth, patriarchy and British nationalism, the heroic performance reveals anxieties aroused by a postmodern child who "has become a threatening, uncontrollable force" (Thacker and Webb 140). The efforts of cultural containment in the narrative underline the troubled nature of childhood in the contemporary world of flux and uncertainty. The identity construction effected by the *marvelous* and its narratives of conventional heroism veil the awareness about the identities and modes of being that are disavowed, abjected and suppressed.

These modes of being are elements like adolescence and magic. As aberrant categories, in their non-normativity and pathological state of being, in the resistance to segmentation and organization, these elements of adolescent fantasy can be approached through the paradigm of the "queer," defined famously by Eve Sedgwick Kosofsky as an "open mesh of possibilities, overlaps, gaps" (*Tendencies* 8). As one of the words used often in coming-of-age fictions,[19] the queer paradigm can be used as an important trope to understand adolescence, especially as presented in the fantasy narrative. Queering the text in this case does not mean pointing out the potential gay or lesbian characters; it involves revealing signs of how a text uses the process of adolescence to explore the disruptive potentials, the disturbing subtexts behind the cultural constructions of a child, development and the accompanying mandatory unidirectional sexual growth. The use of queer theory therefore is not about homosexual representations in adolescent fantasy, though many such signs are represented in the *Potter* series; rather the study is concerned with the queer as a means to explore the categories of the "normal" and the "abnormal" in terms of adolescence and growth. The main project is to study the way in which adolescence and fantasy emerge as points of subversions and challenge despite the overt normative growth into adulthood, marriage and fatherhood.

Queer analysis, derived largely from poststructuralist theories and deconstruction, is an "embodied" critique of any kind of coherent, linear discourse or identity. Bringing together sexuality and culture criticism, queer theory's point of departure is the denial of any schematization of a "normal" or "natural" or "healthy" sexuality — a privileged state bestowed on adult heterosexuality. Destabilizing the notion of identity, the queer paradigm is concerned with sexual expressions that confuse and cut across gendered lines, much like fantasy, which expresses the unspeakable, unnatural, "that which has been silenced, made invisible, covered over and made 'absent'" (Jackson 4). The theoretical paradigm retains its relevance in view of the limitations of traditional identity politics and poststructuralist concern with the "messy" constructions of selfhood. Since adolescence, by its very definition in most cultures depends on biological puberty and the accompanying cultural assumptions regarding the age at which adult responsibilities, including marriage and parenthood, can be undertaken, sexuality, its presence, and more significantly its absence in children's and young adult texts speak loudly about the dominant cultural perception: "children are (and should stay) innocent of sexual desires and intentions. At the same time, however children are also officially, tacitly, assumed to be heterosexual" (Bruhm and Hurley 1).

As mentioned earlier, readers like Michael Bronski have pointed out interesting metaphoric intersections between the story of Harry Potter and the life of a queer adolescent. Harry's entry into the magical world coincides with his "coming out of the (broom) closet." He is supposed to attend the local school called the Stonewall High — a name synonymous with the movement of gay rights in the West.[20] The association of the school meant for the not-so- privileged section of society with the place central to the struggle of a marginalized, and often-demonized section of society is significant, especially in view of the fact that later the Dursleys tell their neighbors that Harry attends St. Brutus' Centre for Incurably Criminal Boys. Harry really attends Hogwarts School in the secret magical world. A.O. Scott points out how being a wizard is close to being queer in the world guided and structured by normativity. The detailed discussion in the coming chapters reveals the force with which the queer subtext impinges on the growth of Harry Potter before the reclamation by heterosexual normativity. Harry's shifting relationships with other characters highlights this gradual movement. Therefore, the trajectory of adolescence and its cultural constructions is replete with a queer subtext that appears insistently and is, in turn, suppressed repeatedly in favor of "normal" development.

Queer analysis of the narrative of boyhood therefore reveals the essentially performative aspect of boy-to-man growth. The elements of fantasy like magic denaturalize this cultural project. The narrative of fantasy revolves around the power of magic, an illegitimate force whose presence in society has been characterized by simultaneous ubiquity and secrecy.

Marcel Mauss describes it as "unauthorized, abnormal, and the very least, not highly estimable," "a kind of religion, used in lower spheres of domestic life" (29). Magic in adolescent fantasy like the *Potter* series appears as a suppressed "abnormality." Its presence exposes the facts of empirical world as consensual "reality." The constitutive nature of the symbolic order is thrown sharply into relief. Like the fantastic, magic signals a crack, an abnormality exposing the hierarchies of the symbolic.[21] Magic as an abnormal excess is central to the growth of Harry Potter, the hero of the community, the redeemer, the savior. The presence of this excess power in adolescent wizards, in the *Potter* series and other such fantasies, points out the "embodied" nature of the critique magic offers:

> Magic is, after all, a queer force — a force that makes one "not normal" (if you happen to live outside Hogwarts), but which can also paradoxically make you fit in (if all our friends are wizards). Like gender, magic seems wholly unverifiable, a collection of disparate influences and physiological coincidences — since magical ability is often passed on genetically — that adults often pretend to understand even when they haven't the faintest clue of what they're looking at. Like gender, magic is a power that confuses children, a power that they are supposed to ascertain clearly but often don't, and a power they would often like to be rid of [Battis, "Transgendered"].

Battis insists that since performativity is an inherent part of magic (for instance, in the magical ritual of spell casting), it is integral to the identity of the wizard. On the one hand, it underlines the performative aspect of identity. On the other hand, since a wizard/witch "embodies" an abnormal power, s/he acts out the "otherness" and its centrality in any construction of selfhood. The wizard hero himself can be seen as a character created "for the figure of the child to be queer." Battis discovers the queer nature of wizards as

> exiled, strange, outlawed, peculiar. They work on the world but not necessarily *in* world, since the world ... refuses to accept them. Even in fantasy, the wizard is queer; so the wizard, in a sense through the sense of her body, makes fantasy itself queer.... The wizard is the ultimate monster, the boundary violation, the fusion of categories [*Queer Spellings* 40].

In his/her queer nature, the wizard hero embodies the essence of adolescence — a state of being that needs to be left behind, abjected out in the movement towards adulthood. Freud in *Three Essays* schematizes the ideal trajectory of sexual development or "growth" in which queerness is the stage normal to the correct patterns of development towards the "final sexual aim." This aim lies in the heterosexual progress over the hurdles of perversities like the Oedipal complex. Steven Brumley and Natasha Hurley point out that

> the utopian projection of the child into the future actually opens up a space for childhood queerness — creating space for the figure of the child to be queer as long as the queerness can be rationalized as a series of mistakes or misplaced desires. In this sense the figure of the child is not the anti-queer at all. Its queerness inheres instead in innocence run amok [xiv].

The figure of an adolescent wizard hero therefore offers a space of resistance to the networks of containment. Even as the narrative follows the linear course that moves towards the end of adolescence and fantasy, towards the world of normalcy and normativity, the presence of a wizard hero at the center signals an extremely peculiar relation to the normal. While the course of the narrative acknowledges the power of the normal, it simultaneously expresses the desire to exceed the normal — a desire that is suppressed and declared illegitimate in the familiar world but can be expressed in the queer world of adolescence and fantasy. Battis points out that "to be queer is, in a sense, to be a part of fantasy, but also to be *fantastic*, somehow different." The performance of a wizard (with its similarities to a drag performance as the numerous examples from the *Potter* series show) creates a queer space outside the normative and conventionally formulated identity. Here it also becomes coincident to the definition of adolescence where rather than total identification with the "normal," the thrust is on the way it falls short of the cultural ideal, leading to the comforting fantasies of wish-fulfillment that re-signify the lack. Hence central to the narrative is a queer adolescent like Harry Potter or a "transchild" like Neville, especially when placed alongside the aggressive physicality of his cousin, Dudley or the insensitive but secure masculinity of his friend, Ron.

The adolescent narratives are concerned as much with exploring the boundaries and pursuing pleasure as with the cultural or parental templates handed top-down. What comes naturally to the children in Rowling's story are not morals and norms but curiosities that drive the narrative — right from the first book where they search for the mysterious object hidden in the school to the search for the parts of Voldemort's soul in the last book. Rule breaking, curiosity against the official imperatives, the feeling of knowing and hiding a secret are important elements through which the narrative moves. Even in the earlier books Harry is hardly a flat character as the characters of fairy tales (Luthi 24; Nikolajeva, "A Return" 127): he is dictated by a variety of motives that range from loyalty to his friends and desire for his parents to a vindictive pleasure in threatening the Dursleys with magic and his "criminal" godfather. Feelings of insecurity, inferiority, persecution, angst — all are important to Harry's characterization in the later books. His world is full of ambiguities and dualities through which he has to negotiate — the good and the evil that mutate into the easy and the right, the pure-bloods and the "mudbloods," the adolescent and the adult. These anxieties undercut the self-assurance that guides the cultural metanarratives on which the series builds. Till the end, Harry remains a flawed hero, a queer schoolboy and a troubled savior. The overt linear movement is undone by the adolescent at the heart of the story. Since at the center of the fantasy *Bildungsroman* is a hero who, unlike an "a-sexual innocent," is at once gendered and sexualized, the variety of shifting relationships with the parents, friendships and love affairs, as well as the relationships between other characters and their legitimate and illegitimate desires that influence the course of the narrative, form an important background. Normativity is problematized in Harry's case through same-sex attachments and also with cross-generational attachments with father figures and cross-cultural liaisons like that with Cho Chang. Theorists like Judith Halberstam locate the queer as a site from where the hegemonic discourses of power can be undermined. "Queer subcultures," she says, "produce alterative temporalities" (314). Queer subcultures, therefore, become communities developed as alternatives to kinship-based systems, institutions of family, heterosexuality and reproduction.

The world of fantasy offers a space to celebrate the dissonance and imperfection as a place of exploration, play and alterity. Like the lack characterized by gendered identification which emerges as the site of queerness, the use of gaps and interstitial spaces of the symbolic in *marvelous* as places of possibilities, alterities, means that this potential hence deconstructs its ideological complicity. Donald Hall argues that to be queer is "to abrade classifications, to sit athwart conventional categories or traverse several" (13). Such queer conceptualizations have significant repercussions for the master narratives of growth. Queering reveals the fragility of the constructions of identity beneath the surface narrative of growth towards marriage and adulthood. The linear development of the hero myth or the school story or the savior narrative is weakened to serve the queer life of an adolescent. While the Oedipal interpretations tell about the struggle against the father, the hero monomyth also tells about the strong friendships between older men and their young apprentices. Such complex associations with traditional notions of authority, legitimacy and correctness locate Rowling's world "diagonally" to the "normal" world. The magical world in a way is an adolescent world, the world of the marginalized and the renegade, a queer world where men wear purple cloaks and high-heeled boots like Dumbledore (Rowling, *PS* 4), or, like Hagrid, carry a pink umbrella and all the paraphernalia of domesticity in their voluminous cloaks (*PS* 40). Destruction of certainties is an important element in the world-creation of popular adolescent fantasy as it opens on to alterity and multiplicity. Phillip Pullman's fantasy series also presents us with multiple worlds existing simultaneously, where what seems to be a minuscule event in one leads to resounding repercussions through the other worlds of the universe. Diana Wynne Jones' *Chrestomanci* series begins with the author's note explaining that "there are thousands of worlds, all different from ours. Chrestomanci's world is the one next door to us, and the difference here is that magic is as common as music is with us." This world construction integrates the alternate orders with the existing reality in a kind of heterotopia, where the worlds "collide, clash and overlap" (Foucault, "Of Other Spaces"). The queer worlds of adolescent fantasy become a means of destabilizing the norms and exploring difference. The story of the hero, as Margery Hourihouran insists,

> does not merely adapt, mothlike, to the environment; because of its omnipresence in our culture, it is a powerful agent in shaping social and political attitudes, and its influence is always conservative. It suggests that existing power relationships are both inevitable and right, that, as Barthes says, they simply "go without saying," and thus it makes the envisioning of different relationships, and different social values, difficult [21].

Rowling's story on the one had can be seen as a product of the same milieu in the sense that the end of adolescence is the end of queer adventures and reassertion of hegemonic positions.[22] The task of this study, and of fantasy, is to locate the points of fragility and rupture that queer these metanarratives.

Katherine T. Bucher and M. Lee Manning in their study of fantasy literature for boys observe that "students who read fantasy are not always those who follow directions. They are often divergent thinkers who use fantasy as a focal point for thinking, creating and imagining" (136). Fantasy, since it embodies this resistance to the patterns prescribed top-down, is a dialogic genre in the sense, that rather than just positioning an adolescent in cultural categories and propelling him/her into accepting them, it also turns around to investigate the cultural categories and becomes a medium of adolescent resistance. The meaning of the text is not fixed as objective or true; through a "pleasurable misreading," the protagonist and thereby the reader negotiates the dynamics between the didactic impulse and wish-fulfillment in fantasy. Freud points out that fantasy for a daydreamer is as serious a preoccupation as play is for a child. In the narratives of those whom Freud calls the "less pretentious writers of romances, novels and stories, who are read all the same by the widest circles of men and women" lies a serious impulse; "every separate phantasy contains the fulfillment of wish, and *improves on unsatisfactory reality*" ("Relation of the Poet" 179, italics mine). Such fantasy can hardly be dismissed as passive escapism. To the contrary, by linking textual strategies at effecting change to future goals, fantasy links action to its purpose.

1

The Hero

Still, I wonder if we shall ever be put into songs or tales. We're in one, of course; but I mean: put into words: you know, told by the fireside, or read out of a great big book with red and black letters, years and years afterwards. And people will say: "Let's hear about Frodo and the Ring!" And they'll say: "Yes, that's one of my favourite stories. Frodo was very brave, wasn't he, dad?" "Yes, my boy, the famousest of the hobbits, and that's saying a lot."—Tolkien, *The Lord* 697

When Frodo and Sam start on their epic journey to Mordor, Sam ponders on their future. He frames the outcome of their quest in a particular type of tale, the heroic narrative. Sam anticipates Frodo's triumph and his epic hero status, because that is the way "the tale they had fallen into" (696) works: after obstacles and hardships, the ordinary hero rises to extraordinary heights and achieves the impossible. The stories of Frodo, "the famousest hobbit" and "Samwise the stouthearted" (697), Sam anticipates, would be a part of hobbit lore—a cultural myth that would be read and told to future generations. In focusing on the bonds of friendship and brotherhood between men, and the ultimate triumph of the fellowship over the forces of evil, the narrative would set a pattern of growth for young boys, the special readers that Sam envisages. Their quest would therefore become exemplary, framing the movement of the adolescent readers from childhood to adulthood.

Sam's description succinctly sums up the reasons the heroic myth is so central to the coming-of-age narratives of adolescent boys. The story of a hero is a transcultural and transhistorical narrative; the readers may recognize their own personal reading of *The Lord of the Rings* implied when Sam imagines others gaining inspiration from his journey with Frodo. For the structuralist studies, the hero monomyth has been one of the main points of entry into cultural narratives. Anthropologists like Claude Levi-

35

Strauss have argued that the sameness of myths across time and cultures comes from their structural similarities; that myths, though they are complex narratives, fundamentally work on a similar pattern as language. Russian formalist critic Vladimir Propp's analysis of folktales highlights the structural functions that the narratives of fairy and folk tales share across cultures. Joseph Campbell, working on similar paradigms highlights the fundamental similarities in what he calls the "hero monomyth": "A hero ventures forth from the world of common day into a region of supernatural wonder: fabulous forces are there encountered and a decisive victory is won: the hero comes back from this mysterious adventure with the power to bestow boons on his fellow man" (*The Hero* 30). It is a myth that has appeared in countless disguises, suggesting a link between the heroic figure and the collective unconscious. Northrop Frye, citing this prototype identified by the structuralist thinkers, insists on the significance of the heroic myth in the study of literature. According to him, the quest myth is the basic myth of literature. It derives its meaning from the cycle of seasons: "the hero is the reviving power of the spring and the monster and the old king the outgrown forces of apathy and impotence in a symbolic winter" (*Anatomy* 188). This close conjunction of the passage of time with the heroic quest highlights the reason the hero myth has been appropriated by narratives enacting the rites of passage out of the liminal world of adolescence into adulthood.

The hero, therefore, is a cultural icon; it is a culturally encoded performance set in a neat structural pattern that reflects the ideologies and values of the society in which it emerges and in which it is disseminated. Written about half a century after Tolkien's epic trilogy and centuries after Homer's *Odyssey*, the story of Rowling's boy wizard, Harry Potter, seems to share several structural similarities with the earlier texts. The mythic narrative, as Levi-Strauss points out, is simultaneously synchronic and diachronic — while the basic structure of the myth is ahistorical, the uniqueness of the narrative lies in its adaptation to the historical moment (*Myth* 17). Rowling's narrative in repeating the archetypal formula taps into a tradition of cultural narratives that precede it. But it is traditional in the dynamic sense, suggested by T.S. Eliot[1]; the emphasis on the continuity that roots it in the past exists along with an orientation towards the present. Thus, the text shares an active relationship with its predecessors as it attempts to reformulate, often undo or modify the formula by relating it to a specific twentieth century context.

The hero monomyth has served as the prototype for most coming-of-age narratives, a kind of Ur story from which most popular fantasy emerges. The central concern of this chapter is the way contemporary fantasy like the Potter series links the transhistorical narrative of the hero with the process of growth in the twentieth century, and the way the fantastic elements in the narrative often seem to undo the linear and teleological nature of such fiction. As mentioned earlier, the heroic narrative, as a traditionally staple genre of coming-of-age stories, textualizes the processes of growth and development. The story of the hero who grows up from a reluctant adolescent to a responsible and powerful member of society seems to enact growth and development as a linear movement from the margins to the center.

Yet on a close look, the hero myth as a template of growth emerges as a narrative full of queer possibilities. The element of adolescence that is central to the narrative often debunks the teleology of growth. Thus, adolescent fantasy like the Potter series centers on a dynamic relationship with the conventional linear narratives surrounding adolescence and coming of age, suggesting alternate meanings even as the narrative overtly adheres to the generic specifications strictly.

Each structural function of the monomyth engages with cultural order and vulnerabilities at a profound level. The Potter series begins *media res*, with a breach in the magical world that comes about with the murder of James and Lily Potter while their one-year-old son Harry miraculously survives. The death of the parents and Harry's subsequent exile from the magical world is cognate with the first Proppian function of *absention*, a significant structural function suggesting a break in order. Each book of Rowling's series begins with Harry's isolation from the magical world, continues with his journey to the school of magic and his adventures there, and ends with his return from life-threatening dangers; the series ends with his reintegration into the magical society following the victory over Voldemort, and ultimately marriage and fatherhood in the epilogue. The central movement of the fantastic narrative follows Harry's growth from an 11-year-old naïve entrant who is prophesied to be the savior of the magical world to a 17-year-old wizard who earns his place in society by his actions.

This rather simple archetypal story operates at multiple levels of meaning; the growth of the adolescent hero progressively becomes a mesh of psychical, social, cultural and political issues. Ruptures at every level reveal as much about adolescence as about the culture confronted by an adolescent orphan hero. The series delineates its preoccupation with the

structures and anti-structures of conventionality and norms with the very
first line.

> Mr. and Mrs. Dursley, of number four, Privet Drive, were proud to say
> that they were perfectly normal, thank you very much. They were the last
> people you'd expect to be involved in anything strange or mysterious,
> because they just didn't hold with such nonsense [Rowling, *PS* 1].

Hence the series situates itself at the peripheries of the conventionally dominant tropes; as a fantasy, it deals with the versions of reality that the com-
monsensical assumptions consider to be "unreal"; as an adolescent fantasy,
it aligns itself with adolescents who occupy an ambiguous position at the
threshold of maturity. The Dursleys are conscious of a world outside their
parameters of "normality," a world that they ignore but it insistently
impinges on their everyday life. It proves that their "normalcy" is a fragile
artificial construct. The morning after the death of the Potters, it intrudes
on Vernon Dursley on his way to work:

> He couldn't help but noticing there seemed to be a lot of strangely dressed
> people about. People in cloaks. Mr. Dursley couldn't bear people who
> dressed in funny clothes — the get-ups you saw on young people! He sup-
> posed this was some stupid new fashion. He drummed his fingers on the
> steering wheel and his eyes fell on a huddle of these weirdos standing close
> by. They were whispering excitedly together.... Why, that man had to be
> older than he was, and wearing an emerald green cloak! The nerve of him!
> [Rowling, *PS* 8].

The same evening Dumbledore dressed in "long robes, a purple cloak
which swept the ground and high-heeled, buckled boots" (Rowling, *PS*
12) leaves one-year-old Harry on their doorstep. And Harry embodies
deviance of the magical world at the level of physical appearance itself.

> Perhaps it had something to do with living in a dark cupboard, but Harry
> had always been small and skinny for his age. He looked even smaller and
> skinnier than he really was because he had to wear old clothes of Dudleys
> and Dudley was about four times bigger than he was. Harry had a thin
> face, knobbly knees, black hair and bright-green eyes. He wore round
> glasses held together with a lot of Sellotape because of all the times Dudley
> had punched him on the nose. The only thing Harry liked about his own
> appearance was a very thin scar on his forehead which was shaped like a
> bolt of lightning [Rowling, *PS* 20].

The description conflates physical, social and cultural alienation: the
physically diminutive status is emphasized by Dudley's old clothes, which,
along with the broken spectacles, point at his social marginalization. At

fifteen, he is still skinny even with a "slightly unhealthy look of someone who has grown a lot in a short space of time" (Rowling, *OotP* 7).[2] This alienation at multiple levels stems from Harry's status as an orphan child. The orphan child or a foundling is a recurring trope in folklore and fairy tales. A foundling is a "quintessential outcast who operates in isolation" due to his or her separation from social and familial roots (Kimball 3). Foundlings in children's fiction from Dickens to Kipling's *Jungle Books*, to popular narratives like Burrough's *Tarzan of the Apes*, often reinforce the myth of a child's innocence. Deprivation, insecurities and disempowerment portray the struggle of children to grow and assert themselves. So Philip Nel points out that a "literary orphan dramatizes the difficulty of being a child" (quoted by Donaghue).

At the same time, the Jungian archetype of an orphan child, especially its variation of the abandoned child, symbolizes new beginnings, change, and volatility along with uncertainty. The motif of the orphan draws its symbolic strength from the greatest foundling story of Western tradition — of Jesus, the Son of God. The image of an orphan at the center of the text locates a point of view that sees the social systems from an outsider's perspective and hence opens a space for critique. Thus, an orphan, rather than a "tangible reflection of the fear of abandonment that all humans experience" (Kimball 1), becomes a position of possibility. The orphan makes for a perfect hero figure.

The scar on the forehead sets Harry even more firmly in the heroic tradition. Harry's scar has interesting literary precedents. In Propp's analysis of the fairy tales, the wounding of the hero by the villain is an important structural turning point. The scar acts as a sort of interpellation, marking the hero out bodily. It is a mark of heroic identity like Odysseus' scar. It is also the mark of rivalry with the father, like Oedipus' clubbed foot. In Phillip Pullman's trilogy, Will Parry, another adolescent, is wounded to mark his identity as the wielder of the Subtle Knife. The wound in all cases is a mark of rivalry as well as of a privileged place in a community.

As soon as Harry turns eleven, he is claimed by the strange magical world despite the desperate attempts of the Durselys to keep any "abnormality" at bay. Instead of misfortune or a lack, whose *revelation*, in Proppian schema, initiates the quest, in Rowling's narrative, it is the power that is strange, "abnormal" and excess of the "normal" powers that a culture "grants" to its adolescents. The expected trajectory of the life is disrupted when the magical forces intervene to reclaim their boy-wonder. The animated and determinedly self-multiplying letter of admission to Hogwarts

School of Witchcraft and Wizardry is what Campbell calls "the herald" of adventure, "the representative of that unconscious deep ('so deep that the bottom cannot be seen') wherein are hoarded all of the rejected, unadmitted, unrecognized, unknown, or undeveloped factors, laws, and the elements of existence" (*The Hero* 52–53). It is the world that draws its power from the "abnormal." In their anxiety and panic, the Dursleys do all that they can to keep the letters from Harry. The refusal to the call of adventure, consciously or unconsciously, is a structural device that rests on "the power of significant action," the power of active choice and agency that would set the plot in motion. Despite all the efforts of his uncle and aunt, Harry chooses to follow Hagrid when he establishes contact with Harry after the letters have failed to do so. Hagrid, the half-giant gamekeeper of Hogwarts, in a way then functions as the "threshold guardian" stationed at the entrance to the magical world, "the zone of magnified power" (Campbell, *The Hero* 77). Rowling introduces him as the "Keeper of the Keys." He guides Harry's first steps in the magical world by taking him to Diagon Alley through the Leaky Cauldron; he escorts children from the Hogwarts Express and, in the first year, he ferries them across the lake to the castle.[3] Living on the periphery of the school grounds, he is one of the few people who can enter and leave the dangerous forest surrounding the school without fear or harm. For Harry, Hagrid, a misfit even in the world of magic, the queer of the queers, is the first guide, mentor and friend. Therefore, the "normal" course of development of an adolescent is contextualized with respect to the deviance and queerness of the "abnormal" magical world in such a way that conventional process of coming of age is destabilized though the narrative moves teleologically towards Harry's maturation.

The composition of the hero monomyth closely follows another central myth of Western culture — that of King Oedipus. The impaired relations with the parents, rivalry with the father and the ultimate usurpation of the father's role and position are the central themes around which adolescent fantastic narratives build. Thus, the structural pattern of the hero monomyth is interlaced with psychoanalytic paradigm to tell the story of adolescence that should end with a successful resolution of the Oedipal crisis through a series of displacements and repressions.[4] This structural pattern from the prophetic birth to the usurpation and the murder of the father is common to several myths — from Oedipus to Moses. It seems to be central to the story of Rowling's boy wizard as well. The very first encounter between the Dark Lord and one-year-old Harry Potter suggests this link between fantasy and psychoanalysis at the level of structural form as well as thematic content. The Dark Lord, bent on taking over the world, kills Harry's parents, unknowingly transfers his powers to the child and creates a permanent link by the act of choosing his enemy.[5] He gives Harry the wound that proclaims their rivalry, that "neither can live while the other survives" (Rowling, *OotP* 741).

Furthermore, Harry's Oedipal narrative parallels Voldemort's own story; the death of his mother and the murder of his father are the decisive moments in Voldemort's life. In the Oedipal version of growth, the son's hostility to the father motivates action. The first act of heroism, therefore, lies in being able to survive against the will of the father; it is the first assertion of self. Interpreted through the Freudian paradigm, Voldemort's obsession with the purity of blood can be seen as analogous to his preoccupation with his non-magical or muggle father. His evil then can be imputed to an Oedipal fixation.

With respect to Harry, the Death Eaters and the magical world at large, Voldemort rises as a daemonic father — demanding, ruthless and vengeful. Like Laertes, he marks Harry in his failed attempt to murder Harry. In the process, Voldemort unknowingly transfers his powers to Harry, giving him the wound that secures his destiny. The prophecy "neither can live while the other survives" secures the link between Voldemort and Harry as the father and son Freud describes in *Totem and Taboo*.

The Oedipal narrative is further complicated during the monstrous "rebirth" of Voldemort in the graveyard. If Voldemort, as a daemonic father, tried to kill Harry in his infancy, the position is reversed during the rebirth: Voldemort returns to life through Harry's blood. While he had transferred his powers to Harry in his failed attempt to kill Harry, now he gains the protection offered by Lily's sacrifice to Harry. The Oedipal motif of rivalry is particularly strong in the entire ritual. Voldemort uses the bone of his own father. For the Death Eaters, as well as for Harry, the return of Voldemort is the return of the primeval vengeful father. If Harry had robbed him of his powers, the Death Eaters too are accused of forsaking him. In *Totem and Taboo*, Freud highlights complex cultural ramifications beneath the neat structural pattern of the Oedipal myth. The killing of the father brings about guilt and anxiety, says Freud, which leads to the prohibition of incest among the exiled brothers, "by which they all alike renounced women whom they desired and who had been their chief motive for dispatching their father. In this way they rescued the organization which had made them strong — and which may have been based on homosexual feelings and act, originating perhaps during the period of their expulsion from the horde" (144). The ritual therefore enacts the early moments of civilization, the time when the central taboos of human society — prohibition of incest and homosexuality — came into being as social networks of family and kinship concretized.

Thus, the anguish of ancestry is central to the story of the hero, in terms of structure as well as the content. Psychic normality lies in overcoming this fantasy of rivalry with the father by giving up the incestuous desire for the mother and identifying with the role of the patriarch. The Oedipal complex and its successful resolution seem to define the stories of coming of age. It spells out the legitimate and illegitimate desires within the social networks and, hence, governs the course of individual development. Separation from parents, socialization and the ultimate entry into the adult world represent the normal course of development of selfhood and individual identity. Bruno Bettleheim, using Freud's theory of psychosexual growth, illustrates the means by which fantastic narratives like fairy tales acclimatize the readers towards their social role.[6] They help in the development of socially acceptable subjectivities and encourage a particular mode of behavior. The theme of separation from the parents is hinted at in the series by the representation of the Dursleys, who can be seen as analogous to the wicked stepparents of the fairy tales. Bettleheim points out how the motif of "wicked step-mother" becomes a means to deal with the changing facets of the mother from a nurturer to a disciplinarian. It also marks the child's response to the imposition of the injunctions of the super-ego. The prime concern of the narrative is the progress towards the world of the symbolic, the movement from the margins to the center of the magical society and the adult world. Thus, the quest of the adolescent hero, framed within the Oedipal structure, is a movement towards independent subjectivity, which is simultaneously validated by the patriarchal frameworks of kinship and family. Otto Rank, in his investigation of the hero myth, asserts that the "the hero should always be interpreted merely as collective ego" (Rank, *The Myth* 52). Therefore the narrative of normalization of the Oedipus crisis becomes a cultural narrative, repressing and displacing desire and its expression in the name of family, state and nation.

Therefore, absent parents, dead parents, neglectful parents and wicked parents are common figures in fantasy. In texts like Diana Wynne Jones' *The Charmed Life*, the story is set in motion with the death of Eric and Gwendolyn Chant's parents. If not dead, the parents are often neglectful, giving space and time for adventures like the Drews in Susan Cooper's *The Dark is Rising* where the parents leave the siblings in charge of their strange Uncle Merry. Lyra in Phillip Pullman's *His Dark Materials* first thinks she is an orphan. Later she has to constantly resist her parents and their ambiguous authority. In the same story, the parents of Will Parry remain absent for most part of the series, though they seem to guide Will's quest. The narrative eludes the neat limitation into the Oedipal structure as Will assumes the role of a nurturer, taking care of his sick mother as he searches for his father. In Anthony Horowitz's *Groosham Grange*, the ridiculously disciplinarian father and weak mother of David Eliot are close to the heavily caricaturized parental figures of the Dursleys. Theirs is a "normal" world, challenged and rendered ridiculous by their adolescent charges who refuse to accept and blend in the system. The (non)representation of the parents in fantasy undercuts the authority of the parents, the Symbolic Other, the agents of the Oedipal normalization. Lurie notes private rather than public operations of subversion in this context: "More or less openly, the author takes the side of the child against his or her parents, who are portrayed as at best silly and needlessly anxious, at worst, selfish and stupid" (*Don't* 9). In most of the above cases, the parents disappear after a short introduction. The parental role is often assumed by diverse characters with varying backgrounds and intentions. In the Potter series, the paternal role shifts from a father figure like James Potter, to bullying Uncle Vernon, to the powerful and wise headmaster Dumbledore and evil, murderous Voldemort.

Hence this loss of the parents symbolizes the psychical distancing from the parental figures that is inevitable and necessary for the normal development of subjectivity — a theme which preoccupies children's and young adults fiction (Coats, *Looking Glasses* 38). It follows the correspondence Lacan institutes between the Oedipal complex at the threshold of a child's maturation and the mirror stage that can be seen as the first psychic encounter between the self and other. The decisive moment when the subject identifies with the reflected other is also the moment when the split within the self is instituted. The unified, coherent mirror image becomes a point of identification; it is also the point of alienation since the very image destabilizes this unity and veils the fragility of the ego. The image of the parents represents the symbolic Other that adds another dimension to the ideal unified self. What is significant is not the parents in themselves but what they represent in a wider context. The subject constructs itself to meet the demands of the ideal-self in the mirror and also with the demands of the symbolic Other who gazes at him. Therefore, with the mirror image,

> the Imaginary register of ideal images has come into being and has determined the only way in which we can know anything — through alienation (knowing oneself though an external image), duality (the result of deep ambivalences caused by the alienation), and identification (the attempt to dissolve the subject into the ideal image and say, "This is me") [Coats, *Looking Glass* 19].

In Rowling's narrative, the encounter with the mirror of Erised (a reverse of "desire") in a disused classroom of Hogwarts illustrates the principal links in the themes of desire, fantasy and construction of selfhood in the process of coming of age. The inscription of the mirror "*Erised stra ehru oyt ube cafru oyt on wohsi*" has to be read backwards to be understood: *I show you not your face but your heart's desire*. In the reflection, Harry sees his parents and his extended family around him. It captures the desires and feelings unbarred, the ideal image of the self, the innermost fantasy of perfect union with the parents.

The reason the inscription is written backwards serves to underline the fact that the Mirror of Erised, or any mirror, only gives a reflection, a mistaken point of identification. The text gives a clear piece of advice on how to interpret the Mirror's content, but Harry, like the subject before the mirror Lacan discusses, fails to notice this warning and is enticed to revisit the vision of his dead parents till the headmaster reveals its secret. It has "neither knowledge or truth" (Rowling, *PS* 157) but an image that is disconnected from reality. What Dumbledore's explanation emphasizes is the imaginary nature of the wish fulfillment that the mirror reflects. There are some similarities to the dream state that, according to Freud, bring the deepest unconscious wishes to the conscious. The trance induces a person to "dwell on dreams and forget to live" (Rowling, *PS* 157). Later we are told that "Harry wished he could forget what he'd seen in the Mirror as easily, but he couldn't. He started having nightmares" (Rowling, *PS* 158).

The encounter with the mirror emphasizes the pattern of growth that entails birth of self through separation:

> If he (a child) can come to acknowledge these things as actually lost or sacrificed in the service of something, then he can complete a process of mourning whereby he disentangles himself from the loved object and asserts his own ego concerns over and against it — in other words, he can individuate [Coats, *Looking Glass* 37].

Thus, Harry needs to come out of the spell cast by the Mirror of Desire, a kind of death wish of perfect union with his long dead parents.

The Mirror of Erised also places the psychic coming of age with the theme of wish fulfillment that lies at the heart of fantasy. The growth of the hero can be seen as a performance that mirrors the social and cultural values systems. The hero therefore offers a point of identification with and within the directives of the cultural collective, a coincidence of the imaginary ideal with the ideal subject of the gaze of the symbolic. As Jackson points out, the crucial aspect of Lacanian theory is "its understanding of the ego as a *cultural construction*" (Jackson 88). The hero, like the image in the mirror, therefore is subject to and is himself a part of an external order, the ideal outside from where one evaluates one's own ego, a vantage point that cements the fragility of ego based on misrecognition. Harry's identification with his parents, his heroism, his quest, for most of the series, is dictated by his desire to belong. The bravery of the ideal hero figure, his obligation towards the community, and his determination to defeat the enemy that threatens the community provide a template for maturation and socialization for the reader — the construction of an ideal image of the self in tune with the demands of the social order to suture the alienation. It fulfills the demand of the social order, the symbolic Other, to be saved by a child. Therefore, "to get back, on to the far side of the mirror, becomes a powerful metaphor for returning to an original unity, a 'paradise' lost by the 'fall' into division with the construction of the subject" (Jackson 89).

The things are complicated further in Harry's second encounter with the Mirror of Erised. In the second encounter, the mirror image is not a point of identification; it is recognized as the other who offers crucial help to fulfill the task of the hero. In the second encounter, the Mirror of Erised does not show Harry his parents or family. Personal desire is replaced by a wider concern of social welfare as Harry seeks to save the Philosopher's Stone from Quirrel. The self who had earlier sought unification with the parents is now initiated into the symbolic networks where it actively seeks to make a place. The encounter with the Mirror at the end of the first year at Hogwarts is set within a wide range of conflicting forces represented by all the key players in the incident. Quirrel as a servant to Voldemort represents the bond of fear and devotion that the Dark Lord commands from his Death Eaters. Voldemort and Dumbledore stand for the two extremes of the thirst for power and its purpose, between which Harry is caught. The presence of the mother, the key object of desire in the earlier encounter with the Mirror, is implicated not only by the presence of the murderer but in Harry's blood itself. Harry's desire, this time to find the stone, is not personal. This time Harry sees his image as the other; it winks at him, emphasizing its otherness and goes on to show him the location of the magical stone.

So the episode of the Mirror of Erised in the first book of the series becomes the occasion to deliberate on the constructions of self, the formations of ego that center on the reflected other, the mistaken point of identification. The reflection seen in the mirror of desire reveals the ever-changing psychical and external components that constitute the sense of selfhood. The Mirror does make Harry's desire come true when he finds the Philosopher's Stone in his pocket. It emphasizes not only the complexities of desire and fulfillment implicated in the subject formation but also the culturally and socially constructed nature of the desire itself. Everybody sees different reflections in the mirror of Erised at different times — Harry sees different things at different points of time; his friend Ron Weasley sees himself triumphing over his charismatic brothers; Professor Quirrel sees himself handing the Philosopher's Stone to his master. The mirror places desire in its specific context; it highlights the changeable nature of desire, its personal as well as contextual nature. Dumbledore explains the nature of desire and the reason it is fulfilled by the Mirror this time; "you see, only one who wanted to *find* the Stone —find it, but not use it — would be able to get it" (Rowling, *PS* 217).[7]

Mirror images appear repeatedly in children's fiction, especially in fantasy, as a means to engage with the issues of self and the other in the process of identity construction. In Lewis Carroll's *Through the Looking Glass* and more recently in Diana Wynne Jones' *Chrestomanci* books, the mirror often becomes a window to other parallel worlds. The double function of the mirror motif— the construction of the self and the awareness of the other that is beyond the understanding and control of the self— coincide with that of fantasy narratives where factuality and the permanence of the here-and-now are always a suspect. In *The Lord of the Rings* the mirror of Galadriel offers visions that show the worst fears of the onlooker. Sam sees destruction of the Shire, and Frodo sees the evil eye of Sauron looking for him. The mirror then shows not just the reflection of "reality," showing the imaginary nature of culture narratives; its (in)version is also a comment on the nature of "reality." In that sense, the function of the mirror is cognate with that of fantasy itself, to show "things that were, and things that are, and things that yet may be" (Tolkien, *The Lord* 377). Therefore, the dual function of the mirror illusions is to reflect "reality" (a function cognate with that of fantasy) and at the same time serve as an entry point into the world of alterity and otherness.

As a "reflection" of ideologically dominant versions of reality, the narrative of the hero expresses not just the growth of the individual but also what Propp calls the "compositional systems," the historical and cultural constituents of the narrative of growth. Subject, selfhood and identity are constructed and deconstructed through interactions between the self and the other.[8] In his later criticism, Propp tied up the formalist analysis of the fairy tales with cultural and historical inquiry insisting that "morphology is sterile if it is not bound directly or indirectly to date from ethnology" (*Theory* 71). The heroic model and the values it represents are shaped by the dominant ideologies of the culture it emerges from. And since it figures prominently in children's and adolescent fiction, the narrative enacts the process of growth and development as envisaged by a specific epoch. A hero's tale is a repository of values and norms that a culture seeks to bestow on its young ones. The role of the fantastic is to unveil these values that are supposed to be natural in a hero's story. As Propp points out: "What needs historical explanation is not individual plots but the compositional system to which they belong" (*Theory* 72). The compositional systems of Rowling's story locate the hero monomyth with the ideals of linear growth into adulthood as told by the dominant psychological and social narratives, the institutionalized rituals of coming of age that include education and schooling, and cultural hierarchies which are influenced by contemporary economics and politics of race, gender and class. The myth of the hero itself becomes a prop to support these ideological networks. The structural and psychoanalytic interpretations of the hero myth in adolescent fantasy like *Harry Potter* are relevant, not just in terms of a generic study or the formula of growth such fantasy engenders, but more significantly, in the way adolescent fantasy deliberates on these foundational paradigms of the hero monomyth, and becomes a means to explore the contemporary narratives of coming of age.

As a heroic fantasy, the themes of growing up coincide with epoch-changing, community-saving and nation-building themes. Critics like Margery Hourihan aver that the compositional system of the heroic formula is about the promotion of the heroic ideal in terms of a white, male savior with its multifarious gender and racial implications. The genre of heroic fantasy primarily has been an export of British children's literature. Critics like M. Daphne Kutzer have pointed out the persistent element of nostalgia in fantasy that had not dimmed even in the twentieth century.

The sense of British history, nationalism and the privileged position of Britain in the world comes across through the narratives framed within English folklore, Arthurian legends and the imperial past of the Empire. In Rowling's series, the names of the characters are loaded with multiple symbolic and historical associations setting the cultural context of the narrative clearly. Roni Natov in "Harry Potter and the Extraordinariness of the Ordinary" points out how Harry Potter, despite being an ordinary name, puts Harry alongside the heroes of English royalty in literature, like Shakespeare's Prince Hal and Harry Hotspur. The name of his father, James, refers to English and Scottish royalty and also brings Christian themes into the narrative. James' animagus form is a stag, which is also the form of Harry's patronus. The stag is an important symbol of divinity in British and Celtic mythology. Apart from being the heraldic symbol of the Plantagenet dynasty, in Celtic mythology the stag is also the symbol of Cernunnos, the God of Plenty and the Lord of Beasts. The appearance of the stag indicates other-worldliness, earthly fertility and cyclic rejuvenation. In Arthurian legends, the stag often appears at the point of transgression of a taboo, leading to a quest. Most of the Weasley family is named after the knights of Arthurian legends. Farah Mandelsohn in "Crowning the King: Harry Potter and the Construction of Authority" also indicates the authority structure in the text which foregrounds the patriarchal heredity of Old England. The name of the headmaster, *Albus* Dumbledore, directly links with the racial aspects of the narrative especially since his opponent Grindelwald is named after Grendel, the antagonist of the great Anglo-Saxon mythic hero Beowulf. This inter-textuality locates the narrative of growth in the culture, history and mythology of Britain. The hero therefore becomes a potent mix of social, cultural and historical ego ideals. The hero monomyth therefore is a national monomyth providing a bridge between an archetypal approach and historical constructions of heroes. Dudley Jones and Tony Watkins insist that in the post-ideal, post-utopian world, heroes continue to be "a necessary fantasy": as mass idols heroes are an inescapable part of the historical narrative "constructed through popular narratives which frame them for public consumption and foreground particular attitudes and values" (6).

The hero monomyth ties processes of individual growth and development with the ideological positions fostering the belief of cultural rejuvenation through the successful maturation of the adolescent boy hero. It is highly context-specific since the hero, even within the formulaic narrative, is constructed through the interaction of conflicting networks of power and ideologies. Therefore Jacquiline Rose, pointing out the impossibility of children's fiction, insists that the desires and narratives of adults contribute a substantial part to the construction of childhood. It makes growth, development and coming of age complicit with the stories of race, gender and class. The quest of the hero with all its obstacles and dangers, which is so central to the hero monomyth, mirrors all sorts of forces emerging from a variety of power networks. The successful resolution of the quest points to a reassertion of dominant value systems. However, the convention of the happy resolution or *eucatastrophe*, as Tolkien calls it, is explored and nuanced by the journey of the quest. The journey in itself can either justify or, as we shall see in the case of Potter series, it can deconstruct the resolution at the end of the narrative.

In adolescent fiction, which, according to Trites, is characterized by its preoccupation with power and repression, the quest is associated with the formation of independent identity and selfhood. Undertaken either by a lone heroic figure who is joined by helpers later or with aides along with him from the start, the movement is grounded by assumptions about relations among individuals and between the individual, society and the world. For instance C.S. Lewis's *Chronicles of Narnia* frames the quest narrative in terms of the neat narrative of Christian harmony. In the Earthsea trilogy, Ged's quest is for the restoration of balance and harmony he had disturbed.

The overt narrative of the Potter series also seems to follows the cultural metanarratives of Christian redemption, of the adventures of an English hero or the growth of a schoolboy. Since the quest is guided by Dumbledore, the headmaster of Hogwarts and therefore an adult in position of authority, the narrative also seems to retain the idea of a helpless child who needs guidance and aid at every step. This seems to be reinforced by the centrality of the space of the school, which is explored in the following chapter. Harry and his friends constantly have to deal with restrictions and rules put in place by the Ministry of Magic, and finally they become important members of the magical community. The quest as a journey of "finding one's self," the notion which underlies the idea of the formation of subjectivity, has clear ideological and teleological goals. At least overtly it does seem that the Potter books do follow the paradigm. Harry's quest is similar to adolescents like Oliver Twist or Dorothy (*The Wizard of Oz*) or Charlie Bucket (*Charlie and the Chocolate Factory*), who are all outsiders and whose narrative gives an insight into the adult world. However, their narratives seldom overturn the actual equations of power and hegemony.

Several readers have illustrated the "incredulity towards metanarratives" built in contemporary fictions like the Potter series or Pullman's *His Dark Materials* trilogy which make for a postmodern myth (Prinzi, Granger). Pullman's narrative deconstructs the metanarratives of theology, science and fantasy by their close juxtaposition in the story of Will and Lyra's coming of age. In Rowling's series, the wizard world is built on metanarratives like the founder's myth, which established the good/evil axis in the form of the Gryffindor/Slytherin divide, racial myths (like the house-elves like slavery, or giants and werewolves are evil) or humanist myths of wise adults guiding innocent children. Rowling's adolescent hero negotiates through the ideological power held by such grand narratives. The neat good/evil axis that Gryffindor and Slytherin rivalry engenders is deconstructed as the source of all divisions and animosity that needs to be bridged.[9] The myth of racial superiority of wizards is, as discussed in the following chapters, destabilized by the political and social narratives concerning other magical races. Harry's search for a stable identity is located within contexts where subjectivity is partial and subject to a variety of socio-cultural discourses and practices. The course of the narrative uses structural strategies of the hero monomyth to deconstruct these grand narratives of the wizard world and hence problematize another grand narrative — growth in terms of the formation of a clear cohesive self-concept through the heroic quest.

In fact, it is Harry's constantly changing and ambiguous relationship with Voldemort, the Dark Lord, that deconstructs some central metanarratives of the heroic quest like the Oedipal framework discussed earlier. Voldemort, who seems to be a vengeful father figure, later becomes Harry's *doppelgänger*, his double, an alternative course of life and being constantly available to Harry. The motif of a double or a *doppelgänger* appears variously in the hero monomyth, as a false hero, a villain or even a fool. The *doppelgänger* motif is an interesting trope to explore the internal split and dialogue within a character. Most heroes of a fantastic narrative have a double or counterpart, internal or external to that character, who is crucial for the construction and representation of that character's subjectivity.

Through the course of the narrative, Harry and Voldemort emerge as literal extensions of each other. Their childhoods follow a similar trajectory. After the death of the parents and subsequent neglect, both find a home at Hogwarts. Due to the attack on one-year-old Harry, Voldemort unknowingly transfers his powers to Harry. The prophecy secures the link. Voldemort later uses Harry's blood to come back to life in the graveyard.

In the subsequent book, *Harry Potter and the Order of the Phoenix*, a mental connection is established between Harry and the "rejuvenated" Voldemort. Harry has access to Voldemort's feelings, thoughts and memories. Voldemort uses this connection to lure Harry to the Department of Mysteries. Towards the end, it is revealed that Harry is the last horcrux; he carries a part of Voldemort's soul in himself.

This close link between the hero and the villainous figure destabilizes the neat good-versus-evil divide that frames most fantastic fiction. For Robyn McCallum the "primary effect of the double is to destabilize notions of the subject as unified, or coherent, or as existing outside of a relation to an other" (75). Voldemort's literal presence inside Harry also symbolizes the fragmented nature of Harry's psyche. He thinks that having access to Voldemort's mind would give him power over the Dark Lord. Voldemort too thinks in a similar fashion but is more adept than Harry in using the connection. Harry also feels the lure of power when he obsesses over the Hallows. Voldemort, therefore, can be read as the He-Who-Must-Not-Be-Named present within the hero. As a double, he is both an other and another aspect of self, the internalized other. Thus the internalization of the intersubjective relation between the self and other is the second function of the *doppelgänger*. Voldemort becomes the other in whose response Harry constructs his selfhood. The choices, the decisions and the actions are undertaken to mark the distance between the self and the daemonic double. Critics like Andrew Blake have pointed out the essential humanism in the construction of Harry Potter, the boy-wizard who is good despite the hardships and neglect he faces in the growing years. However, the presence of Voldemort, within and without, points out the ever-present alternative available to Harry.

For community welfare, the hero myth ensures that the self-centered child grows to take up adult responsibility. Hence Voldemort's quest for immortality in a way represents the fear of growth. Voldemort, in conceptualization of such narrative of growth, seems to be fixated, another boy who does not grow up. He is often depicted as a baby or a child who does not understand things that are bigger than himself or do not concern him directly. He single-mindedly seeks immortality, without considering the wider implications of seeking it through the unicorn blood or the Philosopher's Stone or the horcruxes. During the ritual in the graveyard, he appears as a monstrous baby who returns to life through the blood of his enemy. His shortsightedness during the ritual ensures that Harry survives the killing curse in the end. He is described as a "curious child" (Rowling, *DH* 593) when he pronounces the killing curse on Harry in the forest.

The quest for immortality he therefore seeks to evade the teleological growth which inevitably leads to death. However, as we shall see in a later discussion in the chapter, it is such teleological conceptions of death that fantasy deconstructs.

McCallum, in outlining the dialogic construction of selfhood through the motif of the double, remarks that in the fantasy genre, the double is frequently a symbolic manifestation of a character's alter ego and often represents that character's other "evil" self. Therefore, the death of the double, or the host character, or both establishes a monologic relation where "there is no possibility of either dialogic or dialectic synthesis between the character and its double" (76). However, on a closer analysis of the fantastic narrative, a complex usage of the motif of the double is revealed. In most fantasy narratives, the "evil" *doppelgänger* is a product of human cultural systems, labor or education. It is often associated with industry like Sauron's Orcs, Frankenstein's monster and Dr. Jekyll's Mr. Hyde; the fear they arouse is not merely by the virtue of being the evil alter-egos — they are also products of the much celebrated education and experiments that breach cultural taboos. Similarly, though Voldemort seems to be a problem child from the start as he tortures the other children at the orphanage (there is a hint of genetic evil if one goes by his uncle and Grandfather), his evil nature finds fertile grounds in the decaying, race-obsessed cultural systems of the magical world.

For Harry, whose childhood parallels that of Voldemort, the Dark Lord represents an aspect of the developmental process. Growth and identity construction requires the movement out of childish solipsism into a relationship between the self and the other, a self-concept that exists at an intra-individual or social level. It is repeatedly emphasized that Voldemort, despite his number of followers, likes to work alone. Harry's quest, on the contrary, is at once public and private. It is his private quest to seek out his parents' murderer and come out of the shadow of that fateful event. It is a public quest in the sense that it is located in the networks of power that define the magical world. Ideology of race, authority, schooling — all are implicated in Harry's quest towards adulthood. All the time, he has the choice to follow Voldemort's footsteps. In their very first encounter Voldemort offers to share his powers with Harry: "'Don't be a fool,' snarled the face. 'Better save your own life and join me ... or you'll meet the same end as your parents...'" (Rowling, PS 160).

Thus, the fragmentation or multiplicity that Harry experiences through his *doppelgänger* is conceptualized as a condition of possibility, a potential choice rather than an aberration. The double-motif is therefore related to the exploration of agency, that is, a sense of being consciously capable of action.[10] The possibility of action is located with the self as well as the double; it is Voldemort who, in responding to the prophecy, sets the plot in motion.[11] Harry's choices and actions are determined by his response to Voldemort's choice and actions. Harry's anger at Dumbledore is supplemented by Voldedmort's fear and hatred of him. In this sense, the *doppelgänger* becomes the central point in the construction of identity. It represents the position of the other necessary to complete the self-concept. The threat that the other can take place and efface the self is ever present. In *Harry Potter and the Order of the Phoenix*, Dumbledore insists on Occulumency because there is always the danger of the "voices" in the mind taking over Harry. Thus, rather than focusing on his innate goodness, Rowling's narrative portrays the adolescent quest as an active engagement with the external forces as they impinge on the constantly evolving selfhood.

Harry's relation to the subsequent benign father figures is as complex. The role is taken over by figures like Sirius Black, Remus Lupin and Albus Dumbledore. Though Harry becomes close to the Weasley family, his role is more of a protector than that of a son. He saves Ginny, Ron and also Arthur Weasley, the patriarchal head of the family, in *Harry Potter and the Order of the Phoenix*. Earlier, in *Harry Potter and the Prisoner of Azkaban*, he saves his godfather Sirius Black from the Dementors and helps him escape the prison. Though Sirius seems to confuse him with his father, Harry deals with Sirius and Remus as equals.[12] For Remus Lupin, the werewolf, Harry is one of the few people who accept him without prejudice. Thus, the relationship with the father, which in Oedipal terms is characterized by rivalry and fear, takes on multiple layers; it becomes a mutually reciprocal relationship framed in specific political and social networks. The role of such father figures, indeed of the entire Order of the Phoenix, with respect to their adolescent charges seems to alternate between leading and being led by the children.[13] The role reversal is complete when Dumbledore acknowledges Harry's heroism: "'I am not worried, Harry,' said Dumbledore, his voice a little stronger despite the freezing water, 'I am with you'" (Rowling, *HBP* 306).

Harry's relationship to the headmaster of Hogwarts, Albus Dumbledore, is equally complex. He is the wise old mentor who figures prominently in the hero monomyth. Dumbledore is the classic wizard of the *marvelous* stories: tall and thin, with long, sliver hair and beard, twinkling blue eyes and crooked nose. The Proppian role assigned to him is that of a helper who gives psychological and physical weapons to the hero. In children's fantasy, the stereotype has a dual function — on the one hand, as an old and wise mentor, the adult frames and guides the quest of the younger hero. Thus, though the hero becomes a means of cultural rejuvenation, his quest is placed under the firm guidance of adult authority. Maria Nikolajeva, a prominent critic of children's fiction, points this out in the power equation in the Potter series:

> Thus although, empowered, the child is not given full control; even though it is understood that Harry is the only one to match the evil force of Voldemort, until the ultimate battle Harry has to comply with the rules and laws imposed on him by adults. In the end, Dumbledore, the father substitute, has the final say ["Harry Potter" 127].

Such a reading co-exists with another significant aspect of the stereotype, that is, the strangeness and eccentricity of this mentor figure who is supposed to embody cultural authority. In most cases, the mentor appears as a strange figure who does not fit in with the established modes of being in the world around him. Dumbledore's brilliance and wisdom alternate with his eccentricities. His eccentricities are underscored by the discomfiture of the "normal" teachers like McGonagall. In Susan Cooper's *Over Sea, Under Stone*, the Great-Uncle Merry, the mentor who guides the quest of the Drew children, is hinted to be a descendent of Merlin.

> How old he was, nobody knew. "Old as the hills," Father said, and they felt, deep down, that this was probably right. There was something about Great-Uncle Merry that was like the hills, or the sea, or the sky; something ancient, but without age or end.
> Always, wherever he was, unusual things seemed to happen [3].

This strangeness is characteristic of the "wise old man" of the fantastic tradition including Merlin, the strange magician who interacts with animals and birds on the issues of politics and kingship (White, *The Once*); Tolkien's Gandalf, whose visits are clearly not appreciated by the regular inhabitants of the Shire; and Dumbledore, whose queerness leaves other teachers at Hogwarts embarrassed.

Hogwarts School, though a part of the queer world of magic, under Dumbledore, further becomes home to the deviants of the magical world itself, the queers of the queer world. He admits Remus Lupin, the werewolf, first as a student and later as a teacher in the school. As part animal, part man, Remus Lupin is an outsider in the magical world, shunned due to the prejudice against the werewolves. Hogwarts is one of the few places where Remus finds acceptance. Hagrid, the gamekeeper and later a teacher, as mentioned earlier, is another queer figure living on the peripheries of Hogwarts. As part-giant, Hagrid too suffers prejudice. He is expelled from Hogwarts in his third year under false charges. For Harry, Hagrid, the liminal character of the magical world, becomes a kind of mother figure, bringing him to safety when he is attacked by Voldemort at the age of one; he also brings Harry into the magical world at the age of eleven and, in the last book, he carries Harry out of the Forbidden Forest and back to life and Hogwarts.[14] Dumbledore repeatedly shows implicit trust in Hagrid, something that is paid back with equal loyalty and devotion on Hagrid's part. Dumbledore also accepts Severus Snape, the former Death Eater, despite the incriminating evidence against him. Though his tendency to trust and give second chances is doubted by other characters, the course of the narrative proves him to be right in his judgments. Therefore, under Dumbledore, Hogwarts becomes a refuge of the liminal exiles of the magical world. It becomes a place where the deviant and non-normative co-exists with and within the authoritative and legitimate structures. It is a natural home to children like Harry Potter and Neville Longbottom, the queers and misfits in their own world.

Therefore, in a way, Dumbledore consciously endorses the position of the outsider. Unlike Gandalf, who enters the Shire from the world outside to "incite" Bilbo and later Frodo to leave the comforts of their "hobbit holes," Dumbledore stands for the deviants and misfits at home itself. Under him, as discussed in the following chapter, the magical school opens up as a space to deconstruct the official metanarratives of the magical world from within the establishment.

The interpretation of Harry's relationship to the eccentric headmaster of Hogwarts cannot be confined to the narratives of surrogate parenthood and the Oedipal complex. Dumbledore arranges for Hagrid to deliver one-year-old Harry to the Dursleys after the murder of Harry's parents. He ensures that Harry is safe during his stay at the Dursleys. He comes to Harry's rescue after the battle for the Philosopher's Stone and at the ministry in *Harry Potter and the Order of the Phoenix.* Harry, on his part, reveals himself to be "Dumbledore's man through and through." At the end of *Harry Potter and the Chamber of Secrets,* instead of his mother's sacrificial blood, it is Harry's exceptional loyalty to Dumbledore that brings timely rescue in the form of Dumbledore's phoenix, Fawkes. The phallic symbolism is stressed when Harry fights Riddle with the Sword of Gryffindor drawn from the Sorting Hat brought by Fawkes.[15]

The pedagogic relationship certainly holds room for a platonic but implicitly homoerotic version of desire grounded in giving and receiving knowledge, molding one's character and growth under the guidance of another. Throughout Harry's years at the school, Dumbledore protects and guides him, taking a personal interest in his growth and maturity. In Harry's sixth year, Dumbledore trains him by providing insights into the origins of Voldemort and giving him knowledge of the horcruxes. Such pedagogic relation between the old mentor and young impressionable hero is central to the hero monomyth. It can be traced back to the ancient Greeks and Romans where pedagogy and passionate involvement are closely tied up, producing unique possibilities by queering the masculine hero.

Despite being the most powerful wizard, the narrative reveals the ambiguities that lie beneath the portrayal of Dumbledore as a conventional, stereotypical, wise, old wizard. In his youth, searching for the Hallows, he sought the same power that is later sought by Voldemort. There is almost a Machiavellian element in the way Dumbledore guides and frames Harry's quest towards his own sacrifice. Campbell points out the ambiguity of the supernatural helper as an essential structural feature: "Protective and dangerous, motherly and fatherly at the same time, this supernatural principle of guardianship and direction unites in itself all the ambiguities of the unconscious — thus signifying the support of our conscious personality by that other, larger system, but also the inscrutability of the guide that we are following to the peril of all our rational ends" (Campbell 73). Harry's doubts regarding Dumbledore in *Harry Potter and the Deathly Hallows* are therefore central to the narrative of his coming of age. In his choice to follow the horcruxes instead of the hallows and finally in the last act of self-sacrifice, Harry grows up by surpassing his greatest mentor.

The queer nature of such inter-subjective engagements constructs adolescence as a site of difference and resistance, which become central to Harry's narrative. The adult rationalization of such queerness as a compulsory stage in the process of growing up opens up adolescence as an arena of exploration, of play, of alterity. In Rowling's story, more than Harry and his friends, it is the previous generation, the Marauders who, with their irreverence, portray adolescence as an arena where playful nonconformity can become a serious challenge to the authorities. The Marauders are comprised of four close-knit friends — James Potter, Harry's father; Sirius Black, his godfather; Remus Lupin, the werewolf; and Peter Pettigrew, the hang-along who later betrays his friends. Of the four Marauders, only James and, much later in life, Remus enter into a "normal" albeit short-lived marriage and fatherhood and therefore establish a bond outside the tightly knit group of friends. Yet the most significant relationship for all four, especially in school and, for Sirius and Remus, even after school, is being a Marauder, a part of the adolescent group.

Remus Lupin, since he is a werewolf, is admitted to the school surreptitiously. He is a liminal person, constantly hovering between humanity and bestiality. His condition is a carefully guarded secret, though his friends work out the reason behind his periodic illness. Rather than deserting him due to the widespread prejudice against the werewolves, his friends become animagi, wizards who can transform themselves into animals voluntarily. Since the magical authorities keep a close tab on the complex animagus transfigurations, James, Sirius and Peter are illegal underage animagi. As animals, they keep the werewolf company, spending nights together roaming in the forest forbidden to the students of Hogwarts. Homoeroticism is latent in their intimacy and closeness, in their exploration of the forbidden grounds, in their liminal condition and in the secrecy of the group. Apart from James Potter, none of them evinces any interest in girls.

Unlike Harry, there is no purpose to their rule breaking apart from irreverence and pleasure that lies in hoodwinking authority. They discover secret passages in Hogwarts and hence, draw the Marauder's Map for the future mischief-makers of the school. The map functions with the injunction: "I solemnly swear I am up to no good." Even their magical gadgets are specially designed for the purpose — Sirius owns a flying motorcycle, a threat to the statute of secrecy of the magical world and contravening the act that forbids magicking muggle objects. James' invisibility cloak, a powerful magical object that turns out to be one of the Hallows, is used by them, and later by Harry and his friends to break the school rules. The Marauders flourish in their irreverence, in their play of hoodwinking the top-down powers, for fun. This kind of fun has been defined as the central element of play, something "external to immediate material interests" (Huizinga 9). Play, as exemplified by the Marauders, is free, out of ordinary life and distinct from it. In that respect, their play is close to fantasy as well as adolescence; it is separate from ordinary life temporally and spatially. It begins in the zone of "between and betwixt" where concepts like transgression, seriousness and purpose do not apply. The "play function of fantasy," as Cristopher Nash calls it, rejoices in the "uncustomary" and the "anomalous" as it disengages the habits of thinking by which an adult may feel bound to his context.

But play is not chaotic or anarchic. It has its own rules — the rules of secrecy, of friendship, of loyalty to which each member of the group is bound.[16] These are essential elements of play. Johan Huizinga, one of the earliest scholars to study the play element in culture, insists that play is not an asocial activity; it creates a sense of community and also of order of an alternate kind. The tight-knit group provides a sense of security and belonging. The crime of Peter Pettigrew breaches these absolute and bounding rules of the play. When he says that he was too weak to resist the Dark Lord, Sirius tells him that he should have died for his friends like they would have done for him. This is the order that groups like the Marauders, and later Dumbledore's Army, assert in the face of strife and discord that is the specialty of the Dark Lord. Tragedy strikes once this statute is breached, the group breaks down and dominating powers impinge as forces of evil in the case of James; for Sirius, they become institutions punishing recklessness and disobedience, and for Remus, it is the alienating social setup through which he has to negotiate all his life.

However, in their irreverence, they do reveal the cracks in the authority and officialdom of the society. None of them survive till the end of the series; their disobedience, voluntary or involuntary, is threatening to the official establishment. Thus the free and playful subversion has to be resisted by the dominant agencies to retain control. The threat of the Marauders can be seen as the anxiety with permanent non-conformity and, therefore, the necessity of putting an end to it.

Another set of mischief-makers, the Weasley twins, seem to be the inheritors of the Marauders' mantle at the school. Fred and George Weasley form another tightly knit unit that flourishes in being on the other side of authority. They mirror each other completely, in appearance, in thoughts and in ambitions. On the Quidditch team, both of them are beaters. Such uncanny resemblance and closeness pre-empts the possibility of any other kind of relationship or friendship. Twins, in the structural studies of cultural taboos by scholars like Mary Douglas, represent excess that leads to category crisis. In a narrative concerned with concepts like selfhood, identity and individuality, the twins are problematic in their resemblance and "unnatural" closeness. In Lois Lowry's hegemonic dystopia in *The Giver*, the twins represent a mistake of nature that is "tidied" up by putting the weaker sibling to death. The death of Fred Weasley then, in a way, then enforces the "normal" pattern of growth by putting an end to the "unnaturalness" that the twins represent.[17]

Unlike the Maruaders, the irreverence of the twins is carefully channeled to conventionalized ends. Unlike their brothers, who become head boys and Quidditch captains, they earn the dubious distinction of being the "pranksters-in-chief" at Hogwarts who aspire to set up a joke shop after leaving the school. Yet their defiance and irreverence is channeled into a highly successful commercial enterprise — the Weasley Wizarding Wheezes, which finally makes a place for them in the "normal" order.

For Harry, on the other hand, the non-conformity or the exploration of alterity is always a serious business; each juncture is a crucial step in his growth out of adolescence. His rule-breaking is driven by a serious and grown-up sense of responsibility like protecting others, even in the earlier books — for instance, in sending away Norbert to save Hagrid, saving the Philosopher's Stone, working out the clues regarding the Chamber of Secrets, fighting the Basilisk. Such "games" reward the adolescent by helping him into the adult roles. This link between the mastery of a game and the process of maturation is easily discernible. Play, therefore, is a crucial element structuring the narrative — each victory propels the protagonist out of his subject position as an adolescent, into adulthood; even the insecure and timid Neville Longbottom grows up by surprisingly transforming into a masculine hero figure, by defying authority and assuming leadership of the Dumbledore's Army.[18] Through such sutures, the heroic figure allays anxiety, but at the same time the course that Rowling's narrative emphasizes is the tenuous and fragile nature of such control by juxtaposing it against the polymorphous play and alterity like that embodied by the Marauders. Therefore, as a part of adolescent fiction which deals with power relations, the micro-narratives like the story of the Marauders or the Weasley twins or Neville Longbottom, placed alongside the template of growth offered by the hero, reveals the high cultural stakes in the "normal" end of adolescence.

These close-knit male groups, often with a homoerotic subtext, also serve as an essential background against which the adolescent boy hero constructs his normative identity. Male peer groups appear repeatedly in fantasy narratives mostly in a sexually sanitized form; it marks the condition of adolescence as we see it or would like to see it. The relationship may take the form of rivalry, friendship or a relationship with the mentor figure. Therefore, fantasy epics like Tolkien's *The Lord of the Rings* have been criticized for being "sexually immature" in their fixation on a male peer group and relegating women to the peripheries of the narrative. Anna Smol, in her study of male intimacy in *The Lord of the Rings*, argues that fantasy drew on the medieval literature after it had been "bowdlerized in order to make it fit what was considered suitable for young minds.... The general effect of education was to keep the sexes separate and as innocent as possible, or at least fearful about sexual knowledge" (Smol 950). The narrative therefore coincides with the cultural conception of growth and development seen only in terms of an innocent child growing up to embrace heterosexual normativity. In terms of the adult perception of the narratives of growth and development, the intensity of the male friendships signifies an "unnatural" fixation in the Oedipal stage. For the "normal" and the "natural" course of development, it needs to be sacrificed for the social organization of the community. Smol points out the intimate nature of friendship between Frodo and Sam, though it is "normalized" in the end through Sam's marriage.

Writing about half a century later, Phillip Pullman is more explicit about the homosexual relationship between the angels, Balthamus and Baruch, who guide the quest of Will Parry (*The Subtle Knife*). The transcendental nature of love represented by Balthamus and Baruch is placed within the normative spectrum of Will's growth towards the heterosexual paradigm. The angels, despite their power and status, are subservient to Will and finally sacrifice themselves for him. Male intimacy and the homoerotic subtext represented by characters like the Marauders, the Weasley twins, and even Balthamus and Baruch is therefore depicted as an ellipse — not directly relevant to the story. According to Kirke Fuoss, the politics of containment in YA fiction results in the representation of homosexuality as a "discrete, isolatable behaviour that need not be assimilated as an enduring aspect of identity" (166). As long as homosexuality remains an exteriorized behavior rather an interiorized dimension of identity of the adolescent boy hero, it is manageable, controlable and reversible.

Therefore, in the pattern of growth envisaged by Rowling's narrative, Hermione has an essential though a secondary place in the trio. In boarding-school fiction discussed in the next chapter, the trios were an officially enforced norm to prevent "unnatural closeness" between same-sex students. Therefore, Hermione's presence may solve the problem of "unnatural" closeness between Harry and Ron, especially in view of her and Ron's mutual romantic interest. However, the close friendship between Harry and Ron brings the homoerotic subtext right to the center of the series. It queers the boy hero who is supposed to set the pattern for coming of age. In *Harry Potter and the Goblet of Fire*, Ronald Weasley is progressively "feminized." Ron is fascinated by Viktor Krum, the international Quidditch player; like the girls who follow Krum, Ron lurks in the library to ask for Krum's autograph; he has a miniature model of Krum in his dormitory. In the second task, while it is Hermione and Cho who are taken underwater as Krum's and Diggory's "most precious objects," Ron serves the same purpose for Harry. Thus, for a while then, the goal of the quest is Ron, whom Harry has to save from the underwater world of the merpeople. At the Yule ball, he finally dresses up in "womanly" dress robes and, despite asking girls to the ball, Harry and Ron end up spending the evening together, strolling in the garden in the presence of several other couples.

In a linear narrative of growth, adolescence is seen as a time of ambiguity, non-normativity and "perversion" characterized by the phrase "matter out of place" (Douglas 44). The preoccupation with sexual identity is inbuilt in adolescent narratives, despite the overt construction of a child in terms of innocence and purity. It needs to be overcome on the way to "normal" adulthood. Harry, as the adolescent leader of Dumbledore's Army, is queer not only in his cross-generational attachment to Dumbledore or "unnatural" closeness with Ron; his entire stay at Hogwarts, his friendships and later his relationships undercut the overt narrative of steady linear development. Harry's first relationship with Cho Chang, a girl of East Asian origin, is a cross-cultural alliance, a part of the passing-away phase of queerness on the way to the heterosexual and "correct" adult relationship with Ginny Weasley, Ron's sister.

Therefore, in *Harry Potter and the Goblet of Fire*, following the cultural assumption about the "normal" pattern of growth, the balance is established between the male bonds and relationship with girls. In the three tasks of the tournament, Harry wins over a dragon, saves his friends, and ultimately successfully negotiates a maze full of dangerous creatures and spells. The three tasks integrate motifs that recur in a hero's journey. In each task the complex gender equations are evident. In the first task, Harry steals the golden egg placed among the other eggs of the dragon, thus overcoming the maternal aggression of the beast to save her eggs. In the second task, he fights the merpeople, who live in a matriarchal setup. Hourihan points out that in fantasy, "the hero's triumph over the wild things dramatized the mastery of patriarchy" (107). In the maze, by tasks like fighting dangerous creatures, saving Fleur (the only girl contestant), answering the riddle of the Sphinx, Harry is put in the tradition of male heroes. In other words, the Triwizard tournament marks a crucial stage in progressive "normalization" of the queer adolescent into a male hero.

The most crucial stage in the hero monomyth is the rescue of the

princess; the ascension is accompanied by a wedding and hence the reassertion of communal bonds. Among the seven essential *dramatis personae* in
Propp's morphology of folk tales, the princess is crucial to the quest as a
person sought for, who exists as a goal, who recognizes and marries the
hero. The function, which Campbell terms as "the meeting with the goddess," encloses Oedipal longing for the absent mother and the search for
the unattainable union; it also points towards the normative resolution
that awaits the end of the heroic adventure.

> Woman, in the picture language of mythology, represents the totality of
> what can be known. The hero is the one who comes to know. As he pro-
> gresses in the slow initiation which is life, the form of goddess undergoes
> for him a series of transfigurations: she can never be greater than himself,
> though she can always promise more than he is yet capable of compre-
> hending. She lures, she guides, she bids him burst his fetters. And if he
> can match her import, the two, the knower and the known, will be
> released from every limitation. Woman is the guide to the sublime acme of
> sensuous adventure. By deficient eyes she is reduced to inferior states; by
> the evil eye of ignorance she is spellbound to banality and ugliness. But
> she is redeemed by the eyes of understanding. The hero who can take her
> as she is, without undue commotion but with the kindness and assurance
> she requires, is potentially the king, the incarnate god, of her created world
> [Campbell 116].

Thus, the role of women in the monomyth highlights the cultural conception of gender that inevitably ends in a re-assertion of the normative
sexual roles. In the subsequent books, as Harry's surrogate father figures
disappear one by one, Harry's gradual ascension to the status of "boy who
lived" is complemented by his growing involvement with girls. His first
girlfriend, Cho Chang, is the former girlfriend of his rival Cedric Diggory.
His second girlfriend, and later his wife, is the sister of his best friend,
Ronald Weasley. What is interesting about both relationships is the association of the girls with the men with whom Harry shared close bonds.
Anthropologists like Levi-Strauss in their study of myth locate the Oedipal
bonds within the kinship structures of a social set. The heterosexual marriage system constitutes an exchange of women that checks the incest taboo
and also firms up the bonds between communities. Eve Kosofky Sedgwick
widens Levi-Strauss's principle of kinship and the role of women into a
broader arena of male homosociality, especially as depicted in literature.
In her reading of the erotic triangles figuring prominently in European
fiction, she mentions dynamics of power that structure the rivalry between
the two active members of the triangle — that is, the male lovers — where

the "bond that links the two rivals is as intense and potent as the bond that links either of the rivals to the beloved: that the bonds of 'rivalry' and 'love,' differently as they are experienced, are equally powerful and in many senses equivalent" ("Gender Asymmetry" 524). Heterosexual relationships therefore become the medium through which male bonding is enacted. Sedgwick's study takes this triangle out of the transhistorical Oedipal paradigm and places it in power networks conditioning a particular context. By the term *desire*, Sedgwick emphasizes the affective and powerful social forces as they manifest in a variety of ways, including hostility. Pedagogy, strong male peer groups, friendships and rivalries are instances of socially established confluence between homosociality and homosexuality. In adolescent fiction, especially fantasy, this strong and intimate bond between male rivals signals a continuity of traditional gender relations. The desexualization of the bond, and the element of homophobia that becomes an essential part of it, reinforces the place and role of women, making female sexuality a threat as well as an attraction. The requirements of a normal course of development insist on giving way to the attraction and hence entering the normative heterosexual relationship, but all the while it is the male homosocial bonds that retain their place of prime importance. Triangles figure repeatedly in Rowling's story: Harry-Hermione-Ron, Harry-Ginny-Ron, Ron-Hermione-Krum, Harry-Cho-Cedric, Snape-Lily-James. In each case, intense bonds between the rivals play a greater role. Snape's life and relationships are as much dictated by his love for Harry's mother as by the hatred for his father. Insecurities trail Ron and his relationship with Hermione. Cho Chang seems to reinforce the rivalry between Harry and Cedric during the Triwizard tournament. In the Harry-Ginny-Ron triangle, things are even more complicated. Ginny and Ron in the initial books appear in a similar position. Ron feels inferior and overshadowed by his older brothers while Ginny is ignored since she is the only girl. Ron also feels overshadowed by Harry. Ginny, on the other hand, is tongue tied in Harry's presence when she is young. However, on growing up, she turns out to be more confident and competent than Ron. Yet in the final quest, Ron takes precedence over Ginny.[19] Harry's relationship with Ginny is never a problem, but Harry agonizes over Ron's reaction as her brother and how their friendship might be breached by the relationship. Such homosocial agonizing retains the homoerotic subtext that is veiled by the conventional narratives of heterosexuality and masculinity.

Sexuality therefore emerges as a prominent aspect of the adolescent narrative precisely because it is an ideological minefield. Roberta Trites remarks that "experiencing sexuality marks a rite of passage that helps them (adolescents) define themselves as having left behind childhood" (84). The course of development portrayed by the hero monomyth often approaches heterosexual relationships as the end of the sexual journey that traverses through the queer and deviant regions, ultimately affirming the patriarchal status quo, no matter how libratory the intentions are. However, Roderick McGillis, in his study of writers like George McDonald and Frances Hodgson Burnett, argues that though a fairy tale draws clear distinctions between masculine and feminine according to the norms of the patriarchy, it queers the gender norms by confounding the apparent boundaries (2003). Ximena Gallardo C. and C. Jason Smith point out the prototype of the Cinderella story that co-exists in Rowling's story along with the hero monomyth (196).

The most crucial stage in Harry's growth is the move from active heroism, from the reckless "saving the people thing" to a more thoughtful self-sacrificing passivity. After the death of Dobby, in choosing not to follow Voldemort in the pursuit of the Elder Wand, for the first time, Harry chooses "not to act." It confounds the conventional image of an aggressive male hero. He wins the battle not in a duel but in submitting to death. Since fantasy as a genre defines itself in terms of narratives that upset common expectations, such queering often features in fantasy. In almost a reverse fashion to Rowling's, another contemporary heroic fantasy, Tamora Pierce's *The Song of the Lioness* places Alanna, a female warrior knight, at the center of the knightly tradition. Pierce relates Alanna's story as that of her coming of age, from naïve girl who play-acts with wooden swords to becoming the King's Champion. Her training is structured in many ways like a school undercutting conventional ideas and notions of education and vocation appropriate for girls. The most important lessons for Alanna includes the acceptance that she is female knight, that is the acceptance of her gendered role as it coexists with a more aggressive, conventionally masculine role that she chooses herself. Similarly, in Trudi Canavan's *The Magician's Guild*, the plot is set in motion when the traditional status quo of all-male wizard group is upset by the discovery of magical talents in a girl. The cross-gendering of the stories — that is, placing a boy at the center of a quintessentially girl's story or a girl at the center a traditionally male narrative — queers the foreground pattern of gendered growth. Such queer characters are deeply embedded in a complex network of power relations, especially the relations of power that determine the discourses of growth and development. Foucault remarks that "discourse transmits and produces power; it reinforces it, but also undermines and exposes it, renders fragile and *makes it possible to thwart it*" (*Discipline* 101, italics mine). Thus the point of investigation is not the acceptance or de-legitimization of queer tendencies in young adult fiction, but the way in which the queer subtext so insistently appears in context of adolescent fantasy as a destabilizing function, despite its community-affirming heterosexual resolution. It is this feature rather than the narrative of straight linear development that makes the fantasy the preferred genre of adolescent fiction; fantasy becomes a means of dealing with the dynamics of power and repression, reinforcing, and undercutting simultaneously the narrative of normative development. Complex representations of sexuality frequently occur in coming of age fantasy. The end of Phillip Pullman's *His Dark Materials* enacts the Christian fall from grace in terms of the sexual awakening of its young protagonists. However, in a narrative that overlays theology with discourses of power, repression and resistance, the adolescent enactment of the fall seems to undercut the theological purpose. The fall itself becomes a complex narrative where adolescent sexuality becomes central to restoring the equilibrium of the universe. It becomes life affirming and grants grace, rather than the other way round.

The biblical account also connects the theme of sexuality with the twin theme of death. Sexual awakening and growth signals the end of innocence and also an awareness of mortality, an understanding that death defines existence in terms of limits of the body. The first person to die in the Potter series is Cedric Diggory, the "rightful Champion of Hogwarts," Harry's rival in the Triwizard tournament and also for Cho's affections. The theme of mortality is reinforced by the figure of Voldemort, first a monstrous baby and then the rejuvenated Dark Lord defying death. Structurally, the ritual at the graveyard and the isolation that follows in the subsequent year might be is what Campbell calls the journey through "the belly of the whale," undertaken by heroes like Odysseus in his visit to the world of the dead or by Frodo and Sam in their lonely tract to Mordor after the Fellowship breaks. According to Campbell, "the hero, instead of conquering or conciliating the power of the threshold, is swallowed into the unknown, and would appear to have died" (Campbell 90). The physical body of the hero may be slain or dismembered in the course. Pettigrew cuts Harry's hand to draw blood that will revive Voldemort. Like the hero who dies to be born again, Harry returns after dueling with the Dark Lord. Later on he faces the Dementors, has to defend himself in the wizard court, and suffers Dumbledore's neglect. *Harry Potter and the Order of the Phoenix* ends with the death of Sirius and Harry's self-inflicted isolation.

The subsequent book ends with the death of Dumbledore. The attitude to death is complex and conflicted in Rowling's story. To an extent, death is linked with the theme of separation from the parents, as it is in most children's fiction.[20] Along with the death of Cedric and Sirius, all the deaths are structurally important; most of the heroic figures threatening to overshadow Harry are removed from the narrative to allow the adolescent hero achieve complete freedom. Sirius, the dashing and reckless godfather with a tragic past, often threatens to overshadow Harry. Similarly, Harry cannot make his own decisions or become the most powerful wizard as long as Dumbledore is alive. In the end, he goes to meet Voldemort alone, prepared to sacrifice himself. Death is the ultimate authority; those who die do not come back to life even in the world of magic. Thus the death of Cedric Diggory is the precursor to the emotional maturity that is essential for the *Bildungsroman* of the adolescent hero. According to Trites' reading of sexuality and death themes in adolescent fiction,

> in order to mature, teenagers must understand that sexuality is a powerful tool, that they are mortal and will therefore die, that they must both break free from and accept the authority figures in their lives, and that they are institutionally situated creatures, as all people are. If the use of institutions, if the teenager's rebellion against parental authority, if the adolescent protagonist and the very narrative itself are Being-toward-death in a movement simultaneously designed to admit and deny death's power over the human body — then what is the ideological message of the adolescent novel? With incredible consistency, the answer is this: You shall know your power and that power shall set you free — that is, until you begin to abrogate institutional power or parental power or sexual power or the very power of death itself, in which case, the narrative will remind you of your powerlessness as surely as Harry Potter must return at the end of every school year to reside in relative impotence with his Muggle relatives ["The Harry Potter Novels" 10].

Towards the end of the narrative Harry submits to the power of death voluntarily. The return from the world of dead links entry into adulthood with biblical resurrection. Hope, therefore, comes to fruition only once the hero completes the transition and matures to recognize the limits of his power.

However, adolescent fiction, especially fantasy, seems to problematize such neat resolutions. The Forbidden Forest surrounding the school is often linked to the theme of death and resurrection. It is here that Harry first sees Voldemort drinking the blood of unicorns in order to survive. Harry himself repeatedly enters the forest and returns after life-threatening encounters with giant spiders, Dementors and centaurs. In the last act of sacrifice, he surrenders to Voldemort in the forest and yet survives. Thus, the forest is linked with Harry's repeated encounters with death and return. Lois Lowry's *The Messenger* is another text that links the motif of journey through the forest with the themes of adolescence and death. The protagonist Matty is one of the few people who can negotiate through the "living" forest that surrounds the community dwelling. However, in the last journey through the forest, the forest starts closing up and attacking Matty and his companion. In the life-threatening moments, Matty discovers his special gift of healing, through which he manages to save his companion and also restore the balance of the forest. His last act, like Harry, is to save the community at the expense of his life. Thus the special powers of an adolescent, which help him negotiate with death, are complemented by a wider social and cultural vision. In Pullman's *The Amber Spyglass*, Lyra and Will visit the world of the dead at the risk of great pain and death. They set the souls of the dead free from the eternal torture to become a part of life and nature after dying. According to Campbell, it is in this repeated crossing of the threshold by entering and returning from the zones forbidden to others wherein the power of the hero lies.

Often the narrative seems to defy death, for instance by the means of moving photographs, portraits in which a person continues to live or the choice to become a ghost. Death is described as "the greatest adventure" (Rowling, *PS* 215) in the first book. At the end of *Harry Potter and the Order of the Phoenix*, Harry searches for a means to contact Sirius beyond the veil of death and finally learns to accept the inexorability of death. Yet he meets Sirius again during his final walk to the forest. And the end, Sirius describes it as "easier than falling asleep" (Rowling, *DH* 561). At the end of *Harry Potter and the Prisoner of Azkaban*, Harry sees himself from afar and assumes that he has seen his father. The physical resemblance signifies that his father exists in him, as Dumbledore points out in the exposition at the end of the book. The dead parents return to help him in his duel with Voldemort in the graveyard. Even when dead, Dumbledore continues to aid and guide Harry's quest through Snape. On his walk to the forest in *Harry Potter and the Deathly Hallows*, Harry is able to see and talk to his parents and Sirius and Remus through the Resurrection Stone.

Harry's return from the King's Cross station after facing the killing curse is linked with the structural function of the "crossing of the return threshold" that links hero's return "from the mystic realm into the land of common day" (Campbell 216). Harry's death in the forest, the crossing over to another liminal place like King's Cross Station and the return to the forest completes the heroic adventure. Once again putting the concerns for the community ahead of any personal desire is a crucial moment of triumph for Harry when he surpasses his greatest mentor. If Voldemort is like the first brother in the "Tale of Three Brothers" by Beadle the Bard, who sought to defeat death by the Elder Wand, and Dumbledore is the second brother who tried to bring the dead to life, Harry is like the third brother who willingly chooses to die by coming out of the cloak of invisibility and bequeathing it to his son. He uses the Resurrection Stone as he seeks help in his sacrifice, almost like the way he used the Mirror of Erised when he was eleven years old, without any sense of personal advantage. Dumbledore, on the other hand, looked for the Resurrection Stone to bring back his family, but when he finds it, the cursed Resurrection Stone ring brings about his end. The story of his end is foretold in the story of the second brother in the "Tale of Three Brothers" who recalls the woman he loved from death. Once he discovers that "she was sad and cold, separated from him as by a veil" (Rowling, *DH* 332) he loses his mind and dies. At different moments, Harry identifies with and then distances himself from various father figures in consciously choosing to be different. It is by surpassing Dumbledore that Harry becomes the "master of death," or what Campbell calls the "the master of two worlds" as he

> gives up completely all attachment to his personal limitations, idiosyncrasies, hopes and fears, no longer resists the self-annihilation that is prerequisite to rebirth in the realization of truth, and so becomes ripe, at last for the great at-one-ment. His personal ambitions are totally dissolved, he no longer tries to live but willingly relaxes to whatever may come to pass in him; he becomes, that is to say an anonymity [Campbell 237].

The last act of heroic performance is therefore of complete submission — submission to death which is portrayed as a willing and conscious surrender made with complete control and awareness. Death becomes not a moment of recognition of one's powerlessness, but the moment of realization of continuity into the future. The "freedom to live," the last stage of Campbell's analysis of myth corresponds to marriage and ascension to throne in Proppian formula. In the case of an orphan, with the death of the antagonist coincides with finding a home. However, such freedom and wish fulfillment comes only after "the reconciliation of the individual consciousness with the universal will" (Campbell 238).

Through their dealings with the authority figures of the world of the adult and ultimately with the authority of death itself, the adolescent protagonists ensure that death becomes an important stage in the rejuvenation of life in the universe. In *Bridge to Terabithia*, the death of Leslie Burke depresses Jess Aaron till he shares his fantastic world of Terabithia with his younger sister, who takes the place of his dead friend. Adolescent fantasy, thus, to an extent, seems to negotiate with the power of death as the ultimate authority. The success lies in accepting continuity, in seeing death as the "next great adventure" in the series of events. It is exemplified by Fred Weasley, one of the pranksters-in-chief at Hogwarts who dies laughing at the joke told by his staid and serious brother Percy. It undercuts the teleology of adolescent fiction as being towards death. Death, therefore, becomes an adventure in the playfulness of adolescence. It takes on the fearful aspect of the ultimate hostile authority only when seen as something that puts an end to the narratives of growth, maturity and ambition of an individual. Voldemort, as mentioned earlier, is a model for a potential trajectory of growth available to Harry. In his fear of death, then, Voldemort embodies the humanist narrative of teleological growth.[21]

Fantasy then problematizes that implicit ideological narrative of the hero which seeks to contain the story of growth. It also undercuts the narratives about the limitations of an adolescent's potential power. According to McCallum, "texts which situate characters on the margins of a culture or society can offer positions from which to interrogate the social and cultural boundaries which limit subjectivity, and hence question dominant social and cultural paradigms of identity formation" (118). Narrative strategies that frame the quest of the marginalized adolescent hero in a fantasy also open the interstices of the ideological networks to questioning. The narrative of being saved by the adolescent hero can be read as a narrative of cultural affirmation in which the adolescent saves the community by becoming a part of it, by taking the place of the parents. However, though the adolescent may take the place of their parents, they are not their parents. Adolescent fantasies like the Potter series engages with the issues of power and authority, even that of death, in a way that, while the movement towards conformity and normativity allays the adult anxiety, the idea of being saved by an adolescent who joins the milieu is undercut by the idea of being saved by an adolescent hero who embodies the disruptive and disturbing potential of adolescent non-conformity. In the Potter series, the first step of Harry and his friends towards saving the world is to break away from the decaying official establishments of the magical world. The idea of social continuity and rejuvenation through a conventional end coexists with the break and the figure of an adolescent hero embodies the two simultaneously. In a sense, then, adolescent fantasy has a postmodern impetus at its core. By its queerness and deviance it reveals the incoherence and ruptures in the social, cultural and political power relations. Jacqueline Rose underlines the impossibility of children's literature in the underlying agenda of growth and development. The adolescence of adolescent fiction, or rather the possibility of adolescence in adolescent fiction, lies in the elements that spill over the linear narrative of coming of age. The next chapter explores another template of the growth in young adult fiction — a school boy. As a text centered on the figure of a schoolboy, the Potter series and its predecessor — the boarding-school fiction — become a means to explore the role of education, discipline and instruction that are integral to the discourses of childhood. The chapter examines the role of adolescence and fantasy within the framework of a school that creates space for a dialogue, for potentially disturbing the universe.

2

The Schoolboy

"Do I dare Disturb the universe?"

The famous question of J. Alfred Prufrock captures the dilemma of the middle-aged protagonist when confronted with the structures of his "universe." Prufrock ultimately gives in to the sense of futility and slides into the monotony of everyday life. In Eliot's poem, the protagonist decides not to dare, that he is not Prince Hamlet; rather Prufrock chooses to be Polonius, "the attendant lord" who will be "Deferential, glad to be of use; Politic, cautious, and meticulous." About half a century later, the same question puzzles Jerry Renault, the victimized adolescent hero of Robert Cormier's *The Chocolate War*. The words from Eliot's poem taunt Renault till he decides to "dare" by defying the institutional authority of the headmaster-in-acting and the bullying students body, the Vigils. The story ends with Renault in the hospital, severely beaten and injured. Both texts conclude with the protagonist's realization of the futility of resisting their oppressive universe. However, in Renault's case the realization accompanies a sense of tragedy; the act of disturbing the universe of the school remains heroic despite its failure. In the Potter series, Harry and his friends also decide to "dare"—by resisting the bullying power block of the magical world, the misguided goodness of the benevolent guardians and the dark powers that are on the rise. They emerge as heroes of their world. For Prufrock, Renault, Potter and also for their widely different set of readers, the question reflects the desire to test the limits and the feasibility of such a desire. Trites (who derives the title of her book on the dynamics of power in young adult fiction from the same question) insists that the question is as germane to an adolescent as it is to the aging, balding protagonist of Eliot's poem. The question addresses the issue of "I" with respect to the universe, its (dis)location within it and the anxiety about disturbing the universe. In a way, since adolescence is already in a peculiar relation to the surrounding universe, the question is latent in its very existence. Social discourses of education and citizenship situate the transitional experience of adolescence firmly within its cultural context. Institutions like schools link ideologies with practice, framing the rebellion and angst as a stage within the broader movement towards acceptance and integration, hence attempting to secure the adolescent within the universe with minimal disturbance.

The movement is often expressed by the structural paradigm of the rites of passage that manifests in a variety of ways — in the hero myth or, as we shall see in the present chapter, the school story. The three stages of the ritual — separation, initiation, integration — correspond to the acculturation and socialization of the solipsistic child into the society as an important member, thereby reproducing the structures of his/her social universe. This structural pattern of the initiation rites described by anthropologists like Arnold Van Gennep and Victor Turner is clearly evident in the narratives that deal with growth and education like school fiction. The tripartite division of the rite corresponds to the structure of the boarding school stories. They mostly begin with the preparations to depart from home followed by the journey to the school. The central focus of the text is on essential features of schooling like classes, peer group, teachers, and sports, and finally they end with the journey back home. The ritualistic pattern of the novel of formal education and training, or *erziehungsroman*, is linked with the ideological apparatus that expresses and reinforces the ideational dimensions of adolescence, growth and development.

Rowling's story integrates the two paradigms of coming of age: the hero myth with the school story from which she derives the structure of the seven books of the Potter series. The following discussion deals with one of the central themes of most children's and adolescent fiction — the theme of education, especially on fiction centering on the institution of school, which is interlinked with the themes of fantasy, magic and wizard apprenticeship. By focusing on the school fiction, the study intends to explore the social, cultural and political investments in the pattern of schooling, in the concept of growth and in the figure of a student. The genre is infiltrated by pedagogical ideas like the conception of an ideal citizen, the role of education and, more significantly, the role of school beyond imparting the prescribed syllabus.

As pointed out earlier in the study, the concepts of adolescence, childhood, and also the school are, to a large extent, the functions of the cultural order. The school story, as one of the literary genres specific to children's fiction, textualizes this major cultural preoccupation. The didactic concerns of the culture, which serve as the ideological subtext for most genres of coming of age fiction, become clear and well-defined goals in a school story. Rousseau's treatise on the education of a "natural" child takes the form of an *erziehungsroman*. It ends with the successful integration of Emile in the society — a prototypical school story whose logical end is the entry into the cultural setup, which, though beset with degeneracy, is the inevitable goal of growth and maturation. The hope embodied by the subject, then, lies in upholding value systems and standards in their purity; the childish "innocence," therefore, derives much of its value from its potential to be educated, integrated and thus be made a part of the adult world. The school story, as a narrative emerging from a specific cultural context and being situated in a socio-cultural institution like a school, is doubly bound to ideals and ideologies of its epoch. Beverly Lyons Clark summarizes the context succinctly in saying that a school story thematizes and narrates it own textuality: "the school story self-divides, invaginates itself, is larger than itself. A story about school is a school" (*Regendering* 7).

The *Potter* series, as a coming of age fantasy, conflates these themes of learning and acculturation with the themes of magic and enchantment. In Rowling's story, the education of a schoolboy and his integration into the world is juxtaposed against the fantastical world of an apprentice wizard who begins as an outcast and in whose rebellion lies the hope for rejuvenation of the society at large. The "abnormal" or queer powers of the apprentice wizard exert a crucial and often unsettling influence on the linear narratives of growth. The presence of magic, therefore, adds another dimension to the adolescent question: "Do I dare Disturb the Universe?" Fantasy starts with a disturbance in the pattern of normalcy. As mentioned earlier, magic, the defining feature of the *marvelous* fantastic, is a strange or a "queer" force. Thus, an adolescent wizard is the "other," the doubly marginalized protagonist whose potential to disturb the universe spills beyond the conventional course of angst, acceptance and acculturation. Magic places the act of "disturbing the universe" in ambiguous relations to the norms — rather than a straight acceptance or refusal, it expresses a set of vexed relations with normalcy, calling into question its fixity and rigidity. Therefore, Hogwarts School of Witchcraft and Wizardry offers an interesting framework to locate the moves and the countermoves between the two poles of disobedience and discipline, of subversion and submission — in other words, the journey from the liminality of adolescence to adulthood in a specific social and ideological context.

Hogwarts is carefully modeled on the regular British schools that have appeared repeatedly in children's fiction framing the aspirations of children across the world. Like regular schoolchildren, Harry and his friends attend classes, do their lessons, take exams and so on. The annual progress to the next grade, house rivalries, and tensions among the students are basic to the movement of the plot. The story begins with the journey to the school, an important motif in school stories symbolizing the movement towards isolation from the adult world, entry into a transitional phase of life among the peer group and preparation for subsequent socialization and re-integration in the adult world.

The *Potter* series, then, seems to fit neatly into the genre of boarding-school fiction and its "tradition of providing a moral tale as well as a ripping good yarn" (Steege 151). Critics like David Steege, Karen M. Smith and Charles Elster have provided a detailed analysis of the elements of boarding-school fiction in the Potter series pointing out the close parallels like the code of honor, sticking together with peers and never telling tales, the hostile encounters with the school bully, the "rule of three" that operated in many boarding schools to discourage "unnatural" closeness among the students, the centrality of sports in the life of a schoolboy, and above all, the elitist assumptions that formed the basis of British boarding school. Hogwarts follows a neat system of hierarchy and segmentation, a characteristic of popular boarding schools as portrayed in *Tom Brown's Schooldays*, *Stalky and Co.* or *Eric, or Little by Little*. At the topmost level is the headmaster, followed by a deputy, the heads of the houses, other teachers, the prefects and the sports captains, and finally the students divided according to their seniority. Apart from the educational pyramid, there are other people like Filch, the caretaker; Hagrid, the gamekeeper; and lastly the Hogwarts house-elves who work in the kitchens and remain invisible for most of the narrative. The features, the rules and the history of the school are all well documented in the world of magic. Like the children in the school stories, Harry's rule breaking and punishments do not detract the attention from his overall goodness. These similarities between Rowling's magical school and regular boarding schools have led readers like Pico Iyer (who finds his own experience at British boarding school reflected in the series) to doubt the element of fantasy in the series.

> This kind of writing for children, often misnamed "fantasy," that starts
> from something universal and speaks to some mythic core in us; there is

another kind, of which Harry Potter is a grand exemplar that simply tweaks the particular in a magical direction.

Indeed, Rowling's story of the schooling of an apprentice wizard is peculiar in terms of its socio-cultural specificity onto which it self-consciously holds. In situating her narrative in a school, Rowling's story addresses the cultural concerns not just of the magical world. Nation building and the idea of citizenship have been central to the genre of boarding-school fiction whose emergence coincided with the rise of British imperialism. P. W. Musgrave, in his study of boys' school stories, assigns a precise time of birth and death to the genre: "The genre was conceived around the middle of the last century and was almost dead before the Second World War" (1). The concern with the purity of whiteness is central to the genre that draws its protagonists from the British countryside as the "progenies of the natural winners, inheritors of the fighting stock" (Bonnett 156). In the earlier parts of his story, Thomas Hughes firmly grounds his adolescent schoolboy hero Tom Brown within the English country life. Kipling's Stalky becomes a flamboyant officer in the Imperial Service to India. This ideal of an English citizen encodes the covert message of the superiority of the English Empire and of a certain group within that Empire — and this elitist ideal lies at the heart of boarding-school fiction. Therefore, the historical and geographical specificity of the genres Rowling chooses to write in bring in the themes of power, colonialism and multiculturalism and explores them in the twentieth-century context. Conscious references to issues like racism and terror make for intense political engagements. Therefore, in choosing to write a school story, Rowling's narrative revives the political program that powered the genre since its very inception.

That the schools were first set up for ecclesiastical recruiting itself points out the ideological foundations of the institution (Aries 137). Aries discusses the evolution of the educational institution as central to the evolution of the concept of childhood and later adolescence. Apart from highlighting the social attitude towards children, the educational institutions, despite their much-celebrated ideals and neutrality of knowledge, also reflect, reinforce and reformulate the social ideals and ideologies. The rise of schools, secular education, gradation into classes, the concept of a boarding school and, most significantly, the idea of student discipline all together went into the formation of the modern ideas of childhood, innocence and youth. The passage from primary education in local grammar schools to the university marked the passage from childhood to adolescence and ultimately adulthood.

Boarding schools, which figured prominently in British children's fiction over the last two centuries, came into being, from what Aries calls pedagogicas, annexes to the colleges where the students lodged. What were once merely lodging houses later changed into places where an eye was kept on the studies as well as on the moral principles and leisure interests of the pupil. Thus, school learning clearly has wider implications than simply training a student for future vocation. Melanie Klien, in her essay "The Role of the School in the Libidinal Development of the Child," asserts that school and learning are from the first *libidinally* determined for everyone. The nurturing environment of home is replaced with a strict and rigid system of institutional authority that compels a child to sublimate his/her instinctual energies. In a way, the transition to adulthood through the process of schooling can be taken as the second phase of entry into the *symbolic* order of society. If fantasy of union with the parent, as argued in the previous chapter, coincides with the imaginary phase of the mirror stage, then deviance that coincides with adolescence is another phase that needs to be overcome during the course of normal growth. The function of the school is to guide an adolescent to overcome his/her "abnormalities" or deviance and gradually merge into the symbolic networks that define the adult community. This is the only "normal" course of growth available within the cultural networks. In the cultural narratives of boyhood, repeated emphasis lies on the need for guidance and instruction to reign in boisterousness and indiscipline. Thus, the genre of adolescent fiction centering on schools is extremely self-conscious. Dr. Arnold, the famous education reformist of Victorian England and the headmaster in Thomas Hughes' *Tom Brown's Schooldays*, sums up this view of education in one of the first school fiction novels published for boys in 1857[1]:

> The object of all schools is not to ram Latin and Greek into boys, but to make them good English boys, good future citizens; and by far the most important part of that work must be done, or not done, out of school hours. To leave it, therefore, in the hands of inferior men, is just giving up the highest and hardest part of the education. Were I a private schoolmaster, I should say, Let who will hear the boys their lessons, but let me live with them when they are at play and rest [64].

The conventional heroes of school stories are boys like Tom Brown and Stalky, depicted as adolescent rebels, defying authority through their larks and escapades. The narrative of the adolescent protagonist, therefore, follows the dictum "boys will be boys" who will, as they grow, give up rebellion in favor of integration and maturation. Jefferey Richards locates the significance of the genre in its gender code: "books tell us something about the boy's mind and the experience of boyhood. For it is a remarkable fact that the best school stories have been more often than not written for boys; that is to say the authors have been literally or metaphorically boys" (*Happiest Days* 6). The books, therefore, serve as a kind of psychological insight into "the phenomenon of the boy-man, the permanent adolescent" (6).

However, the co-existence of novels of education and training for girls illustrate the ideological subtext of boarding-school fiction that links education with sexuality and gender. In Sarah Fielding's *The Governess; or the Little Female Academy*, a story about the education of young girls published in 1749, the principle aim of the tutor, Mrs. Teachum, is to "improve their minds in all useful knowledge; to render them obedient to their superiors, and gentle, kind and affectionate to each other; yet she [Mrs. Teachum] did not omit teaching them an exact neatness in their persons and dress, and a perfect gentility in their whole carriage" (1). Two centuries later, in 1946, the headmistress of the Malory Towers, Enid Blyton's fictional school, announced a similar agenda to the newcomers in the school.

> One day you will leave school and go out into the world as young women. You should take with you eager minds, kind hearts and a will to help. You should take with you good understanding of many things, and a willingness to accept responsibility and show yourselves as women to be loved and trusted. All these things you will learn at Malory Towers — if you will. I do not count as our successes those who have won scholarships and passed exams, though these are good things to do. I count as our successes those who learn to be good-hearted and sensible and trustable, good, sound women the world can lean on. Our failures are those who do not learn these things in the years they are here [*First Term at Malory Towers* 7].

Learning is expressed through the motif of a student as a receptacle; the language is often replete with aggression. The metaphors in the above examples range from gentle but firm handling in girl's school stories ("to render them obedient to their superiors," "All these things you will learn at Malory Towers — if you *will*") to almost aggressive violence in the boy's fiction ("the object of all schools is not to ram Latin and Greek into boys"). In conventional terms, then, education becomes an exercise of domination, structured in terms of a student-teacher relationship that is one-directional. Power dynamics at the core of an educational institution make it a central ideological apparatus of a community where "an apprenticeship in a variety of know-how (is) wrapped up in the massive inculcation of the ideology of the ruling class" (Althusser 156).

Michel Foucault therefore describes the school, along with the hospital and military organizations, as a panoptical society, a society in which "it is possible for the authority to maintain control and power by simply presenting the idea that individuals are constantly under observation" (*Discipline* 197). Such psychological manipulation is an effective instrument of discipline in schools. For instance, in Rowling's series, at Smeltings, the school Harry's cousin Dudley is slated to attend, the peer group itself is converted into a panopticon through "the knobbly sticks, used for hitting each other while the teachers weren't looking. This was supposed to be good training for later life" (Rowling *PS* 29). Therefore, disciplinary policies, isolation and physical confinement in schools reinforce the social codes like honor, competition, elitism and the thrust on tradition and rituals. The flip side is the ensuing sense of claustrophobia and sense of physical incarceration in a boarding school (all of which Orwell discusses at length in his anti-school essay "Such, Such Were the Joys"). The rules and codes of discipline that generate conformity are complemented by the punishment meted out to the transgressors.[2] The clash with authority results either in submission and hence "normalization" of deviant elements, or, if the adolescent refuses such normalization, into a kind of monsterization of the deviant protagonist and his/her eventual elimination. Therefore, school stories not only serve as ideals of conformity but also as moral lessons, full of warnings. Frederic W. Farrar, in the preface to the first edition of *Eric, or Little by Little*, writes:

> The story of "Eric" was written with but one single object — the vivid inculcation of inward purity and moral purpose, by the history of a boy who in spite of the inherent nobleness of his disposition, falls into all folly and wickedness, until he has learnt to seek help from above. I am deeply thankful to know — from testimony public and private, anonymous and acknowledged — that this object has, by God's blessing, been fulfilled.

Dudley's "knobbly stick" therefore seems to be a metaphor for the education system that seeks to impose control. The arbitrary nature of the rule to hit each other when the teachers are not looking highlights the symbolic violence, which, according to Pierre Bourdieu and Jean Claude Passerson, is inevitable in pedagogic apparatus that seeks "the imposition and inculcation of a cultural arbitrary by an arbitrary mode of imposition and inculcation (education)" (6). More recently, the disturbing subtext of the school stories has been explored in an offshoot of school fiction that includes books like J. D. Salinger's *The Catcher in the Rye* and the Robert Cormier's *The Chocolate War*. While Salinger's Holden Caulfield undergoes a complete nervous breakdown, Cormier leaves Jerry Renault critically injured. Ironic comment on the issue is Anthony Horowitz's school, the Groosham Grange, an institution for drop-outs and misfits which is manned by monsters like werewolves and vampires. Groosham Grange, therefore, as its brochure tells the parents, is the only school with its own cemetery. Similarly, the motto of Lemony Snicket's Austere Academy is equally bizarre — "Memento Mori" — "Remember Death" — dark words especially when inscribed on the gates of a school. If school fiction is another form of the coming of age story that ends with the adolescent subject entering in adulthood, then this is the warning to the deviants, the students who refuse to submit to the normal pattern of growth and choose to remain outsiders.

Thus, the "correct" pattern of growth in school fiction is a complex of dominant positions on a variety of cultural concerns — sexuality, gender, class and race. These are the "real" themes of education which unite to form the social system of a boarding school in fiction. Marxist scholar Ivan Illich highlights the logic of economic capital that dictates the entire institutional structure of a school, the way economics and class systems become conflated with scholarship and degrees. The self-replicating hierarchies of power were the usual norm in single-sex boarding schools where admission requirements favored students whose parents have been alumni, the cost of tuition precludes lower-income applicants, and the elitist and privileged peers marginalized the scholarship students. Therefore, Smeltings, the school Dudley attends, was also attended by his father, reminding one of the prized families patronizing Eton, Rugby or even Enid Blyton's Malory Towers, or St. Clare's. A school like Smeltings then represents a social microcosm, complete with its divisions and hierarchies.

Culture therefore centers its energies on maintaining the "innocence" of a child by discipline and constant monitoring through the means of school authorities, peer group and parental control. What is at stake is the image of a schoolboy as the breeding ground of the future generations. The concerns of normative sexuality are transmuted in the concerns of race and class that surround a schoolboy, especially in context of same-sex boarding schools. Thus boarding-school fiction, with its pedagogic impulse, comes with ingrained homophobia and homosociality. The greatest insult is a term like "fairy"; in *The Chocolate War* it ends the passive resistance of Jerry Renault.[3] The reason, as Foucault points out, is that the deviant schoolboy, "the child surrounded by domestic servants, tutors, and the governess, who was in danger of compromising not so much physical strength as his intellectual capacity, his moral fiber, and the obligation to preserve a healthy line of descent for his family and social class" (*History* 121).

These disturbing implications of boarding-school fiction become even more complex in the story of Harry Potter, a school story of an apprentice wizard. At Hogwarts, the talent of magic is common. It is the talent that grants entry into the school of magic and is honed to perfection by its curriculum. Margaret Oakes sees it as a form of alternate technology, which enables wizards and witches to work in a faster, abler and more efficient manner than their muggle counterparts. Therefore, Harry, in possessing magical skills, is same as the rest of his peers at Hogwarts though his history of violence and fame precedes him.

But, as pointed out in the introduction, adolescent fantasy establishes a difference between magic as a common talent and magic as a power wielded by those on the sidelines of society. The essence of magic as a power lies in its inherent subversiveness — the secrecy, isolation and element of threat that characterize it. It is in the sense of being a threat to the status quo that magic is cognate with the power of the adolescent protagonists. Its threat is embodied by the bottom-up power that upsets the hierarchy and therefore needs to be controlled. In the Potter series, as discussed in the last chapter, it is embodied by the Marauders, by the Weasley twins, by the strange headmaster, and most of all, by Harry Potter in his constant refusal to follow rules and submit to authority. As an other of the dominant paradigm of knowledge, magic serves as an adolescent's answer to the adult power systems.

Therefore, most adolescent fantasy focuses on exceptionally gifted youngsters — "gifted" not merely in terms of possessing a "different" set of skills but in their potential to wield those skills as their unique form of power, in their willingness to engage in the wider socio-political discourses rather than submit to the paradigm of adult-child relationship that seeks to relegate children outside such discourses. Though Phillip Pullman's trilogy *His Dark Materials* celebrates the complicated technologies of the alternate worlds with inventive devices like Lee Scoresby's balloon, the "intention craft" and the gyroptors, these adult inventions are easily destructible. On the other hand are the marvelous instruments of the young protagonists: the golden compass or the altheiometer and the subtle knife. These are something more than mere technical inventions. Useful only to the specially gifted children, they give them insights to the future, and access to alternate worlds. This complex association of magic with adolescence comes to an end with the entry into adulthood where similar powers can be recovered only by years of diligent study and hard work.[4] The point then is not that these youngsters can do magic, but rather that they use it as a form of their power as outsiders. The youthful subversion that the school stories seek to neutralize is acknowledged as a powerful force and hence, the need for apprenticeship under the wise old wizard who guides the educational quest. Therefore, unlike "he knobbly stick," the instrument of discipline in Dudley's uniform, Harry's wand symbolizes the power of the other, the magic that lies outside the rules of normativity or official authority.

As a school of apprentice wizards, the Hogwarts School of Witchcraft and Wizardry embodies a dialogic tension between the ideals of schooling that underlies school fiction and its magical syllabi. Though elements like institutional structure, the method of instruction, and the goals of education are similar to regular school education, growth is patterned not just on the structure set up by the educational institutions; it is complemented by the strange and "uncustomary" power of magic. Hence, as a school of magic, Hogwarts is central to the magical society. As the series progresses, Hogwarts becomes a place of "uncustomary" even within the magical world, especially in its relation to the authority structures of the magical world.

Thus the story of an apprentice wizard in a school of magic serves a dual purpose. Firstly, it schools magic, that is, reflects the institutionalization of the strange "abnormal" talent of magic in the magical world. The second function is paradoxical to the first. As a school of magic, it exists in a complex relationship with the dominant agencies of a society. Although as a school, it serves to institutionalize and control the youngsters, as a school of magic, it reflects on and often upturns the power equations that characterize a regular school.

Magic in the wizard world is situated in the networks of power, politics and economics. There is a clear demarcation between the "right" and "wrong" or dark magic. Children as well as adult wizards live according to the set of rules and laws laid down by the establishment. Despite the presence of unconventional teachers like Dumbledore, Lupin or Hagrid, the official establishments like the Board of Governors and the Ministry of Magic make rules that constrain the adolescent wizards. The wizard community is careful to safeguard its rights as wand carriers, keeping wands away from other magical races such as centaurs, goblins and the house-elves. The first legal punishment in the magical world is the breaking of the wand. Children are not permitted to do magic outside school. There are rules and punishments in place to prevent the abuse of magic by children and adults. Such official establishment of magical society is not peculiar to the Potter series. In the Chrestromanci world, Diana Wynne Jones underlines the importance of a government in the magical world: "The job Chrestomanci has is to make sure witches don't get out into worlds where there isn't so much magic and play havoc there. It's a big job" (*Charmed Life* 104). In LeGuin's Earthsea, Roke Island with the school of magic is protected by potent spells, magical wind and fog. Yet apart from being a center of learning, Roke Island is also the seat of government for the archipelago of the Earthsea world. Therefore, even as it serves as a space for the outsiders of the world, the magical society itself works through a neat system of rules and laws that keep the prevailing power dynamics in sway and the school of magic, in a way embodies this social and political power differential.[5]

At the same time, magic is synonymous with the power of agency and action, and hence, to an extent it embodies a threat since the agent of action always has the power of going against the rules and norms decreed by the dominant agencies. It is evident in the students' resistance against the decrees imposed by Dolores Umbridge, the representative of the Ministry of Magic at the school. Despite its isolation as a boarding school, in the later books, Hogwarts first becomes the center of an ideological tussle between the Ministry of Magic and the Order of the Phoenix, the dissenting underground group led by the headmaster, Albus Dumbledore. Later, it becomes the center of resistance against the Death Eaters, as the only institution that resists complete takeover by Voldemort. If magic is a queer, non-normative and deviant force as argued earlier, then a school of magic, which houses adolescents, the exiles and the dissenters — the marginalized in the hierarchy of power — is appropriately the center of the magical society. Due to this volatile paradox on which it stands, Hogwarts, unlike the regular schools which epitomize security, order and hierarchy, is a place of danger, strife and uncertainty.

The first reference to Hogwarts comes in the form of a strange letter addressed to "Mr. Harry Potter, The Cupboard under the Stairs, 4 Privet Drive, Little Whinging, Surrey" (Rowling *PS* 17). When the Dursleys choose to ignore it, a flurry of letters arrives from all possible places in the house — the post box, owls from the windows, the fireplace. The letters follow them even as they leave the house. The Dursleys are finally forced to face the strangeness when confronted with Hagrid, the half-giant emissary of the magical world. Thus, the letter of admission from Hogwarts itself upsets the normal power equation in the Dursley household, privileging Harry over his surrogate family. The preparations for the school mix the ordinary with the extraordinary. Nowhere is it more evident than in the list of books and supplies sent by the school.

> HOGWARTS SCHOOL OF WITCHCRAFT AND WIZARDRY
> Uniform
> *First-year students will require:*
> *Three sets of plain work robes (black)*
> *One plain pointed hat (black) for day wear*
> *One pair of protective gloves (dragon hide or similar)*
> *One winter cloak (black, silver fastenings)...*
>
> Other Equipment
> *1 wand*
> *1 cauldron (pewter, standard size 2)*
> *1 set glass or crystal phials*
> *1 telescope*
> *1 set brass scales*
>
> *Students may also bring an owl OR a cat OR a toad*
>
> PARENTS ARE REMINDED THAT FIRST-YEARS ARE NOT
> ALLOWED THEIR OWN BROOMSTICKS
>
> "Can we buy all this in London? " Harry wondered aloud.
> "If yeh know where to go," said Hagrid [*PS* 52–53].

Hagrid's reply directly links knowledge with power; Diagon Alley represents the seat of magical power that is denied to the muggles. The list draws the contours of the magical education; rather than a chaotic world of the unreasonable, the abnormal, or the strange, magical education is a highly organized affair. The availability of all these items in London itself hints at a secret society active within the metropolis, accessible only to those who "know." The school curriculum includes subjects like Transfiguration, Potions, Charms, Defense against Dark Arts and so on — branches of knowledge traditionally associated with magic and subsequently discredited. The subjects arouse discomfort and unease in their associations with the occult or illegitimate branches of knowledge. Transfiguration, for instance, as a magical subject subverts the Christian associations of the term. It deals with shape-shifting or metamorphosis. The students start with turning animals into inanimate objects and slowly graduate to more complex transfigurations like animagi, that is, wizards who can change into animals voluntarily. The subject complicates issues like selfhood, body, identity and so on. Thus shape-shifting has been a common trope to explore the darker aspects in the dynamics of selfhood, consciousness and identity in fantasies like *Dr. Jekyll and Mr. Hyde*. The subject of Potions, as described by Severus Snape, is clearly an occult offshoot of alchemy.

> As there is little foolish wand waving here, many of you would hardly believe this is magic. I don't expect you will really understand the beauty of the softly simmering cauldron with its shimmering fumes, the delicate power of liquids that creep through human veins, bewitching the mind, ensnaring the sense.... I can teach you how to bottle fame, brew glory, even stopper death [*PS* 102].

The Philosopher's Stone, which is central to the plot in the first book, combines the two best-known goals of the alchemists: transmutation of common metal to gold and the creation of the elixir of life that can "stopper death." One of the renowned scholars of the subject is Nicholas Flamel, a real, historically discredited alchemist who is said to have found the way to make the Philosopher's Stone.[6]

Therefore, Hogwarts sets itself up as the other of the dominant paradigm of the "legitimate" branches of knowledge. Hogwarts, the magical school, is meant to train and hone the rare inborn magical talents of the adolescent novices, and, therefore, it is a place of constant tussle between the institutionalization of magical talent into a routine skill and the flexible and open-ended paradigm of magic as knowledge and power.

Often, the knowledge essential to the wizard apprentice lies beyond the structures of formal education; it lies in the unorganized chaotic moments outside the timetable — in the dangers and obstacles of the quest. Apart from the practical education at Roke Island, LeGuin's wizard Ged also grows with his encounter with the dragon (when he becomes the dragon lord), and ultimately when he defeats the dark shadow that he had released from the underworld while boasting of his magical prowess. The shadow represents the darker aspect of self and Ged's ultimate victory lies in defeating it and thereby restoring the balance of his world. Therefore, in the paradigm of magic and fantasy, knowledge itself becomes a quest that is undertaken outside the classroom. In T. H. White's *The Once and Future King*, Merlin specially trains Arthur, the boy who would be the king, by transfiguring him into fish, birds and animals to learn "natural history." Commenting on later-day English education, Merlin even expresses distaste for normal conventions of boy's education like the focus on games and sport. Wynne Jones, in *The Lives of Christopher Chant*, establishes a clear dichotomy between the two kinds of knowledge.

The school that Chant attends prior to the discovery of his magical talent and which his friend from another world, Milie, aspires to attend is the school as it figures in boys' and girls' fiction. Milie is even given books by Angela Brazil, a well-known writer of girls' school stories. However, the text clearly separates the issue of wizard apprenticeship and regular schooling.

The queer nature of wizard's apprenticeship in coming of age fantasy constantly upsets this overt trajectory of linear growth and the institutionalized education of school story fiction. The process of growth in the Potter series is portrayed as a constant process of negotiation between social, cultural and political projects of growth and the power that rests with the adolescent subject. Such subversion in the *Potter* series, which starts with peculiar letters of admission, becomes more and more profound as Harry's education progresses. The strangeness is embodied by the headmaster Albus Dumbledore, to whom "normal" school teachers like McGonagall and Snape are subservient.[7]

So, in its troubled relationship with the impulses of containment that drive a school story, Hogwarts emerges as a space of adolescence. As a magical school, Hogwarts offers space for the adolescent wizard to exercise the power of choice. Like regular schools, the students are sorted in four houses that have a deep symbolic significance. The four houses of Hogwarts offer four distinct value systems, distinct set of ideologies to endorse and follow. The fact that most dark wizards are a product of Slytherin does not result in any official regulation against the house. In Hogwarts, the ideology of the Slytherin house, its belief in cunning and ambition is as valid as the bravery and courage that Gryffindors value. Harry's stay at Hogwarts begins with his choice of being a Gryffindor and not a Slytherin. Such choices are hardly made in isolation. The act of making a choice is a moment of active decision-making, a reflection on the alternatives and a deliberation over the consequences; it reflects on the agent, on what s/he wants and the way the choice helps to achieve that. Thus the moment of choice making is the moment of agency when the subject actively endorses or rejects a specific role model or ideology. Harry chooses to belong to the house that his parents belonged to, the house that Ron tells him "sounds by far the best, I hear Dumbledore himself was one" (*PS* 79); he rejects Slytherin knowing that "there's not a single witch or wizard who went bad who wasn't in Slytherin. You-Know-Who was one" (*PS* 61).

In a way then, despite the prophecy, Harry consciously follows the course that makes him Harry Potter, "the chosen one." At every crucial juncture, every character has a choice to follow an alternate course; each choice, each spur of the moment decision, has unforeseen repercussions.

Growth and identity formation are therefore shaped and reshaped constantly by the process of active negotiation with social, cultural and political structures. The initial books seem to endorse the liberal humanist framework that, according to Robyn McCallum, dictates most children's literature. Such assumptions are particularly true in fantasy literature where the emphasis is on the innate goodness of the protagonist, which makes him and only him worthy of undertaking the quest. However, though the narrative, as a fantasy and also as a part of the project of schooling, begins with an emphasis on the innate self, it constantly hints at the process of identity formation which is dialogic between an individual and his social and cultural position. While Peter Pettigrew belonged to Gryffindor, he is weak and disloyal; Hermione reveals that the Hat had debated about putting her in Ravenclaw before deciding on Gryffindor (*OoTP* 353). In the last book, Dumbledore, in talking to Severus Snape, the head of the Slytherin house and one of the most complex characters in the series, muses that sometimes Hogwarts sorts too soon (*DH* 545). What is emphasized is the constant state of dialogue and change in the constructions of identity. The process of maturation spills beyond the unidirectional growth towards the fulfillment of social expectations.

The nature of magical knowledge is essentially related to the power differential that being a wizard brings into being. The magical prowess, especially in the hands of the adolescents, constitutes a bottom-up force that reveals the gaps beneath the ideological didacticism. In Rowling's series, the two paradigms constantly complement each other. The annual encounters with danger are an essential part of apprenticeship that spills over the technical instructions in the classroom. They fill in the gaps in the technical nature of the formal magical education at Hogwarts. In his very first year, the encounter with Voldemort tests Harry with the lure of power. Every subsequent year, the annual encounters teach him about the power of love, sacrifice, loyalty and mercy, equipping him with the magical knowledge and hence magical power essential to defeat Voldemort. What defeats Voldemort then is the stunted nature of this *magical* knowledge. While Tom Riddle, one of the brightest students of Hogwarts, cares only for the things that concern him and his ruthless quest for immortality, he ignores other forms of magic and knowledge which become Harry's greatest protection. After the battle at the Department of Mysteries, Dumbledore tells Harry,

You would be protected by ancient magic of which he [Voldemort] knows, which he despises, and which he has always, therefore, underestimated — to his cost. I am speaking, of course, of the fact that your mother died to save you. She gave you a lingering protection he never expected, a protection that flows in your veins to this day. I put my trust, therefore, in your mother's blood. I delivered you to her sister, her only remaining relative [*OotP* 736].

As the school passes over from the Order of the Phoenix to the Ministry of Magic and finally the Death Eaters, the ideological tensions latent in the school are reinforced through the tussle between adolescent rebellion and adult authority. While other institutions like the press succumb to the ideological agenda of Cornelius Fudge, the Minister of Magic, Hogwarts resists the authority of Dolores Umbridge, the representative of official authority. Later even under the brutality of the Death Eaters, the rebellious Dumbledore's Army holds forth. Therefore, unlike the other official establishments, the school of magic as a space of the subordinates becomes the fount of resistance. As the Ministry and the Death Eaters become one in the last book, the last place of resistance to the official powers is appropriately the space of adolescents, the school of magic and witchcraft. Timmerman points out the presence of such sacred space is central to fantasy fiction: "the locus of order in the affairs of the kingdom, a center from which forces of darkness and disorder may be driven back, and a spiritual harmony arranged by supernatural powers but revealed in the affairs of men" (68). Hogwarts as a *school* is such a space; it is the focus of the world that surrounds it, an institution which subverts and re-orders the magical community. However, rather than a space of "spiritual harmony," it is a space of political turmoil, of resistance and subversion against the powers of containment exerted by the dominant agencies.

Therefore, Hogwarts, the *school of magic*, is crucial to the narrative of resistance and regeneration. There are innumerable spaces within the school of magic that embody the "treason within." In most school fiction, a school is also full of territorial spaces that embody resistance and tensions of the adolescent maturation process. These are places that escape the panopticon set up by the school authorities. In *Tom Brown's Schooldays*, it is the ground used by the boys to wrestle to settle scores; for Stalky and his friends, the woods around their academy are places to escape control, break rules and play pranks on the teachers. These spaces manifest the dialectical construction of identity through an interaction between a newly evolving sense of selfhood and the conflicting multiple strains that go into its construction.

In Hogwarts, such places exist within and around the castle. These are spaces that are hidden, like the Room of Requirement or the Chamber of Secrets, or out of bounds, like the Forbidden Forest or the Shrieking Shack. Much action takes place in the bathrooms and toilets of the school. In the first book, Harry and Ron, despite being forbidden to go wandering in the school, enter the girls' toilet to save Hermione from a troll, thereby forging a strong tie of friendship. Later they overcome the obstacles placed by the teachers to enter the secret room where the Philosopher's Stone is hidden. The toilet is once again an important site in *Harry Potter and the Chamber of Secrets*: again in the girls' toilet, Harry, Ron and Hermione brew the Polyjuice Potion illegally to disguise themselves to enter the Slytherin common room; the same toilet also conceals the entry to the Chamber of Secrets, the underground chamber where Harry kills the Basilisk and the destroys the first Horcrux — the diary of Tom Riddle.

There are underground passages known only to students; Harry uses them to visit Hogsmeade village surreptitiously when denied permission. The Marauder's Map, which appears to be a harmless bit of parchment till the student swears that s/he is "up to no good," epitomizes the irreverence and subversion that Hogwarts stands for. It is an unofficial architectural layout of the school, telling secrets about the school unknown to the teachers. It writes abuses when Severus Snape tries to force out its secret. Another place to figure prominently in rule-breaking escapades is the Room of Requirement; it is the meeting place for the illegal Dumbledore's Army, the place where Harry hides the book of the half-blood prince with its "unofficial" instructions on potion making. It is the room that hides the mutinous students in *Harry Potter and the Deathly Hallows*.

Even the official spaces within the school are ambiguous in their symbolic import. The main rival houses — Gryffindor and Slytherin — are the houses of the male founders. But as Gallardo and Smith point out, the tower of the Gryffindor, despite its phallic symbolization, is a common symbol of Virgin Mary, a feminine element reinforced by the head of the house, Minerva McGonagall, and the portrait of the Fat Lady that guards the entrance of the Gryffindor common room. The association of Slytherin house with the dungeons sets up a contrast

> between the visible and virginal power of the tower and the hidden dark femininity of the dungeon or cave actually completes the traditional feminine dyad of virgin and crone. (Hufflepuff and Ravenclaw are rarely a part of the equation.) Thus Hogwarts castle itself constitutes a feminine space, full of secret passages and secret chambers, all of which Harry must

explore; indeed his father would be disappointed, Professor Lupin tells us, if he *didn't* [Gallardo 198].

The unstructured places outside the boundaries of the school often impinge on the school life of Harry and his friends. In the third year, the students are permitted to visit the nearby Hogsmeade village. In the climactic moments of *Harry Potter and the Prisoner of Azkaban* at the Shrieking Shack, all the official versions that surround the death of Harry's parents are revealed along with the truth of Sirius, Remus and Peter Pettigrew. The forest at the peripheries of the school ground is an important place where Harry and his friends escape school authorities. Forest figures prominently in fantasy for children and adolescents, pointing out the close association between child-like innocence and nature. But unlike the secret garden of Victorian fiction which the children tame and which in turn relieves their pains, the Forbidden Forest has a life of its own — derived from its inhabitants like the angry Centaurs, dangerous spiders and, in later books, the destructive giant, Grawp. In *Harry Potter and the Order of Phoenix*, Harry and Hermione are finally able to get rid of Dolores Umbridge by using these powerful dwellers of the forest.

Though the action moves out of the school in the later books of the series, coinciding with the growth of the children into the adult world, Hogwarts with its mysterious surroundings remains a prominent character. The interstitial or external spaces offer only a temporary respite. The communal space of school is ultimately what the students return to and fight to preserve. During the last battle, the school itself seems to join the fight against Voldemort with its suits of armor, gargoyles, and moving pictures shouting words of encouragement.

Troubles of Gender and Race

The elements of magic and fantasy, therefore, question and often undercut the ideological conditioning inherent in boarding-school fiction. Magic and fantasy become cognate with the power of adolescents disrupting and resisting the attempts of containment by the dominant power networks. It is important to analyze the effect that these elements exert on the themes of gender, race and nation — the themes that have been central to boarding-school stories, especially the British school stories. The Potter series explores these norms rather than adopt them unquestioningly. It is the very troublesome nature of these issues that creates tensions and drives the narrative.

The fundamental aspect of being a co-educational boarding school goes against the belief in the essential role of gender segregation in development of boys and girls. Lesko points how the early scholars of adolescence from Rousseau to Stanley Hall "sought to get older boys into the hands of men in order to make them strong, courageous, honest, and disciplined. This could only be done by getting them away from women, both mothers and teachers, and the soft, feminizing, emotional influences" (57). The gender-specific school stories and series followed from the ideology of gender segregation and expounded different sets of educational instructions and values for boys and girls.

Though the course of Harry Potter's education follows the same assumptions about boyhood and masculinity favored by the earlier boarding school stories, the norms are modified and complicated by various elements, complicating the overt narrative. Charles Elster points out that education and training at Hogwarts is a highly gendered affair. For instance, in tune with the traditional image of the boisterous boyhood, Harry and Ron are little interested in the classes. The highlight of their time at the school (apart from the encounters with the dark wizards) is Quidditch, the wizard sport played on broomsticks. Harry is one of the best Quidditch players in the school. Following the tradition of boys' school fiction, Quidditch as a sport retains its central importance in the narrative.[8] Games, especially as depicted in the school stories, are a test of character and strength and hence central to a boy's growth. The fight for the Quidditch cup at Hogwarts emphasizes that it is not merely a matter of play. The identity of the houses, their winning qualities, their heroism — all are proven in the game of Quidditch. The ideologically loaded nature of the sport event in a school makes Harry's entry onto the Gryffindor Quidditch team in his very first year at Hogwarts extremely significant. Harry is the youngest player in a century to have made it to the school team. His entry to the team turns the fortune in favor of the Gryffindors, who had been losing to the Slytherins for years. His position as the Seeker of the team reflects on the larger theme of quest. For Harry, Quidditch is the first place to prove himself worthy of the heroism that has been assigned to him.

Games, in the boarding-school tradition, instill respect for authority, self-confidence, fair-mindedness and self-control. Therefore, it is only natural that while Harry Potter, the hero, turns out to be a natural in the sports field, his arch enemy, Draco has to buy his way into the team. The game, therefore, becomes another form of articulating the fight between what is considered good and what is deigned evil. The rivalry reinforces the identity and social relationship pattern of the school, especially the Gryffindor/Slytherin rivalry off the field. The dyadic nature of the rivalry with the specific other, the archenemy, heightens the sense of drama. Later, with most of the Weasley family in the team and Harry as the captain, the Gryffindor team seems to reinforce the social relations on which the series turns. Such dyadic rivalry goes into creating a group identity among the spectators, too — an identity which lasts beyond the match itself. It culminates in post-match celebrations inviting everybody of the group to participate in the victory. Hence, a sport event becomes a vehicle of identification and assimilation. Situated strategically near the end of the term before the declaration of the winner of the House Cup, the Quidditch match becomes an arena where identities are made and modified. Just as Harry is the youngest player in a century to join the Gryffindor uidditch team, in Book 4, we are told that Krum is the best and the youngest player in the Bulgarian national team. Such legends and myths are important since they underline the prowess and enhance a larger-than-life image of the players.[9]

Quidditch therefore cements the connection between the game, the house, the school and the nation. The link shared between sports and recreation with intangible ideals like loyalty, courage, and physical stamina signaled a new kind of heroism in nineteenth-century fiction. In *Tom Brown's Schooldays*, Tom as well as Harry East, though average in academics, are ideal students due to their extra-curricular merits. They are important members of the football team. Tom goes on to captain the "noble" game of cricket which, in his paean to the sport, he describes as "more than a game. It's an institution" (288). The regimentalized nature of the sports, with strict rules and associated ideas like team spirit, loyalty and courage, fitted neatly with the kind of education conceived for boys through institutions like the Boy Scouts. When a part of the school stories, games played an essential role by linking growth and development with the ideas of masculinity and nationalism.[10] The subtext of territorial, sexual and economic conquest behind the abstract ideals turns the sport events into dramas that inform a kind of institutionalized identity. A sport event is therefore a cultural narrative that holds chief place in a school story. Sports becomes a field of apprenticeship in masculinity, offering young men a way into a world of masculine values and relationships and linking it with the themes of nationalism and citizenship.

Sport therefore is crucial to the story of Rowling's boy wizard. The

Triwizard Tournament progressively becomes centered between the three male players and later between the two English players from Hogwarts. Harry's rivals in the Triwizard Tournament, Victor Krum and Cedric Diggory, are his rivals in the Quidditch pitch and also his rivals in the arena of sexual relations. Viktor Krum is an international sports star, followed around by girls. During the Yule ball he develops a relationship with Harry's friend Hermione which threatens the budding romance between Ron and Hermione. Later on, he shows interest in Ginny Weasley, Harry's girlfriend and later his wife. Diggory, on the other hand, is Harry's rival for Cho's affections. Even before he starts dating Cho, Diggory threatens to overshadow Harry in the Triwizard Tournament. He is handsome, he is the only Seeker in the school who managed to catch the Snitch before Harry in Harry's third year, and he, according to popular opinion in the school, is Hogwart's legitimate participant in the tournament. Harry, on the other hand, is young and inexperienced. Despite his feats in the previous books, he has yet to acquire a definite individual heroic status in the community. At each task of the Triwizard Tournament, the figures of older and more legitimate heroes, Diggory and Krum, are undone by the victory of Harry Potter, the underdog. Winning the tournament therefore appears to be a metaphor for the attainment of individual identity and personal distinction over rivals who are much higher up in the hierarchy, a turning point in the movement from the peripheries to the center.

Rowling does try to overcome the gender bias by writing Quidditch as a gender-neutral sport. For instance, though the chief Quidditch equipment, a broomstick is a conventional phallic symbol, it is simultaneously "a slight modification of the housewife's tool" which "still operates in connection with the transgressive magic world of (female) witches" (Gallardo 196). In tracing the history of Quidditch, Rowling recounts the first reference to the game in a place called "Queer Ditch Marsh" (Whisp).[11] A Quidditch team is comprised of male as well as female players. In Rowling's story, though Viktor Krum occupies the center stage in the Quidditch World Cup, the winning Irish team has several female players. At Hogwarts, the Gryffindor team, the best Quidditch team, has several marginalized students including Harry, who unlike other athletic heroes, is small and skinny. Cedric Diggory, the Hufflepuff Seeker and later the Triwizard champion, is "a lot bigger" (Rowling, *CoS* 91). As the youngest player and one of the most talented Seekers, the status and prestige offered by Quidditch is the greatest wish fulfillment for Harry, who had spent eleven years as an underprivileged and outcast child with the Dursleys. For a boy who seeks closeness, the rule-bound structure of organized sport promises to be a safe place in which to seek attachment with others. The sport also offers status and prestige to the Weasleys who are often taunted for their poverty. Most of the siblings find a place in the team, including Ron, despite his nervousness and erratic performance. His sister Ginny becomes an important member of the team, though she was never allowed to play with her brothers at home. An excellent addition to the team, she is confident and useful since she can play in different positions, even replacing Harry in the times of crisis. Unlike Ginny her brother Ron turns out to be a nervous and an average player. The only all-male team in the school is that of the Slytherins. It is a team where members can buy themselves a place. Draco Malfoy's father buys new brooms for the team in return of his son's inclusion in the team. The team is composed of an aggressive male peer group that seems to go for "size rather than skill" (Rowling, *PoA* 161). Their captain, Marcus Flint, who "looked as if he had some troll blood in him" (Rowling, *PS* 100), constantly needs to be warned about playing rough and cheating. Aligning such qualities with the Slytherin team shows narrative disapproval of the kind of sportsmanship represented by the team. Thus, to an extent, Harry's heroism at the Quidditch pitch seems to overcome some social and cultural hierarchies of the world outside.

Thus, the theme of male rivalry and solidarity through sports is complicated by the traces of some unconventionality of Rowling's playground vision. There are further fissures in the gender subtext. While Quidditch alternates between being a gender-neutral sport and an arena for the spectacle of masculinity, it looses importance as the series progresses. The gap is filled in by the political activism of Hermione Granger, endorsed by characters like Dobby and Lupin, who reveal the biases and prejudices common in the magical world. Thus a stereotypical protagonist of a girl's school story known for her appetite for knowledge and love of rules, Hermione Granger's presence undoes many ideological assumptions that underwrite conventional school stories. As the smartest witch at Hogwarts, Hermione's place and importance in Harry's quest derives from her intellectual resources. It can also be seen as a constant attempt to prove her place in the magical world, since, being a "mudblood," she faces an increasingly hostile atmosphere at Hogwarts and the magical world at large. But in the tradition of the boarding-school fiction, while the features of "ideal" boyhood center on energy and activity, conformity is the key to girls' education. In her article "Hermione in the Bathroom," June Cummins comments on the crucial scene in *Harry Potter and the Philosopher's Stone* when Hermione is saved from a troll by Harry and Ron. Highlighting the gothic elements in the scene, Cummins comments how the scene feminizes the heroine by saving her from her monstrous self, the aggressive bossy girl, and, therefore, fitting her neatly into the role of a powerful but subordinate helper — a position that Hermione accepts early in the series.

> "Harry — you're a great wizard, you know."
> "I'm not as good as you," said Harry, very embarrassed, as she let go of him.
> "Me!" said Hermione. "Books! And cleverness! There are more important things — friendship and bravery and — oh Harry — be *careful!*" [Rowling, *PS* 208].

Conformity, for a variety of reasons, therefore, seems to be essential to Hermione; in *Harry Potter and the Half-Blood Prince*, while Harry follows the instructions on the old Potions book successfully, Hermione steadfastly insists on "ploughing on with what she called the 'official instructions,' but becoming increasingly bad-tempered as they yielded poorer results than the Prince's" (*HBP* 184). The stereotype is further strengthened in context of her relationship with Ron, her dramatic transformation during the Yule Ball and the advice on relationships she dispenses to others. Hermione, in seeking to conform, thus fits in with the paradigm of the "ideal" girl student.

However, as the story progresses, Hermione appropriates the stereotype to use it as her power. She is the first one to voice the idea for a secret student's defense group and the one to work out the way to guard its secrecy. She is the only one in the group to question Harry's dream regarding Sirius' torture in the Ministry of Magic. She saves Harry more than once during crucial moments in *Harry Potter and the Deathly Hallows*, once right from the clutches of Voldemort at Godric's Hollow. Despite the threat to her relationship with Ron, she refuses to abandon Harry's quest.

While the initial books of the series show Hermione endlessly cramming to be on the top of the class, she seems to come of age in the later books as she uses her knowledge to supplement Harry's superior but impetuous magic. Though she breaks rules with Harry and Ron, her ideals about house-elves, giants and other races provide the moral and ethical framework for Harry's quest. They are reinforced in the culmination of her relationship with Ron, when she is finally able to "convert" him.

"Hang on a moment!" said Ron sharply. "We've forgotton someone!"
"Who?" asked Hermione.
"The house-elves, they'll all be down in the kitchen, won't they?"
"You mean we ought to get them fighting?" said Harry.
"No," said Ron seriously, "I mean we should tell them to get out. We don't want any more Dobby's, do we? We can't order them to die for us —"
There was a clatter as the Basilisk fangs cascaded out of Hermione's arms. Running at Ron, she flung them around his neck and kissed him full on the mouth [*DH* 502].

If magic is the subversive power that lies outside the status quo, then, as Gallardo and Smith point out, Hermione as a girl, as a "mudblood" and also as a champion of the underdogs, appropriates the slanderous connotations of the term "witch": "Hermione appropriately recognizes the injustice of the house elves' servitude because as a 'Mudblood' and political minority, but also as a woman, she can see discrimination where others see tradition" (202). Her knowledge is not dedicated to the maintenance of the stereotypes of gender and race but to the reformation of the status quo. Her quest, despite its subordination, places Harry's story in a wider perspective of the racism, gender bias and class prejudices present in the magical world. Hermione's vocal activism, her political views and her openness to the culture of the others upsets the conventions of the British boarding-school story. It places the history of the individual hero in the context of the history of the community; without Hermione and politically active characters like her, the narrative could have been just a story of Harry's revenge on Voldemort.

Similar complexities characterize Rowling's engagement with other significant themes of boarding-school fiction such as that of imperialism. In the context of its generic history, the existence of the liberal framework and a multicultural society in Rowling's fantasy-school narrative reveal interesting insights about contemporary Britain. While Rowling's story owes several of its stylistic motifs to its predecessors in the field of fantasy and school fiction, it differs in this important aspect. Hogwarts School of Witchcraft and Wizardry, unlike its fictional predecessors, is a multicultural institution. Unlike the depiction of conventional racial elitism of the English boarding schools that coincided with Britain's empire-building phase, Hogwarts has people from Asian and African origins. Harry's first girlfriend, Cho Chang, is from East Asia, while the Patil twins are of Indian origin. Dean Thomas, Angelina Johnson and Lee Jordan are other people of color in the school. Therefore, despite situating the text in the British boarding-school tradition, the ideological implications of Rowling's por-

trayal of gender and nationalism are informed by twentieth-century political and cultural trends. In "The All-White World of Middle School Genre
Fiction: Surveying the Field for Multicultural Protagonists," a study con-
ducted on the youth fiction, Denise Agosto, Sandra Hughes-Hassell and
Catherine Gilmore-Clough find out that about 84 percent of texts featured
only white protagonists. In such a scenario, Rowling's series does stand
apart. In recreating the school fiction genre for the contemporary world,
Rowling induces twenty-first century concerns of nation and race in a
genre previously dominated by all-white educational institutions. The
series' representation of ethnic minorities and non–Europeans might pre-
empt any inquiries into racial or ethnic biases. Hogwarts does have Asian
and African students studying along with English ones. Parvati and Padma
Patil, as their names suggest, could be from India. Similarly Cho Chang,
an important character as she is Harry's first love interest, could be of East
Asian origin. Due to the reference to dreadlocks, Lee Jordan, has been
assumed to be of African origin.[12] And so is Angelina Johnson, a Gryffindor
Quidditch player, who, Rowling tells us, is black (*GoF* 230). Most of them
are brave enough to belong to Gryffindor house, the house to which Harry
and his best friends belong. Cho and Padma are witty enough to belong
to Ravenclaw house, known for selecting only exceptionally intelligent students. The logic of the narrative follows a liberal line on the question of
ethnicities, and this logic shapes the student interactions and thought
processes. Neither Harry, Ron or Hermione nor Cho, Parvati or Padma
see themselves located in a specific cultural and historical horizon vis-à-
vis each other. They meet and deal with each other as equals, according
to Rowling's text.

However, problems with Hogwarts' liberalism become evident on
closely looking at what Said calls the "strategic formation" of the text that
analyzes the "relationship between texts and the way in which groups of
texts, types of texts, even textual genres, acquire mass density, and refer-
ential power among themselves and thereafter in the culture" (20). It is
evident that all the names mentioned above come loaded with surplus
meaning in the social and historical context — something that the series
does not seem to take into account. South and East Asians represented in
the series bear a specific relation with Britain — that of colonial domination.
Most of these characters come from the parts of the world which had been
under colonial rule of the British till the last century. What is dubious is
that neither Parvati, Padma, Cho, nor even Angelina has any anxiety caused
by uprootedness, or any sense of alienation due to cultural difference. The

sense of anxiety and alienation, which characterizes the diaspora and its cultural expressions, is completely absent in Rowling's representation of the diasporic Asians and Africans adolescents.

Fantastic cross-cultural encounters can be a means to study and engage with the theme of otherness — a corollary to the central concern of identity construction in YA literature. Diasporic writers like Lawrence Yep use fantasy and myths to highlight the experience of otherness that characterizes the diasporic ethnic groups and links to the project of selfhood which comes into being in a particular set of social and cultural relationships. While the Potter series also seems to do justice to the contemporary ethnic diversity of Britain, the confusion and tension that inevitably characterizes the cross-cultural encounters is absent. While the narrative describes the life, thoughts and adventures of Harry Potter, he shows no awareness of cultural differences when it comes to Cho Chang. That an English boy is unaware of these complexities even though burdened with the enormous task of saving the world seems highly improbable.

So, if one takes the series as subversive with the presence of a magical adolescent super hero and fantasy, then one needs to ask how subversive it remains in its flirtations with the multicultural environment of growth, especially since it shares some cherished values of its predecessors that supplemented the discourse of colonial bondage with institutional logic.

> In stressing the liberal humanist message of "we are all the same beneath the surface," and asserting that race and ethnicity should not be important in judging another person, Rowling's text conveys the message that race and ethnicity are not important for those who experience life from this position — hardly true of late twentieth/early twenty-first century Britain, Canada, the United States, or much of the rest of the world [174].

The multicultural associations are further called into questions by the presence of stereotypes. In fact, stereotyping is carefully used to further the distance between the central coterie and the peripheral characters. Cho Chang is important only as a part of the romantic subplot. Her romance with Harry ends abruptly because, as we are told in the last few pages of Book 5, Cho "cried too much," thereby fitting into the gender stereotype like the Patil twins who often behave in a "silly" manner. On the other hand, Ginny Weasley and Hermione Granger are important because of the aid they can provide in Harry's quest. Though romantically involved with Harry and Ron, the central male protagonists, they are crucial to the main narrative as they fight along with Harry to save the world. In the Yule ball held during the Triwizard Tournament — most of the couples are interracial — Cedric and Cho, Fred and Angelina, Ron and Padma and Harry and Parvati. In each case, cultural otherness is assigned to the female characters. Despite the cross-cultural love affairs, an endogamic principle is reflected in the happier romantic liaisons of Harry as well as Ron. Therefore, on a closer look, the racial and gender ideologies are intricately bound.

The differences are typecast according to the older power differentials. For instance, Beauxbatons Academy of Magic, probably located in France, is represented by Fleur, who has a touch of a Veela. The attraction of Veelas is not genuine; it is magical and fatal. They symbolize the fatal attractiveness of a foreign woman, especially in context of Ron's fascination with her. Drumstrang, on the other hand, probably located in middle Europe, is represented by sinister characters like Viktor Krum and Igor Karakoff. Though Krum is not evil, he is often described as stealthy and secretive. During the last task of the Triwizard Tournament, he comes under Imperious Curse (which Harry is able to resist easily) and starts attacking the fellow players.

Thus, though the multicultural education of Hogwarts embodies easy sharing of different perspectives, the series betrays the ideological weight by its (non)representation of the power differentials among the groups. Radical particularity of cultures is devalued. This "we are the world" kind of multiculturalism ignores the complex tension behind the cohesive image of the young wizards and witches fighting under Harry's leadership to save Hogwarts and the magical world.

It should, therefore, be easy to dismiss Rowling's "boutique multiculturalism" as tenuous and superficial; the attempts at depicting the issue of race in a politically correct manner are undercut by the historical and cultural unconscious that underpins the genre of boarding-school fiction. Yet at the level of fantasy, things become even more complicated. In the context of fantasy, Harry is the Other with respect to his surrogate muggle family, the Dursleys. Harry and his world of magic represents a revolt against the conventional, normal life, the rule-bound life of the muggles like the Dursleys, who belong to the middle class of "normal" grown-up England. Like the traditional bad penny of the Victorian narratives, he is banished from the ordered English society to the distant lands or the colonies. In such a context, as Giselle Liza Anatol points out, Hogwarts and the entire wizard world seems to be a colony of the "normal" city. It is meant for non-conforming adolescents. Hogwarts, as a school of witchcraft and wizardry, as a place of education for witches and wizards, is at once a refuge for exiles and an elitist institution. Since it is a place of magical education, the exclusion of non-magical people or the muggles is justified. But the exclusion is complicated by the power differential that exists in the relationships between wizards and muggles and which underlies the common wizard sport of muggle baiting. Even among magical beings, the institutions chooses to educate only witches and wizards; centaurs, goblins, especially the house-elves who, despite their own kind of magic, are not only excluded from the magical education at Hogwarts but used directly as labor in the school.[13]

The cultural issues left unaddressed in the multiculturalism of the text are brought to centerstage by the fantastic creatures. The self-proclaimed superiority of the wizards and the power of the magical wand is a source of resentment for groups like the centaurs and the goblins. In peaceful times in the wizard world, there is no project to separate or exterminate the other groups. Yet they live in their separate spheres. The resentment and bitterness is common among groups like the centaurs, werewolves and goblins. The series reveals the disturbing subtext of the "inclusive" world by its engagement with the social and political history of the magical world. The references to the giant wars and goblin rebellions point to a turbulent political context of the wizard community. Anatol also points out actual racial characteristics given to the fantastical races like the giants in terms of their tribal organization, the werewolves where the attitude to the problem (whether it is medical or racial) is ambivalent.[14] The lens of fantasy distances the issues of ethnicity and race offering a perspective that debunks the overt representations of the text.

Ron is an important character in this respect since he comes from a middle-class English family. Harry and the reader learn about other magical races from Ron. He has been living in the magical world all his life. He has imbibed not only a thorough knowledge of its institutions but also its prejudices, which he mouths in an extremely unself-conscious fashion: "Harry, they're just vicious, giants. It's like Hagrid said, it's in their natures, they're like trolls" (*GoF* 374); when Hermione confronts them with the idea of setting house-elves free, he insists, "They. Like. It. They like being enslaved" (*GoF* 198). When Remus Lupin, the best Defense against Dark Arts teacher, turns out to be a werewolf, Ron cannot bear being touched by him even when he is saving Ron's life. While Harry treats Lupin's lycanthropy as a medical problem, Ron's attitude hints at the socio-historical attitude of the wizards to other races. What he cannot see is that the prejudices leveled against various fantastic races are social, political or cultural. The mythic narratives about the cruelty of giants and werewolves are challenged by the very presence of characters like Grawp and Lupin. While Ron insists that house elves like slave labor, Dobby likes his freedom and wages. The presence of these characters at the borderlines of the text challenges the apparent solidity of an authentic center by juxtaposing unexpected alternate narratives. It leads to a crisis for the player from the dominant field like Ron, a fear of decline that leads to the reassertion of the "fund of historical and cultural reference ... the elements of non-social identity which is negative for the Other — classed as evil and inferior — but positive for the racist actor" (Wieviorika 50). Thus Dobby is a "freak," while the normative behavior for the house-elves is espoused by Winky, Hokey and even Kreacher, all of whom are loyal to their masters unquestioningly. Dobby's individuality is an anomaly in such collectivity. Yet Kreacher's story undercuts such simplistic notions. The text holds up Ron's point of view for criticism, particularly when set against the political stance of Hermione Granger, Dobby and Kreacher's stories of ill-usage, and Lupin's self-pity. One of the defining moments in the relationship between the two characters is when Ron is able to think of the house-elves in the kitchen unaware of the dangerous battle raging among the wizards.

Rowling's text thus emerges as a palimpsest of its predecessors — complexities of the empire, its racist ideology, its downfall all seem to be reflected beneath the representation of the post-colonial globalized world. Text's multiculturalism therefore seems to lie in the way that it constantly negotiates between its cultural history and twenty-first-century racial politics. Arnold Krupat characterizes multiculturalism as a battleground of power:

> Multiculturalism refers to an order of instruction concerned to present that which a dominant culture has defined as "other" and "different"— usually, of course, minor and inferior as well — in such a way that it may interrogate and challenge that which the dominant culture has defined as familiar and its own — and so, to be sure, major and superior [107].

As mentioned earlier, the presence of the politically vocal group of characters like Hermione, Lupin and Dobby lifts the narrative from being a mere personal history of Harry Potter and his revenge, and situates it in a wider political, social and cultural debate. Yet all this does not detract from the fact that Harry's growth is located in the paradigms that are essentially masculine and English. The genre in which Rowling situates herself manifests the cultural investment in the process of growing up. The figure of a schoolboy reflects cultural concerns regarding race, class, and patriarchy and therefore any deviance is a cause of anxiety and threat. To an extent,

Rowling's multicultural liberalism fails to notice the paradox it rests on. Tison Pugh and David L. Wallace, in exploration of the essential heteronormativity of the series, insist that though on the conscious level the narrative allies itself with the deviant and the queer, normativity is inbuilt within the genres in which Rowling chooses to write — the hero myth and English boarding-school fiction. "Early in the twentieth century," says Karen M. Smith, "when boy's public schools began to be regarded as training places for the administrators of the British Empire, school story fiction celebrated the manliness, athleticism, and ethnocentrism considered necessary qualities for the tribunes of the Empire" (Smith 83). The narrative, through sport, athleticism and rule flouting, links Harry's transition to adulthood with the themes of masculine heroism, nationalism and sexuality.

At the same time, the story of Harry Potter, the apprentice wizard, by centering on a school, de-centers it in turn. The narrative of his coming of age in a magical school challenges the conventional narratives of schooling and acculturation. The binaries like child-adult or male-female are preserved but problematized. A child in Harry's narrative is not helpless when confronted with repressive agencies of the adult society. He is marked not just by Voldemort but also by Dolores Umbridge, embodying the official political establishment of the magical world where he becomes "Undesirable No. 1." By organizations like the DA, the otherness is put to effective use; it becomes a position of alternate power whose potential is acknowledged when Rufus Scrigmeour asks him to join the Ministry. Similarly though Harry's masculinity is reinforced with motifs like the scar, his Quidditch prowess and his boyish non-conformity, it is different from masculinity as embodied by Dudley. It includes the "feminine" values of interpersonal relationships, sacrifice and perseverance. Beverly Lyons Clark, in her discussion of Louisa M. Alcott's school stories for boys, points out the complexities in the cross-gendered nature of such texts written by women authors. According to Clark, the women writers, though they adopt the accepted codes, are not able to internalize it and hence "at times proceed to contradict it, or are at pains to justify and contextualize it, or maybe transform it" ("Domesticating" 323). Though Rowling's narrative falls short of any kind of radical transformation of the cultural codes of school fiction and its traditional racial and gender equations, the pains taken by the author to justify, contextualize and modify are clearly evident. It is in these efforts that the narrative reveals the fissures of the dominant ideological positions. The elements of fantasy and adolescence seem to defamiliarize the system of schooling, thereby unearthing the troublesome issues that underlie the institutions of education and training. By exploring what is marginalized through the story of an orphaned magical adolescent, fantasy reveals the process of subversion as well as containment through which contradictions are suppressed and displaced as the orphan in integrated into the social setup. The quest of the apprentice wizard therefore places a story of the psychic growth of an adolescent within a socio-political institution like a school. The next chapter further widens the focus by turning to another template of growth that often recurs in children's and adolescent fantasy fiction — the scriptural story of the savior. As it resonates with the story of the savior, young adult fantasy adds a metaphysical dimension to the idea of regeneration embodied by the figure of a child. The chapter focuses on the postmodern elements in the narrative that textualize the scripture and open it up for exploration.

3

The Savior

"Whosoever shall not receive the kingdom of God as a little child, he shall not enter therein." — King James Bible, Mark 10:15

In the Gospel, Jesus warns his disciples that in rejecting the children, they are shutting themselves from the Kingdom of Heaven. In Gospel of St. Matthew, there is corresponding advice: "If you do not change you hearts and become like children, you will not enter the kingdom of heaven" (Matthew 18:3). In the story of redemption and hope, of the Kingdom of Heaven, a child is situated centrally. What does it mean to "welcome the kingdom of God like a little child"? It could refer to the innocence, spontaneity and openness that we associate with the figure of a child. It could also refer to a complicity between the Kingdom of God and a child: welcoming a child means welcoming a promise, the same way that the Kingdom of God remains a promise for the future. In the gospel of man's redemption by the sacrifice of Christ, Tolkien finds the source of all fairy stories: "The gospels contain a fairy story, or a story of larger kind which embraces all the essence of fairy stories" (Tolkien, "On Fairy-Stories" 62). The story of the savior is the metanarrative that leads to the happy endings of fantasy. It offers recovery, escape and consolation following the fall of humankind:

> The Christian has still to work, with mind as well as body, to suffer, hope, and die; but he may now perceive that all his bents and faculties have a purpose, which can be redeemed. So great is the bounty with which he has been treated that he may now, perhaps, fairly dare to guess that in Fantasy he may actually assist in the effoliation and multiple enrichment of creation ["On Fairy-Stories" 63].

Fantasy, therefore, according to Tolkien, is an art of sub-creation — a creative activity that follows the primary act of divine creation. The acts of magic, readers like John Granger point out, imitate the creativity of God. Fantasy is linked intricately with Christian miracle stories and morality plays.

And a child protagonist holds an important position to this Christian project of fantasy.[1] While the hero monomyth and the school story situate an adolescent in relation to society and politics, the story of a savior is an overarching narrative of hope and promise that a culture posits in its youth and in its ability to lead everyone to the "Kingdom of Heaven." In the "holy family," Christ himself appears as the child of mysterious origins, growing up to save the adult world from its self-inflicted catastrophes, and so becoming the father of man. Being saved by a dispossessed and innocent hero, therefore, is a metanarrative in which religion and fantasy overlap. The present chapter analyses the role and centrality of an adolescent savior in fantasy texts, its relevance to the projects of growth and, most significantly, its importance in cultural constructions of childhood.

The Potter series has been denounced on the charges of luring children to magic, occult and paganism. And yet the greatest magic according to the series is love: in the first book itself Dumbledore tells Harry,

> If there is one thing Voldemort cannot understand, it is love. He didn't realize that love as powerful as your mother's for you leaves it own mark. Not a scar, no visible sign ... to have been loved so deeply, even though the person who loved us is gone, will give us some protection forever. It is in your very skin [*PS* 216].

It is the emotion that Christianity divinizes: "Whoever does not love does not know God, because God is love" (John 4:8). The Christian subtext in the series is hardly subtle. The series begins with a mother sacrificing herself for her son. Lily Potter's act of love and sacrifice has repercussions that resonate through the series. It saves Harry on the night of the murder attempt when he was one year old; the sacrifice re-surfaces again and again to save Harry till he in turn sacrifices himself for love and communal welfare. The story therefore comes a full circle when Harry puts an end to the terror of Voldemort, not by fighting or dueling, but by embracing death in a Christ-like fashion. John Granger, highlighting the essentially Christian nature of Rowling's text, insists that

> the fundamental reason for the astonishing popularity of the Harry Potter novels is their ability to meet a spiritual longing for some experience of the truths of life, love, and death taught by Christianity but denied by a secular culture. Human beings are designed for Christ, whether they know it or not. *That the Harry Potter stories "sing along" with the Great Story of Christ is a significant key to understanding their compelling richness* [*How Harry* 2, italics in original].

Stories of child savior serve as a background of most young adult fantasy — from C.S Lewis to Phillip Pullman. The involvement of children in the battle between good and evil also seems to underlie Tolkien's conception of the Hobbits or halflings, the "little people" caught unwillingly in the great quest for power. The figure of a child savior, therefore, is of special concern given the cultural anxieties and insecurities that underpin the figure. A child in fantasy fiction stands on a volatile cusp of innocence and power. On the one hand is the romantic conception of child, the "noble savage" the Wordsworthian notion of a paradisal innocence that "lies about us in our infancy." It is the conception of child that informed fantasy fiction of writers like George MacDonald and C.S. Lewis. MacDonald's fantasy emphasizes the child-likeness of God claiming that theology consistently misrepresents God when it portrays him as the great king ("The Child" 14). The angelic infant and his redemptive qualities, according to Thacker and Webb, are the romantic inheritance of children's literature that has persisted "beyond the shocks of history" (41). This "desire to idealize childhood as a time of 'one-ness' with the spiritual contributed to a literature proposed by Wordsworth and his peers, which sought to reconstruct the child's subjectivity as an ordered, legible, normative and moralized text in its own right" (Thacker and Webb 18).

At the same time, another crucial function of religion in children's literature is of social ordering (Woods 1). It is worth noting that the child in biblical thought has been constructed through the discourses of helplessness and vulnerability, the need to discipline, mainly due to the original sin bequeathed by Adam and Eve to the future generations of mankind. The discourses of childlikeness, innocence and humility that build on the biblical narrative emphasize simplicity and not the superiority of a child in the Christian model. Judith Gundry Wolfe points out that the elevation of child in the New Testament presupposes the inferiority of childhood; though a sharer in the Christian faith, a child is the meekest, lowest and humblest and, therefore, close to Jesus. Adolescents receive a stricter treatment since they are accountable for any violation of rules and precepts. Thomas Aquinas insisted that children past puberty were adults in ecclesiastical and moral matters. Adolescence, despite its potential to "save" human kind, is defined in terms of incontinence, fallibility and immaturity.[2] Therefore, the notion of the angelic infant is constantly debunked by the narratives revealing the amorality of childhood, a potential of destruction inherent in its innocence. Stories like *Lord of the Flies* and *A Clockwork Orange* revolve around the destructive child, unconditioned and uncontrolled by social and cultural institutions. The cultural meta-narratives like schooling, discussed in the previous chapter, or religion, which the present chapter is concerned with, seek to control and frame the child protagonist, thereby soothing the discomfort and anxieties aroused by the figure. Trites also points out the role of religion as an institutional discourse of containment: "Children and adolescents taught to believe in the omnipotence of an unseen patriarchal deity who must be obeyed are indeed receiving ideological training that represses them" (41). Adolescent rebellion against religion gives way to the acceptance of "some variation of the status quo that is socially acceptable" (45). In fantasy, as mentioned earlier, children not only possess special talents but are powerful in terms of their willingness to wield those skills to upset the status quo. A close analysis of fantastic narratives reveals a variety of ways in which the institutional discourse of religion attempts to contain the process of growth. A variety of subversion and sub-versions of religious status quo make it crucial to study the role of religion in fantasy narratives.

Insofar as the narrative merges the idea of an adolescent's growth with the progress of a Christian pilgrim towards salvation, it invokes Christianity — the cultural narrative of a savior is linked intricately with the narrative of growth. In exploring this link, the study is not concerned with the debate whether the Potter series sends out a Christian message or debunks it (at the same time, it would serve well to remember the continuity that is evident between Christianity and earlier belief systems can also be seen in the series). Rowling takes elements from Greco-Roman mythology along with secular narratives like the tales of knighthood and ideas of chivalry and links them with Christian elements. For instance, though the end of the series tells the story of Christ's sacrifice, the battle can also be compared to the battle of Ragnarok, the mythic destruction and renewal of world in Norse canon.

These sacred stories of culture are central to the rites of initiation for its neophytes. Tracing these religious and mythic roots of the fantastic takes the neophyte on a journey to the time of origin of mankind, of society and cultural system. In early societies, the stories of heroes and gods were a part of a child's growth and initiation. Mircea Eliade classifies the stories of the heroes and legends as "true stories" next only to the myths of gods. Revelation of these stories is an essential part of the ceremonies like the initiation rites because, as Eliade insists, in the re-enactment, the neophyte is able to repeat what gods and heroes did *ab origine*:

In imitating the exemplary acts of a god or of a mythic hero or simply by recounting their adventures, the man of an archaic society detaches himself from profane time and magically re-enters the Great Time, the sacred time [*Myth* 6].

This sacred time is also a communal or shared time — away from the everyday life and its routine. Hence, in *The Elementary Forms of Religious Life*, French anthropologist Emile Durkheim argued religion is nothing more than "Society Divinized." Its themes and symbols serve as a binding force holding the social order together.[3] The genre of fantasy echoes this notion of the sacred. Eliade defines sacred as "a reality of a wholly different order from 'natural' realities" (*The Sacred* 10). A fantastic narrative can be seen as a *heirophany*, the moment when "*something sacred shows itself to us*," manifestation of another order of reality different from our lived one (*The Sacred* 11).

The sacred functions at a dual level of existence — it becomes something else even as it continues to participate in its surrounding milieu. Since, as argued previously, popular fantasy can hardly be divorced from its temporal milieu, it juxtaposes sacred narratives with profane concerns. A fantastic narrative is oriented towards the contemporary socio-political milieu even as it works at another level where its immediacy is transmuted to a supernatural level. The Potter series engages with the lived reality of terrorism, capitalism and postcolonial power networks, in placing these elements against themes like love, sacrifice, death, and all this in the backdrop of the battle between good and evil, the story is linked deeply to the metaphysical concerns of Christian religion.

In the *fantastic-marvelous*, as in religious and cultural narratives, laws and precepts are instituted to veil the strangeness, incoherence and instability of human knowledge and power. The uncanniness and strangeness is explained away by the supernatural. Here Tolkien sees further similarity between the Christian gospel and stories of magic and wonder. For Tolkien, a fairy story is the gospel of human salvation and re-creation. Its highest function is *Eucatastrophe,* "a sudden joyous turn," a "miraculous grace," "never to be counted on to recur," necessary for deliverance and denying universal defeat ("On Fairy-Stories" 60). Therefore, "the birth of Christ is the eucatastrophe of Man's history. The Resurrection is the eucatastrophe of the story of Incarnation. This story begins and ends in joy. It has pre-eminently the 'inner consistency of reality'"("On Fairy-Stories" 62–63).

Magic in a sense, then, seems to be a part of religious discourse. John Granger highlights the Christian nature of *incantational* magic in the *Potter* series as it "sings along with" or "harmonizes" with the notion of creation through the creative word of God. In Genesis, the world comes into being with the miraculous word of God: "God said, Let there be Light: and there was Light" (Genesis 1:3). Since *incantational* magic harmonizes with God's word, this magic is "in conformity with both literary tradition and scriptural admonition" (*How Harry* 6). In *The Chronicles of Narnia*, Narnia is gradually created through the music invoked by Aslan. In the Potter series, the main magical devices are the spells, the most essential part of magical syllabi at Hogwarts. They form the crux of the educational content. They are a part of the *incantational* magic in the series. In Ursula LeGuin's *Tales of Earthsea*, knowing and naming are synonymous with the highest magical power. This *incantational* power of the word is pitted against *invocational* magic, the darker form of magic through which Ged summons the amorphous shadow from the underworld. The *incantational* magic actually characterizes the writer's creation of the fantastic universe, as "one that has no reality outside language; the description and what is described are not a different nature" (Todorov 92). Like the scriptural universe, the world of fantasy is primarily a logocentric world, a world that comes into being by the imaginative creativity of man.[4] Thus, if fantasy is seen as a postmodern genre with its focus on the breach in the structures of the known world, then the theological core of fantasy seems to reinstate the concerns with teleology and coherence. Repeatedly, the stories return to the central myths of religion — creation powered by the word of God, the savior dying and then returning from death, thereby enacting the story of redemption. The "otherworldliness" of fantasy then can be seen as "theological abstraction of faith, the willing embrace of the numinous, the unknown, the immeasurable, the unquantifiable" (Todorov 92). Kath Filmer, therefore, argues that

> the literature of fantasy and science fiction has a significant part to play in the religious concerns of the late twentieth century, and that the discourse of religion, marginalized not only by the consumerist and materialist society, but also by the anti-theological discourse of certain contemporary literary theories, is legitimized by these genres [5].

The figure of a savior here can be seen as a cultural fantasy; the hero of a Christian narrative, a culturally encoded icon, an amalgam of symbolic representations that promise redemption and therefore direct the collective desire towards the modes of being that fit with the value systems of the religious symbolic, in the present case, the Christian symbolic. In this context, stories of being saved by a child seem to serve as an opiate which both satisfies and oppresses much like religion in Marx and Engles tradition — a way to escape the grim day-to-day realities of "primary" world into the joys of the "secondary" world. Hence, following Jackson's theory of ideological conditioning of the *fantastic-marvelous*, the other worlds and alternatives as reflections of gospel stories present coherent metaphors that do not effectively problematize reality or open space outside the dominant.

However, though opiate can relieve pain, rarely would a healthy person need it. Fantasy can therefore be seen as a symptom of something very wrong in the "primary" world. Jack Zipes sees a kind of revolutionary desire in fantasy, that the fantastic world, though it remains dependent on the primary world, exists to transform that world: "there is a quality of hope and faith in serious fantasy literature that offsets the mindless violence that we encounter in the spectacles of everyday life. If fantasy is subversive, then it wants to undermine what passes for normality, to expose the contradictions of civil society, to right the world out-of-joint in the name of humanity" ("The Spectacle" xi). There is skepticism built into the very concept of fantasy, in its desire to explain the incomprehensible, in its escape from the contingencies of reality. But this skepticism, especially in the *fantastic-marvelous*, is linked to hope — it is not about rendering the reader passive or inactive but hopeful.

It is in this revisionary aspect that fantasy has the potential to postmodernize theology. Todorov, as he installs fantasy in the zone of hesitancy, insists that the fantastic requires "near belief" (31). It brings out the genre's postmodernist preoccupation with indeterminacy: "The fantastic becomes a sort of anti-mythic, deconstructive power, threatening the coherence of narrative, and the ambiguous and complex relation between fantasy and religion is highlighted, not resolved" (Aichele and Pippin, *Violence* 4). According to George Aichele, the postmodern view of fantasy foregrounds scriptural narrative as a narrative of fragmentation. Unlike the modernist theology based on the politics of meaning and revelation in the scriptural text, the postmodern core of fantasy reveals theology itself as a text. It is anti-apocalyptic; it reveals the canonical scripture as a metanarrative that authorizes judgment and is open to question. Aichele notes that while modern theology sees temporal wholeness and an ultimate destiny in the kingdom of God, postmodernism reveals this to be a fiction, an illusion that conceals fantastic discontinuities and multiplicities ("Literary Fantasy" 327). Since fantasy works by making a conspicuous presence at the moments of instability, in case of religion, it textualizes the metanarrative, the supernatural elements, the moralistic framework of good and evil, right and wrong, and holds them up for examination and modification. In a fantastic narrative like the Potter series, religion is not just a mythic framework underlying the narrative and revealing its "true" meaning, Christian or otherwise; the religious framework itself emerges as a text to be explored, examined and reworked.

An adolescent, with the openness and fluidity that characterizes his/her position, becomes a central figure in this theological debate of fantasy. The narrative of coming of age can be read in coincidence with the story of a pilgrim's progress to the kingdom of God. In either case, the state of being is characterized by its liminality. Hence the motive of a journey — the quest for selfhood in the Christian framework is linked to the transcendence of the self and, as we shall see, to the forging of radical relations between the self and the other — a concern that coincides with the primary theme of adolescent fiction. Given the didactic role of children's and young adult fiction, the biblical themes of obedience and free will, of autonomy and agency also find an echo. The disobedience of Eve in the Christian tradition is the starting point of the story of man's fall and redemption. Themes and symbols surrounding disobedience and its metaphoric reflection on the moral status of mankind have been appropriated by fantasy as means to explore the Christian metanarrative from multiple perspectives and at different historical junctures. Rowling's narrative belongs to this complex zone of overlap between adolescent fantasy and religious discourse — a zone which has been explored in great detail by her predecessors like George MacDonald and C.S. Lewis.

Lewis' Narnia series uses Christian allegory to place the growth of a child in context of the religious metanarrative. Christianity and its role that Lewis envisages in shaping a child are all clearly presented. It serves as an important point of reference and contrast for the later fantasies like Rowling's and Phillip Pullman's series. Writing in the aftermath of World War II, C.S. Lewis' *The Chronicles of Narnia* posits the divine order of Christianity, upholding its hierarchical framework and its theological doctrine, where the Creator is good and benevolent and, hence, submission to his authority is good and sensible. Obeying Aslan is aligning oneself on the side of good. Divine prohibition therefore becomes an opportunity to obey. Disobedience becomes a perversity. There is a direct reconstruction of "man's first disobedience" in *The Magician's Nephew*, where Digory is ordered by Aslan to fetch the apple of eternal youth from the forbidden tree in the newly born Narnia. The white witch Jadis incites Digory to take the apple for his dying mother without permission, but he demurs and decides to bring back the apple to Aslan, giving up the hope of saving his mother. As a reward, Aslan lets him pick another apple for his mother, pointing that if he had taken the apple without permission "it would have healed; but not to your joy or hers. The day would come when both you and she would have looked back and said it would have been better to die in that illness" (100). This incident elucidates Lewis' position on the fall, death and obedience. Obedience to authority is a means to be virtuous. Since authority is benevolent, disobedience becomes more heinous. Timmerman points out that "since Lewis believes in the ultimacy of the good, incarnated in Aslan, the good responds to and assists the protagonist in his heroic endeavors. In high fantasy, there is no such clear response. Since the protagonist controls the magical powers, the crisis is laid on his shoulders for action" (81–82).

Contemporary narratives, like Rowling's series or Pullman's, also engage with the metanarrative of redemption but in a more complex and ambiguous manner. For John Granger, the Christian nature of Harry's *Bildungsroman* can be traced through the three steps of the alchemical process — purification, dissolution, and reformation. The end is almost an allegorical reconstruction of Christ's sacrifice for the redemption of mankind. Yet, as it has been pointed out, the series constructs childhood in a postmodern sense. The children take agency and find means "to extend their power and control outside their prescribed roles, unlike traditional child characters who are more at the mercy of their world's institutions and rule(r)s" (Chappell 282).

Rather than seeking a divine intermediary, then, the children take on the task of redeeming the faltering world. Harry, for all his magic and power, is human. Most of the miracles that save him are wrought not by him but by others who love and protect him, by the magic that emanates from the acts of friendship, love and sacrifice. The sacred story, out of scripture and in a popular fantasy, becomes a means of active political engagement between an individual and his/her milieu. At each turn the "divine plan" or the prophecy depends on individual acts and choices. Unlike the modernist conception of destiny and linear movement of history towards the day of judgment, the conception of magic and its uncertainties or incomprehensibility foreground the forking narratives which repeatedly return to past choices as they anticipate the future. The sacrifice of Harry's mother, the mercy shown to Peter Pettigrew, the cruelty of the Dark Lord to the underlings — these are the deeds that configure and re-configure the story repeatedly. Individual choices play a decisive role at each turn. Harry's growth is a journey from naiveté of a fantasy hero to responsibility, from "Why me?" at the first revelation of the prophecy to "Only we can stop him" after the death of Fred Weasley. At the end of each book, Harry emerges from the abyss of death. At the end of the series, he embraces death willingly to save the magical world, renouncing friends, love and future for communal welfare. Therefore, though set in the scriptural framework, Harry is an adolescent protagonist who embraces the qualities of postmodern childhood — "ambiguity, complexity, agency, resistance — rather than accept the binaries promoted by and constructed in traditional literature. These qualities facilitate the questioning of injustices established by and through the adult world of control" (Chapell 292).

Similarly, Phillip Pullman's trilogy takes its precedent from the book of Genesis, the dramatic point of Eve's transgression. Divine prohibition in Pullman's series is seen as a means of restraining man from being autonomous, free and adult. The end of the narrative re-works the dramatic forking point of Christian history — the divine authority is revealed to be a "puppet" in the hands of powerful archangels. The adolescent protagonists reinterpret the biblical myth of creation by revealing the tyranny and fragility of the divine authority, destabilizing it, and putting an end to the kingdom of God by instituting a new order, that of the "republic of heaven." In a reversal of the Christian narrative, in Pullman's story, the moment of man's first disobedience becomes the moment of grace, of creation and continuity of human order.

Therefore, the Manichean theme that runs through the Old Testament occupies the center stage of fantasy. It has been argued that one of the enduring appeals of the Book of Revelation is to the human taste for the fantastic and an underlying psychological attraction of the conflict of opposites (Doty 93). In the Potter series, the rivalry between Harry and the Dark Lord builds on the historical metanarratives of the magical world, mainly on the rivalry between Godric Gryffindor and Salazar Slytherin. The symbolic associations of the two houses are not hard to decipher. Gryffindors (the house named after mythological beast, the griffin, half-lion and half-eagle), with a lion on the banner, are the "natural" antagonists of the Slytherins, with their serpentine images complete with a snake symbol on the banner. The central conflict of the series is consistent with the Christian view of the world as a battleground between God and Satan, between good and evil. The story of this cosmic conflict provides a dramatic setting for fantasy. The apocalyptic imagery of the battle between good and evil involves humans, non-humans and part-humans.

This conflict between good and evil has been resolved in different ways. Rowling's predecessors like C.S. Lewis resolve the conflict through the victory of God over the blasphemous opposition. This resolution leaves the theological and psychological dualism of good and evil intact. God is never mentioned but there is a reference to "the Emperor beyond the Sea" who orders and re-orders the world, and whom Aslan represents. Narnia's destiny, though sidetracked by doubt and evil, nevertheless consistently follows the track laid out by the Christian framework. The stories narrativize the necessity of maintaining order, indeed a constant struggle to do so, in the cosmos that could at any moment turn to chaos. In this sense the fantasy remains open ended despite the generic convention of a closure. The Potter series offers further complexities — the closeness that links good and evil, the narrative of adolescent abjection and its displacement in the figure of Christ, the essential theme of coming of age, and the construction of selfhood with respect to the other. Together these complicate the religious symbolism that saturates the narrative. The universe is not inert, the "universal" narratives like the victory of good over evil are not fixed, unchanging precepts. An adolescent needs to find and negotiate a place for him-/herself constantly, the way he or she places himself vis-à-vis the powers of creation and destruction. Each decision becomes an act of will, which can either abet or control the constant threat of chaos and evil. Coming of age through painful and frightening events produces emotional, intellectual and spiritual growth. Each event therefore becomes a symbolic rite of passage.

The idea and the ideal of love, as a manifestation of the relation between the self and the other, are central to the narrative of growth as well as to the idea of Christianity. In Lewis's Narnia, love is the command that comes from Aslan in his song of creation: "Narnia, Narnia, Narnia, awake. Love. Think. Speak" (Lewis, *Magician's Nephew* 64). *The Lion, the Witch and the Wardrobe* establishes the existence of a moral law: "Deep Magic from the Dawn of Time." Edmund is forfeited when he breaks it. Aslan dies in Edmund's place, showing that this "deeper Magic from *before* the Dawn of Time" represents divine love and grace that saves the erring humans.

Therefore, love, especially divine love, is repeatedly emphasized as the highest form of magical power in fantasy literature. It is frequently mentioned in the *Potter* series, and in the fantastic narratives like Pullman's.

This idea of divine love sits uneasily next to the idea of love and sexuality that is central to adolescent fiction where it is imbricated with the theme of construction of selfhood and intersubjective relationship with the Other.[5] In Christianity, as mentioned earlier, love is a hallowed concept. The Christian God is the God of love. The worldview rests on the idea of the Holy Trinity: at the top is God, the supreme creator who fathered all things and ordered their being; the Son who redeemed the wayward world by sacrificing himself; and, the Holy Spirit which binds the Father to the Son. For Singer, the idea of the Trinity works at overlapping levels, binding the cosmos into a tight unity: within the divine "Holy Family," then among men and his fellow beings, and thirdly, joining the two levels of reality — the divine and the human, the creator and the creation. The Christian tradition, therefore, situates man centrally in the network of love — in a position where he or she is at once sinful and redeemed by the power of love. It can be seen in operation in a fantastic narrative where a child savior is placed in the context of his earthly family, his friends, peers and aides — all bound by the principle of love. In the Christian sense the highest form of love, *agape*, is divine bestowal, the unconditional promise of salvation. It is freely recognized by "believers" like Lucy Pevensie (who plays and romps with Aslan) and grudgingly accepted by Edmund once he is transformed from spiteful and self-centered child to self-sacrificing, brave and mature individual. Unlike in Freud's account of the violent relationship between God, the father and the sons in *Totem and Taboo*, the Christian concept of Trinity bound by love, mirrored in fantastic narrative, solves the problem of generations, obedience and authority at once.

This godly model is carefully purged off its earthly aspects like sexuality.[6] In the final Narnia volume, *The Last Battle*, earthlings return to Narnia and travel to Aslan's country: all except for one. Lewis leaves Susan on Earth since she is preoccupied with fashion, physical appearance, in lipsticks and nylon stockings. Polly suggests that Susan's is the case of arrested development — during childhood she longed to be older and now that is she is, she will spend rest of her life trying to remain that same age. However, Polly and Digory, the adults who retain the ability to re-visit Narnia, remain strangely child-like — single and untouched by the cares of this world. For Lewis, secular interpersonal relationships between human beings should not be an end; they are to serve as stepping stones towards the eternal divine love, or charity, as he calls it. Sexuality hardly fits in with the scheme; for Lewis, the body is a joke played upon man by the gods (*Four Loves* 142).

In contrast to Lewis, love in fantasy like Rowling's and Pullman's is not just a divine power meant to save erring mankind. It emanates from human actions and has repercussions in the human sphere. It forms the core of interpersonal relationships. It is secular love rather than the divine that holds sway. In Pullman's series, it is love and sexual attraction between the adolescent protagonists that leads to the "fortunate fall." In Madeline L'Engle's *The Time Quartet*, especially in the first book, *A Wrinkle in Time*, Meg Murray, a misfit adolescent, learns that she can rescue her father and brother from the totalitarian "utopic" community guided by a disembodied, all-controlling brain, "IT," only by love and compassion, which can overcome her anger.

Equally complex is the concept of love in Rowling's series, which begins with the love of a mother for her son, the love which makes Lily sacrifice herself; it lives on in the son and becomes Harry's greatest protection: "to have been loved so deeply, even though the person who loved us is gone, will give us some protection for ever" (Rowling, *PS* 216). Christ's story is easily discernible in Harry's story. To an extent, Lily's act of sacrifice emulates the immaculate conception of Christ by his virginal mother.[7] After being rescued by Hagrid, Dumbledore becomes Harry's protector, magically securing him in the house of his mother's sister. Dumbledore becomes a God-like figure watching over Harry. He saves Harry from difficult situations, guides him, and prepares him for the final encounter. Harry, on the other hand, reciprocates by being "Dumbledore's man through and through" till the end of the narrative, following and trusting him even in the face of surmounting doubts and slander. Right after Dumbledore announces love as Harry's weapon against the Dark Lord, love and attraction in a variety of disguises — legitimate and illegitimate, requited and unrequited, misplaced, denied or perverted — become the plot of the penultimate book of the series, *Harry Potter and the Half Blood Prince*. And since the essence of magic lies in its subversive nature, especially significant is love that is unsanctioned, illegitimate and extreme. Embodied in a variety of figures and forms — between Dumbledore and Grindelwald, Snape and Lily, Merope and Tom Riddle Senior, and, in an obsessive form, even between Bellatrix and Voldemort, love is an amoral force refusing to submit to the understanding based on morality or conventions of legitimacy. The comic moments of romance — Hermione attacking Ron with a flock of canaries and Romilda Vane's single-minded pursuit of Harry by love potions — frequently resonate with the tragedies in the main plot. Morfin laughs at his sister Merope's besotted pursuit of the handsome muggle Tom Riddle, till it becomes a dangerous obsession. Riddle's marriage to Merope under the influence of love potion, his subsequent desertion, the birth of Voldemort and the death of Merope are the background to the rise of the Dark Lord. Slughorn echoes Dumbledore when he tells his students that Amorentia, the love-potion, "is probably the most dangerous and powerful potion": "when you have seen as much of life as I have, you will not underestimate the power of obsessive love" (Rowling, *HBP* 177).

Growing up involves initiation into the complexities of love, sexuality and mortality — a sacrifice of innocence that is essential to regaining paradise, even though in the religious narrative, it signifies the final loss of paradise. This process of growth does not end with the renunciation of the world or any kind of transcendence of materiality. The child savior emerges into the adult world through his/her active political engagement. This is related to the "messianic" potential of fantasy to envision and establish a more just and humane order. In other words, fantasy becomes an adolescent narrative that can lead from a divinely offered "kingdom of God" to a politically active "republic of heaven," and the conception of love as an active, intersubjective force is central to it.[8]

In the crucial moments of conflict at the end of each book, the growth of the adolescent protagonist is linked directly and intricately with the figure of the savior through the themes of love, sacrifice and death. Each conflict is a metaphoric descent to death and rebirth. The climactic adventure in the first book begins with a kind of renunciation: "Losing points doesn't matter any more, can't you see? D'you think he'll leave you and your families alone if Gryffindor wins the House Cup? If I get caught before I can get to the Stone, well, I'll have to go back to the Dursleys and wait for Voldemort to find me there. It's only dying a bit later than I would have done, because I'm never going over to the Dark Side" (Rowling, *PS* 197). Therefore, the decision to save the Philosopher's Stone begins with a renunciation of all the things that have come to mean a lot to Harry in his first school year — the house, Quidditch; indeed Harry is willing to be expelled from Hogwarts, — the place that matters most to him.[9]

Sacrifice links the theme of love with the theme of death, in religion as well as fantasy. Christ's love for mankind and his sacrificial death is the central narrative of Christianity. The Potter series returns and explores this scriptural element at multiple levels. Once the above outburst decides the course that the three friends are going to follow, it is time to descend into the abyss of death. In each book, the confrontation with death takes place in underground chambers or in isolated, forsaken places. In the first book, the children descend under the school through the trapdoor guarded by Fluffy, a ferocious three-headed dog. Fluffy, whom Hagrid bought from a "Greek chappie," is linked to Cerebrus, the mythical beast guarding the gates of hell. It is the obstacle that Quirrel takes the longest time overcoming. While Harry is able to renounce the world, Quirrel, with Voldemort, who is searching for immortality, in his head, struggles against Fluffy for the longest time before he learns the secret of putting him to sleep by playing a harp like Orpheus. In the subsequent Potter books, the encounters take place in the underground Chamber of Secrets, the Shrieking Shack, the graveyard, the Department of Mysteries under the Ministry of Magic, in an isolated seaside cave and, in the last book, in the Forbidden Forest itself. The theme of descent can be traced back to the classical motif of the hero's journey to the Land of the Dead. The space of encounter itself can be seen as a liminal space where life encounters death. These non-organized places outside the reach of school authorities become zones of ritualistic action. For Eliade, the zone of sacred encounters is important since

> it opens communication between cosmic planes (between earth and heaven) and makes possible ontological passage from one mode of being to another. It is such a break in the heterogeneity of profane space that creates the center through which communication with the transmundane is established, that, consequently founds the world, for the center renders *orientation* possible [*The Sacred* 63].

The encounter between the living and the dead, the victory over death, the sacrifice — these sacralize the action and also orient it according to the Christian point of view. Though the encounters can be compared to the classical motif of the journey to the world of the dead, the ritualized action in each encounter re-enacts Christian cosmogony. In the classical parallel, heroes like Odysseus descend to the land of the dead to gain information and insights into the future. In the Christian version, Christ's descent into Hell or the "harrowing of the hell" is undertaken to liberate the dead. It marks the victory of Christ over Satan on his own ground. Rowling's text interlaces the classical formalist motif with Christian content. Harry mostly undertakes his journey to save the innocent victims of the Dark Lord. Each "transmundane" encounter, therefore, becomes a ritual that orients the action in line with the central Christian dogma of love and sacrifice as the only way to overcome death; at the same time, the dogma is complicated in multiple ways.

Rather than love that reflects the glory of God, the bond of love in a fellowship is based on the interpersonal relations between man and his fellow beings. Each obstacle commands teamwork — it is a test of fellowship for the three friends. Unlike Voldemort, who likes to work alone, a large part of Harry's strength comes from his allies. The idea of fellowship that characterizes the quest of fantastic heroes could be linked to the Christian notion of *philia*— the idea of Christian brotherhood based on the divine love that is bestowed equally on everyone. Ron, during the game of chess, is the first who enunciates the idea of fellowship in his willingness to sacrifice himself for his friends in the chess game.

> "We're nearly there," he muttered suddenly. "Let me think — let me think..."
> The white queen turned her blank face toward him.
> "Yes..." said Ron softly, "it's the only way ... I've got to be taken."
> "No!" Harry and Hermione shouted.
> "That's chess!" snapped Ron. "You've got to make some sacrifices! I take one step forward and she'll take me — that leaves you free to checkmate the king, Harry!" [*PS* 205].

Later, in *Harry Potter and the Prisoner of Azkaban*, when he believes that Sirius is about to kill Harry, Ron tells him,

> "If you want to kill Harry, you'll have to kill us too!" he said fiercely, though the effort of standing upright was draining him of still more colour, and he swayed slightly as he spoke [*PoA* 249].

Though none of the obstacles could have been overcome without her, Hermione too makes way for Harry. The idea of fellowship therefore remains central to fantasy. Timmerman points out that though the hero of a fantasy performs the heroic task alone, his quest is always placed in a group. Helpers and aides are essential. In all the ordeals, Harry and his friends posit themselves as antitheses of all the things that Voldemort and his Death Eaters stand for.

When Harry faces the last obstacle, he seems to be on his own. If it is the love for others that helps Harry finds the Philosopher's Stone, he, in turn, is saved by the sacrificial love of his mother. According to Dumbledore, the happiest person in the world is the one who looks into the Mirror of Erised and sees himself: the Mirror in a way re-configures Christian *eros*—the mystical ascent towards perfection, wholeness which guides man to love the promise of perfection incarnated by divinity.[10]

Yet in the series, so replete with Christian imagery, God himself is absent. Though it is linked to the idea of a Christian pilgrimage, it is an account of human journey following Christ. It is a pilgrimage that has to be undertaken in the present, in this world with all its power politics, social tensions and cultural shortcomings. In the second encounter with the Mirror, Harry is able to use the Mirror to get what he wants only because he wants to find the stone, but not use it. The desires that are reflected by the mirror, this time, are configured towards communal welfare, towards service for others before personal advancement. Quirrel, on the other hand, is burned once he tries to touch Harry. Love and sacrifice become the fire of hell for the one obsessed with power and evil. According to John S. Morris, "the journey or quest undertaken always involves a moment which discovers the enormity of the struggle — one in which the travelers may participate, but in which they are deeply aware of the clash of forces which are completely beyond them" (81). Harry, despite being the chosen one of the magical world, is always aware of and defers to the social, magical and cosmic forces that lie beyond his grasp and understanding.

And since his pilgrimage is placed in the context of the community, the expanding network of friends and aides is crucial to his victory. In *Harry Potter and the Chamber of Secrets*, showing fealty to Dumbledore, the surrogate god-like figure of the series, saves Harry. Granger points out morality play–like elements evident in the encounter with Voldemort disguised as Tom Riddle at the end of the next book. Harry, a kind of "everyman" character, descends to the underbelly of the school, the hidden Chamber of Secrets, to rescue Ginny Weasley, innocence duped by evil. Tom Riddle, who had also succeeded in deceiving Harry Potter into believing that he is a friend, turns out to be a Satanic figure. Harry is saved by the Phoenix, the "Resurrection Bird" who not only wounds the serpent and brings the sword that can kill it, but also heals Harry's mortal wound by its tears, an analogy of Christ suffering for mankind.

In the succeeding book, Harry discovers two of his greatest friends and supporters — his father's friends, the escaped convict Sirius Black and the werewolf, Remus Lupin. Both are outcasts in the magical world. Sirius is even believed to be the cause of his parent's death. For the first time in the figures of Sirius and Remus, Harry, Ron and Hermione encounter the cost that their quest against evil can exact.

Therefore, if a ground is being prepared for ushering in the kingdom of heaven, it does not seem to be via a return to literal childhood, its easy and blind trust, its naivety. Growth embodied by the fantastic pilgrimage is towards a more discerning kind of trust. It rests on a maturity of judgment rather than the helplessness of a child. At the beginning of *Harry Potter and the Prisoner of Azkaban*, Harry "blows up" Aunt Marge for maligning him and his parents. In a crucial scene of denouement, he is able to show mercy to Peter Pettigrew, the person who betrayed his parents and led to their death. Pettigrew becomes indebted to Harry — it is the magical order of justice against the human order that is wrongly bent on punishing Sirius. But this magical order functions via human choice and actions. The mercy shown to Pettigrew can be equated to the idea of divine justice and grace central to Christianity, but the narrative portrays it as a choice available to Harry. His decision to spare Pettigrew is free, unforced and spontaneous. As he does so, he emphasizes the link between him and James, his father: "I'm doing it because I don't reckon my dad would've wanted his best friends to become killers — just for you" (*PoA* 275). At the time that the narrative of the savior is put in the context of the family, it is also put in the context of human community — its legal and political systems. When Harry regrets freeing Pettigrew, Dumbledore's explanation reminds of wide ramifications that a simple act may have:

> "Pettigrew owes his life to you. You have sent Voldemort a deputy who is in your debt. When one wizard saves another wizard, it creates a certain bond between them ... and I'm much mistaken if Voldemort wants a servant in the debt of Harry Potter."
> "I don't want a bond with Pettigrew!" said Harry. "He betrayed my parents!"
> "This is magic at its deepest, its most impenetrable, Harry. But trust me ... the time may come when you will be glad you saved Pettigrew's life" [*PoA* 311].

This emphasis on human emotions, thoughts and feelings is further explored through the figure of the Dementors. The battle with the Dementors is central to the book. The Dementors incarnate despair and depression. They crush humanity by feeding on hope and happiness. In the wizard prison Azkaban, they trap the prisoners inside their own heads in a state of depression and doom. The ultimate weapon in their arsenal is the kiss — "an expression of a 'consolation' found in despair" (Granger 147). The Dementor's kiss signals the damnation for the soul, a soulless existence. Harry, in their presence, relives the trauma of his parents' murder; the memories of the eventful night buried in his mind, resurface. In Pullman's series, those who have lost their "daemon," similar to souls in our world, become mechanical and lifeless. In *The Northern Lights*, the children whose "daemon" is "severed" die soon. In *The Amber Spyglass*, Will and Lyra visit hell on the condition that they leave behind their souls, an extremely painful experience for both. The soul and its journey through the cycles of life is a significant preoccupation of the religious discourse. In Rowling's world, there is a charm to fight the Dementors — "Expecto Patronum." According to David Colbert, it means "I throw forth a guardian." John Granger, on the other hand, deciphers it as "I look out for a guardian." Rowling associates the charm with happy memories and faith. Harry's patronus takes the form of a stag, the animagus of his father. The gospels tell us that the Son's relationship with the Father and ours to the Father through the Son and the Holy Spirit of love are the essential relationships of Christian salvation. Harry's father appears in the form of a stag, a Christ symbol.[11] His deliverance (as son) comes at his realization that he is his father. It expresses the essential union of Father and Son: "I saw me but I thought I was my dad!" Through the symbol of a stag, Rowling unites the father, the son and the God. Before escaping, Sirius tells Harry that he is truly his "father's son" (*PoA* 303). Later Dumbledore mentions it again: "I expect you're tired of hearing it, but you do look *extraordinarily* like James" (*PoA* 312). The repeated emphasis highlights the centrality of the Father-Son relationship to the text and its resonance with the Christian context of the series. The first chapter highlighted the numerous surrogate father-son relationships in Harry's life. The relation is central to the series, since it places the orphan in the family at the same time as it places Man in relation to Christ and God. A relationship, conditioned by the spirit of love, ultimately places the growth of the hero with respect to the journey of Christ towards the ultimate sacrifice.

And what is the goal of the sacrifice? In the first book, Harry's greatest desire is for his parents, standing between his father and mother, over-looked by his ancestors. By the end of the first book, he is able to transcend this personal desire. The desire for communal welfare that he shows in saving the Philosopher's Stone is not pitted against love and attachment to any specific person. In the subsequent books, Harry becomes more and more involved in networks of attachment. Ron and Hermione become important — the times spent with them become the happiest memories that help him conjure a patronus. He saves Ginny Weasley, Ron's sister and later his own girlfriend. The Weasley family and the Burrow become his "home" apart from Hogwarts. Sirius and Remus become surrogate fathers, protectors and friends. His friendship with the "monsters" and "freaks" of the magical world like Hagrid, Dobby and Lupin, explored in the following chapter, signals a new kind of alliance which is based on a kind of equality with the abject.[12] The movement out of childish solipsism is accompanied with an identity that rests on concern and sympathy with the other. As an adolescent grows, the pilgrimage gets tougher with each passing school year. Unlike the renunciation in the first book, the sacrifice that comes at the end of the series is much harder. This time Harry is not renouncing examinations, Quidditch or the House Cup. It is greater renunciation — giving up the joys of friendship, love and family in order to save them; the sacrifice is not transcendence from earthly desire like that of Bunyan's pilgrim, it is the final act of belonging, loving, being one with the community.

The expanding network of friends and loved ones starts coming to a kind of climax with the mounting death toll, fourth book onwards. Though none of the characters die in the first few books (apart from the offstage murder of Harry's parents) the shadow of death is always close. Quirrel attempts to murder Harry. Tom Riddle leaves Ginny on the verge of death; Harry and Sirius themselves comes close to being "killed" by the Dementors. In *Harry Potter and the Goblet of Fire*, for the first time the theme of death comes to fore. Three characters — Barty Crouch Sr., his son masquerading as Alastor Moody and Cedric Diggory — succumb to death. As the adolescent hero realizes the importance of friends and family, as he forms his sexual attachments and discovers new friends, he realizes the complexities that accompany them. The discoveries are interlaced with a sense of loss that permeates the strongest attachments. Even as he is coming to trust Sirius as a father, he witnesses another tragic father-and-son relationship — that of Barty Crouch and his son. He ascribes them to Voldemort: "It was Voldemort, Harry thought, staring up at the canopy of his bed in the darkness. It all came back to Voldemort.... He was the one who had torn these families apart, who had ruined all these lives..." While Harry's growth is placed in the context of relationships, friends, guardians — an entire gamut of secular relationships — Voldemort's growth is an opposite direction. His first act of evil is the murder of his own father. Thus Harry's victory over Voldemort is the victory of love whose power comes from its secular context, from the intersubjectivity of the self directly rather than a divine transcendental source.

In the narrative of growth out of childhood solipsism into intersubjective relationships, sport events like the World Cup and the Triwizard Tournament mark a definitive stage. Sports and combat have been metaphors for "inner" life in the Western literary tradition, right from the Greek epics. As pointed out in the previous chapter, the tradition found its space in the literary genres like the school fiction and the hero's story.

The knightly tradition spiritualized the theme of sports by adding a Christian dimension. The Triwizard Tournament begins with the magical cup, the Goblet of Fire, selecting the participants from the three schools. The Goblet is made of wood. The flames in the wooden goblet spew forth the name of those worthy to enter the dangerous contest that promises money, fame and glory. Granger compares them to the flames of purgatory. Dumbledore calls the Goblet of Fire "an impartial judge." Moody describes it as "powerful magical object." Readers and critics have drawn parallels with the Holy Grail (Colbert, Granger 164). It symbolizes the covenant of Jesus — his promise to die in exchange for the forgiveness of sins committed by mankind. And indeed, the two winners of the tournament do face death, both of them fair and believing that the other deserves to win — Cedric dies, while Harry escapes narrowly.

The quest for the grail, a prominent motif in the tournament, links it with the tales of knighthood and Christian faith. In the tournament, the contestants fight a dragon and rescue innocent hostages. In the second task, Harry insists on saving all the hostages because Hermione, Cho and Gabrielle are important even if they are not meant for him to save. None of the other players show similar concern. Though Harry feels like a fool, he is rewarded.

> "Harry Potter used gillyweed to great effect," Bagman continued. "He returned last, and well outside the time limit of an hour. However, the Merchieftainess informs us that Mr. Potter was first to reach the hostages, and that the delay in his return was due to his determination to return all hostages to safety, and not merely his own."
>
> Ron and Hermione both gave Harry half-exasperated, half-commiserating looks.
>
> "Most of the judges," and here, Bagman gave Karkaroff a very nasty look, "feel that this shows moral fiber and merits full marks. However ... Mr. Potter's score is forty-five points" [*GoF* 440].

The virtues are tested and rewarded literally through the points that he wins at the end of each task. The knightly tasks are followed by the Christian ones — the maze can be seen as a representation of the quest for self. The contestants need to help each other and forge a bond of kinship rather than rivalry. Cedric wins because his "growth" through the tournament is consistent with these ideals. He tells Harry about the clue in the egg. He refuses to take the cup because he feels he is not worthy of winning. However, in the encounter with Voldemort, Harry as a Gryffindor, set apart by his "daring, nerve and chivalry," wins (*PS* 88). In overcoming Voldemort and bringing back the body of Cedric Diggory, Harry proves himself worthy of carrying on the pilgrimage. The tournament, therefore, becomes a spiritual warfare — the martial virtues like bravery and courage place the narrative in the context of a masculine tradition of initiation. At the same time, the thrust on sacrifice and morality link it with the Christian themes of the series.

However, another dimension that links the Triwizard Tournament with the Christian journey in an ironically inverted manner is Voldemort's "resurrection." It has been compared to a witch's Sabbath or the "Black Mass" — an inversion of the Eucharist in Christian liturgical tradition (Kjetil Kriglebotten). The things that bring him back to life — "Flesh, Blood and Bone" — desecrate the Christian symbols of Eucharist. Voldemort's birth is a reversal of Christ's sacrifice: the grave of the father he murdered is re-opened — "Bone of the father, unknowingly given, you will renew your son!": the sacrifice of flesh is painfully wrenched from the servant — "Flesh — of the servant — w-willingly given — you will — revive — your master"; the spell is completed by the blood of the enemy — "B-blood of the enemy ... forcibly taken ... you will ... resurrect your foe" (*GoF* 556). Even as they bring about his "rebirth," these objects become the cause of his final destruction. Rather than love, it is fear, evil and deceit that hold sway. The ritual in a way secures Voldemort too in a network of relationships, but these are relationships of fear, animosity and murder, relationships that turn on exploitation and demand rather than reciprocity. Like a vengeful master, he demands absolute obedience from his followers and promises a frightful fate for the Death Eaters who deserted him. In Voldemort's return, life takes on a daemonic aspect.

Harry, on the other hand, is saved by Voldemort's victims, by those who literally stood in the Dark Lord's way, including Harry's parents. Voldemort himself feels "livid with fear" at the unexpected rise of those he had put an end to. The light and the phoenix song hint at a supernatural presence.[13] The phoenix feather wand works in an unexpected and unforeseen way, raising the spirits of the dead. Often the magical order of justice and its unseen ways seem to work in a kind of karmic cycle. What saves Harry repeatedly is not external preparations, though they help, but the acts of courage, love, and virtue — performed by him and by others for him. It is these acts that determine the receptivity of the graces.

The later books complicate the notions of love and death. There is a gradual shift in the attitude towards love, especially parental love. In the early books of the series, the emphasis is on the "presence" of

Harry's parents despite their death, on their greatness and bravery, which is a living influence on the life of the son. The first incident with the Mirror of Erised shows that it is based in and sustained by the imaginary unities of the mirror phase. The parents are literally "magically" incorporated into the self. Coats points out that the parental love that looks back for the "lost" unity is regressive:

> The love involved in developmental mourning entails the birth of self-love through separation. The child posits the mother or mother substitute as idea, the ideal inevitably fails or is lost, and the child's ego takes on the characteristics of the lost ideal in order to render the loss acceptable to the desiring id [*Looking Glasses* 38].

So, according to Coats, to grow, a child must develop an identity that is separate from that of the parents. This forms the central theme of children's literature. If in the early books of the series, Harry consciously identifies with his parents, especially with the father, the later books complicate the process.

The fifth book of the series, *Harry Potter and the Order of the Phoenix*, is a kind of climax, where all the earlier ideals, securities and comforts are questioned and found wanting. As the book progresses, Harry loses most of the things that had come to define him. Rather than the boy who lived, he is projected as a deranged lunatic telling tales about the return of Voldemort. He is even subjected to a trial for unauthorized use of magic. His relations with Dumbledore become strained. The father, the "ego-ideal" till now, turns out to be "every bit as arrogant as Snape had always told him" (*OotP* 573). By the end of the book, he can no longer play Quidditch, he is no longer in love with Cho and learns that he is tied to Voldemort inseparably by the means of a prophecy. Sirius's death is the final straw. John Granger describes the book as "the dark night of the soul": "*Order of the Phoenix* is a book length disillusionment for Harry to rid himself of his self illusions and to prepare him for the revelation of who he really is at the bottom: the destined vanquisher or victim of the Dark Lord *as we all are*" (*How Harry* 174).

If till now Harry had occupied the privileged positions like the youngest Quidditch player, the best Seeker, the boy who lived, a great wizard, the son of brave and popular parents, in *Harry Potter and the Order of the Phoenix*, he is closest to Sirius, the outlaw on the run, forced to hide in the house he hates, constantly at odds with the members of the Order and yet unable to act on his own. Both Harry and Sirius are misunderstood and isolated and made to suffer unjustly. They occupy the position of the abject, the outsiders in the magical world. Only in death is Sirius able to prove his innocence and recover some of his lost position in the magical world. Only in death is he absolved of the crimes he was charged of. After his tryst with infamy and collapsing ideals, Sirius' death also severs Harry from the position of the abject and helps him to re-enter communal ties. He is no longer obliged to be an image of his father. Though the prophecy burdens and isolates him, it also places the ultimate responsibility on his shoulders.

To Harry, then, Sirius's death marks a break in his life: "the week that had elapsed since he had last seen Sirius seemed to have lasted much, much longer; it stretched across two universes, the one with Sirius in it, and the one without" (*OotP* 763). Death to Harry means an ultimate finality, a complete termination of his relation to the loved one who is now no more. Indeed, the failed communication through the two-way mirror proves it to be so. Later, when Ron doubts Dumbledore's death, Harry's assertion is emphatic: "Dumbledore's dead,' he said. 'I saw it happen, I saw the body. He's definitely gone'" (*DH* 317). With the mounting death toll, especially of his loved ones, the later books find the adolescent hero struggling to find meaning in death, and in life in the face of death.

Trites explains that "in adolescent literature, death is often depicted in terms of maturation when the protagonist accepts the permanence of mortality, when s/he accepts herself as a Being-towards-Death" (*Disturbing* 119). Attitude to death in fantasy seems to be more complex and ambiguous. In fantasy, death is seen in terms of a crossing over from one level of existence to another through a threshold like the archway in the Department of Mysteries. It is not a permanent closure. The dead like Harry's parents repeatedly return and assert themselves. In this repeated return of the dead, fantasy ties the central concern of adolescent fiction with the Christian idea of life after death.

The narrative is full of people who cast shadows beyond the grave — Harry's parents, Voldemort's victims, talking portraits, ghosts in Hogwarts; the dead return in the magical world in a variety of forms. Fantasy therefore becomes a means to explore the implications of death on life and afterlife, a crucial theme outlined on the gravestone of Harry's parents: "The last enemy that shall be destroyed is death" (Corinthians 15:26). The ambiguous attitude of the series towards death is embodied in Harry's encounters with the Dementors — though he relives the trauma of his parents' murder, he also wants to hear his parents' voices, even in death throes. If, as Trites notes, that in adolescent literature, acceptance of death becomes a point of maturation, then fantasy, in disturbing the teleology, complicates the closure affected by death. Tamora Pierce's *The Song of the Lioness* features a villainous wizard who repeatedly returns from the dead. Garth Nix's *Sabriel* is concerned with the struggle of an adolescent necromancer against the spirits bent on returning from the gates of death to the world of living. In Pullman's *The Amber Spyglass*, the liberation of the dead parallels Christ's harrowing of the hell in the Bible. Lyra and Will enter hell, where all dead souls are trapped, and release them to become a part of the cycles of life. Rowling's series builds around the villainous figure who goes to great lengths to "conquer" death and yet remains unable to do so while the hero who submits to death becomes the "Master of Death."

Death in all these narratives is envisaged as a point of regeneration, a moment of grace itself. In the first book, Dumbledore tells eleven-year-old Harry that "to the well organized mind, death is but the next great adventure" (*PS* 297). His friends Nicholas Flamel and his wife choose to die after a long life. Indeed he himself plans and chooses the right moment to "depart" from the world. In the *Goblet of Fire*, when Harry tells him about the return of Cedric and other victims of Voldemort, he insists "no spell can reawaken the dead" (*GoF* 605). When Moody shows Harry the picture of the earlier Order of the Phoenix and lists the causalities of the first war, Harry is disturbed. Similarly, nothing can alleviate the agony of the arbitrariness and meaninglessness of Sirius's death. *The Order of the Phoenix* ends with Harry insistently questioning "What happens when you die, anyway? Where do you go? Why doesn't everyone come back? Why isn't this place full of ghosts? Why —?" (*OotP* 759). For the first time, he questions the presence of ghosts in Hogwarts. Ghosts, in the series, are the pale imprints of their living selves. Nearly Headless Nick tells Harry that they are those who were afraid to die and therefore, chose to remain behind, "neither here nor there": "I know nothing of the secrets of Death, Harry, for I chose my feeble imitation of life instead" (*GoF* 759). A brave wizard like Sirius would choose "to go on," he tells Harry. When Harry at last meets Sirius in *Deathly Hallows,* he tells Harry that death is easier than sleeping.

It is through sacrifice that meaning emerges in death. Dumbledore chooses to drink the potion in the cave to save Harry and thus in the very act of dying helps to bring about the end of the Dark Lord.[14] He rushes to Hogwarts when he discovers that the school is under siege. He shows mercy to Draco, who was responsible for the presence of the Death Eaters at Hogwarts. Even in his last moment he saves Harry. It is in sacrifice that meaning emerges. In Pullman's fantasy, Lyra's parents atone for their cruelty and selfishness by sacrificing themselves for Lyra. In the Christian tradition, death, on the one hand, represents the "wages of sin" (Romans 6:23). In the Garden of Eden, God warned Adam and Eve: "of the tree of knowledge of good and evil, thou shalt not eat of it: for in the day that thou eatest thereof thou shalt surely die." Death, thus, came about as the result of man's first transgression against divine will. On the other hand, triumph over death came about with the incarnation of Jesus, who showed that the way to destroy death is by dying, sacrificing himself for the love of mankind. In death, we are born again (Jesus in John, chapter 3, tells Nicodemus). This powerful magic is the greatest mystery even the world of magic:

> "There is a room in the Department of Mysteries," interrupted Dumbledore, "that is kept locked at all times. It contains a force that is at once more wonderful and more terrible than death, than human intelligence, than forces of nature. It is also, perhaps, the most mysterious of the many subjects for study that reside there. It is the power held within that room that you possess in such quantities and which Voldemort has not at all. That power took you to save Sirius tonight. That power also saved you from possession of Voldemort, because he could not bear to reside in a body so full of the force he detests. In the end, it mattered not that you could not close your mind. It was your heart that saved you" [OotP 743].

Dumbledore tells Harry that he needs to stay at the Dursleys because it is the home of Petunia Dursley, sister of Lily Potter: "While you can still call home the place where your mother's blood dwells, there you cannot be touched or harmed by Voldemort. He shed her blood, but it lives on in you and her sister. Her blood became your refuge" (OotP 737). It brings in mind the symbolism of Eucharist: "whoso eateth my flesh, and drinketh my blood, hath eternal life; and I will release him up at the last day" (John 6:54).

Yet when we see Voldemort for the first time, in the shadowy form that he was reduced to after his first encounter with Harry, he is drinking the blood of the unicorn — the symbol of Christ.[15] Firenze, the centaur, tells Harry that "it is a monstrous thing to slay a unicorn."

> Only one who has nothing to lose, and everything to gain, would commit such a crime. The blood of a unicorn will keep you alive, even if you are an inch from death, but at a terrible price. You have slain something pure and defenseless to save yourself, and you will have but a half-life, a cursed life, from the moment the blood touches your lips [PS 188].

Granger points out that Firenze seems to be directly quoting from *The Bible:* "For he that eateth and drinketh unworthily, eateth and drinketh damnation to himself, not discerning the Lord's body" (Corinthians 11:29). In a way it sums up the sin of Voldemort. In shedding the blood of the innocent, though he evades death, his life is cursed. Granger deciphers "horcrux," the pieces of his severed soul as "the horrible cross"—it is the cross the Dark Lord has to bear for murder of the innocents. Rather than gaining immortality through the lifesaving sacrifice of Christ, he accomplishes the task by splitting his soul through the ultimate act of evil against the fellow beings. Yet for Voldemort, it is a "successful" experiment.

> I was ripped from my body, I was less than spirit, less than the meanest ghost ... but still I was alive. What I was, even I do not know.... I, who have gone further than anybody along the path that leads to immortality. You know my goal-to conquer death. And now, I was tested, and it appeared that one or more of my experiments had worked ... for I had not been killed, though the curse should have done it [*GoF* 568].

In a variety of ways, the narrative repeatedly returns to its central concern-that "there are other worse ways of destroying a man" (*OotP* 718). In Azkaban, the wizard prison, the greatest punishment is not death but the soul-destroying kiss of the Dementors. Death follows soon after. Peter Pettigrew, who betrays his friends to save himself, lives as a rat for years and eventually is killed by the Dark Lord. Dumbledore tells Voldemort: "Indeed, your failure to understand that there are things much worse than death has always been your greatest weakness" (*OotP* 718). Voldemort's fear of death and his obsessive ambition to escape it in a way stands for the fear of the natural cycle of growth and development, of thinking of death as a closure, as the ultimate negation of life rather than part of the life cycle. His quest is exploitative; he is not concerned with things that do not matter to him; he murders most of his own family; there are no friends, only followers. In his last attempt to kill Harry in the forest, Voldemort appears to be an overgrown baby, in its solipsistic state, "a curious child, wondering what would happen if he proceeded" (*DH* 564).

As mentioned earlier, Voldemort, Dumbledore, and Harry can be seen as the three brothers in the tale of Beadle the Bard — all seeking ways to overcome death. Voldemort's quest for immortality is linked with his thirst for power. It is symbolized by the death stick or the wand of elder. Folklore wisdom points out its futility: "Wand of Elder, never prosper" (*DH* 336). But it is the kind of wisdom for which Voldemort has no time. The three unforgivable curses in his arsenal are imbricated with the notions of power, control and suppression of otherness which become progressively horrifying with each curse. Imperius is subjection of will, Crucio (derived from the word "crucify") is the torture curse, while Avada Kedavara is the ultimate curse of murder, of snuffing out the enemy, the other. In *Deathly Hallows*, he tortures the wandmakers, kills wizards and finally desecrates the tomb of Dumbledore to gain the most powerful wand. Yet its power remains elusive.

Dumbledore's search for the Resurrection Stone is linked to his guilt of letting down his family in his quest for power even though he conceived it "for the Greater Good." Taken from the Gospel of St. Matthew, the epitaph on the grave of his mother and sister sums up his error — "Where your treasure is, there will your heart be also." It refers to the lasting treasure that Christ asks his disciples to seek by giving away the worldly pursuits as they wait for the Kingdom of Heaven. In his pursuit of power and ambition, even when meant "for the Greater Good," Dumbledore is guilty of negligence that led to the death of Ariana, one of the most tragic characters in the series. In a way Rita Skeeter is right in asking "Is it possible that Ariana Dumbledore was the first person to die for the greater good?" (*DH* 293). Once Dumbledore returns to his senses, his greatest desire is to undo the wrong: to bring his sister back from the dead. In Plato's *Symposium*, Phaedrus discounts a similar search of Orpheus for his wife Eurydice and the attempt to win her back from Hades as an act of cowardice. What Orpheus gets back, like the second brother of the tale and Dumbledore himself, is "apparition only of her who he sought," because "he showed no spirit; he was only a harp-player, and did not dare ... to die for love, but was contriving how he might enter Hades alive; moreover, they [gods] afterwards caused him to suffer death at the hands of women, as the punishment of his cowardliness" (4). Dumbledore suffers death at the hands of the Resurrection Stone, the Deathly Hallow through which he wanted to revive his family. Love and death therefore interlace the political implications of Dumbledore's quest of power with his familial history and also tie them up with the scriptural and mythological elements. The narrative intertwines the personal and spiritual aspects with political dimensions. To a large extent, Dumbledore does conquer his earthly ambitions but in the desire to recover his dead family by the means of the Resurrection Stone, to re-awaken them in their human form, he forgets the destiny of the second brother of the tale.

Harry unwittingly achieves what Voldemort as well as Dumbledore desire. If, in the earlier books, Harry is saved repeatedly by the sacrifice of the others, at the end of *Deathly Hallows*, he accepts death to save others. The book begins with the attack on Harry and the members of Order escorting him to the Burrow. The death of Moody once again brings out the danger he poses to his friends. Though friends, aides and helpers continue to guide Harry's quest, the number is constantly diminishing. When he becomes obsessed with the Hallows, Dobby's death brings him back. Dobby's friendship, his growth in love, and his sacrifice serve as an example. Despite the sense of loss and tragedy that accompanies the termination of life, death is repeatedly portrayed as a part of a greater struggle, a loss on the way towards the next goal. Fred Weasley's death with "the ghost of his last laugh still etched upon his face" embodies this attitude towards life and death.

Hermione points out the real message behind the two inscriptions on the graves of Dumbledore's family and the Potters: "It means ... you know ... living beyond death. Living after death" (*DH* 269). Harry still cannot comprehend: "But they were not living, thought Harry: they were gone. The empty words could not disguise the fact that his parent's moldering ruins lay beneath snow and stone, indifferent, unknowing." It makes him wish for death — death that is an escape from responsibility and pain. Yet once Harry decides to sacrifice himself, face death not as an escape but as the only means to save his friends and the world, he meets his parents, Sirius, and Remus; they are neither "mouldering ruins," nor are they indifferent and unknowing. The dead are the symbols of the past who continue to have a stake in the present. Unlike Dumbledore who sought to bring back his family from the dead by the Resurrection Stone, Harry brings back his family as he seeks to join them in death. Even though dead, Harry's parents have looked after him beyond the grave. Sirius points out the place of the dead: "'We are part of you,' said Sirius. 'Invisible to everybody else'" (*DH* 561). Similar idea occurs in Pullman's series also. In Pullman's story, the dead become a part a part of nature, of the endless cycle of regeneration. Rowling's dead live at a more personal level — in their loved ones, in the magical deeds wrought in their lifetime: this is what Dumbledore meant when he asked Harry, "You think the dead we loved ever leave us? You think we don't recall them more clearly than ever in times of great trouble? Your father is alive in you, Harry, and shows himself plainly when you have need of him" (*PoA* 312).

However, death does put an end to something; it is the thing that Harry is most conscious of in his final walk to the forest. "He felt the heart pounding fiercely in his chest.... He felt more alive, and more aware of his own living body than ever before. Why had he never ever appreciated what a miracle he was, brain and nerve and bounding heart? It would all be gone ... or at least, he would be gone from it" (*DH* 555). There is an understanding that there is a part of him beyond the body but materiality of body, corporeal pleasures and sensations, define humanity — a condition that Pullman's Authority envies and seeks to destroy. On his way to the forest, the last friend Harry sees is Ginny and the future that he is renouncing. His last living thought is kissing her. The body and bodily pleasures are not abject and sinful. The human incarnation of Christ itself can be seen as the redemption of the body. Corporeality, for a human being, is a necessary condition, a condition that he sacrifices.

It is the sacrifice of this "human-ness" that is the final act of being one with his human community. In sacrificing his corporeal body for the redemption of mankind, the sacrifice of Christ unites body and soul. The Eucharist symbolizes this mingling of the body and the spirit made possible by Christ. In the text, it can be done only by following the calls of love and responsibility, even as they draw one to the abyss of death. Like the third brother, Harry does not seek to conquer or deceive death but willingly meets it as a friend. Unlike Pullman's protagonists, Will and Lyra, who bring about the death of death itself, by the act of sacrifice, Harry submits to death as an equal who can still escape but surrenders to it willingly. The sacrifice is an embodiment of love in terms of being a person for others.

The aptly named King's Cross railway station is the place from where the dead journey on. Once again, it is the return to the liminal space between the worlds. In submitting to death, Harry's arrival at King's Cross coincides with the cessation of the link between him and Voldemort's soul residing in him. Unlike Lewis, who bans Susan from the Kingdom of Aslan, there is grace available even to Voldemort on the condition of painful penance. The soul, bawling like a newborn, waits for Voldemort to make his final choice on earth. Despite the prophecy, the availability of choice even in death emphasizes the insistence on free will.

The sacrifice in the forest thus is linked to the liturgical time of Christ's Passion, death and resurrection. In the recreation of the sacred narrative, the series returns to the sacred time of Christianity, the time of purification, of expulsion of the past and its sins. Girard also relates the violence of sacrifice with communal regeneration. The sacrificial process furnishes an outlet for those violent impulses that cannot be mastered by systems and hierarchies of society. The sacrifice is therefore a "mixed" ceremony resulting from a complex nuanced relation between crisis and restoration of order. Unmarried adolescents hold a special position among the sacrificial victims due to their location at the fringes of the society. By dying out of the dangerous liminal position, in the act of sacrifice, they finally become central to the community.

Sacrifice, therefore, takes into account the continuity seen in the theme of regeneration, as well as discontinuity or rupture seen in the violence of the sacrifice itself. In recounting the death of Harry within the scriptural framework of Christ's sacrifice — as means of communal regeneration of the magical world, the narrative itself seems to participate in the sacrificial violence that characterizes the scriptural narrative. According to Eliade, the sacred time that reactualizes the myths of origin is the "starting time over again at its beginning" (Eliade 78). Harry's sacrifice is meant to purge the community of its injustices and begin it anew. It lifts the narrative out of the profane level where the responsibility towards himself, his friends, and his murdered parents is transformed into a responsibility on a cosmic plane. At one level, Eliade points out that such a return may appear to be a refusal of history, of creative freedom and spontaneity, a continual repetition of a limited pattern that shows "man paralyzed by the myth of eternal return" (93).

In Rowling's narrative, however, the sacred time of sacrifice is integrated with the historic time. The narrative is located in the present contemporary milieu. The problems of the wizard world, as readers and critics have pointed out, are suspiciously like our own. *Harry Potter and the Order of the Phoenix*, published in 2003, the first book of the series to come out after 9/11 is important in this regard. But even before that, in *Harry Potter and the Goblet of Fire*, published in 2000, the readers witness a realistic terrorist event on the grounds of the Quidditch World Cup celebrations. The unexpected transformation of post-match merriment to swift onslaught of terror leaves not just the characters but also the reader startled much like the effect of a real terror attack. The Ministry is in denial, negating any sense of urgency or insecurity. It is only when terror strikes close at home, at the very heart of the most powerful institution of the wizard world, that the Ministry of Magic accepts the existence of the threat. Judith Rauhofer points out the close similarities of Ministry's directives on "Protecting your Home and Family Against Dark Forces" with the UK government's "Preparing for an Emergency" pamphlets delivered in 2004. The Ministry takes "telling" steps in tackling the death-eaters: arresting innocent people like Stan Shunpike in hope of staving off panic and creating the impression that the ministry is taking action. Harry refuses to become a poster boy of the new minister, who feels that in the war against terror perceptions matter most: "'If you were to be seen popping in and out of the Ministry from time to time,' he tells Harry, 'that would give the right impression.... It would give everyone a lift to think you were more involved.'" (*HBP* 324). The dismal tidings in *The Daily Prophet*, parental panic, the escalating death toll — all evoke the fear that readers have already seen and felt. Julia Turner, a television producer, notes the effective use of the strategy in the later books:

> This new approach is powerful. In 1998, when the first Harry Potter book came out, Voldemort was a fantastical villain, a symbol of evil in the abstract. Today, however, as we substitute for our abstract fear of Voldemort the very real fear we've felt in our own immolated cities, the new book resonates in ways that the old ones have not.

The narrative insistently foregrounds the social and political context of the act; the themes of love and death co-exist with the concerns of race and terror. The narrative makes it clear that the violence and tension simmering beneath the social fabric of magical community have reached the point of no return. The community can be saved only through the violent act of sacrifice — sacrifice that is "designed to suppress all dissension, rivalries, jealousies within a community" (Girard 8).

At the same time, the course of Rowling's narrative, especially in its historicity, in its relation to the references to contemporary politics, renders the regenerated "redeemed" magical world more and more suspect. The awareness of the insufficiency of the religious sacrifice is something that preoccupies the entire course of the narrative. The overt text of the conventional battle between the "good" and "evil" is deconstructed through the seven books at various levels. The persistence of the problems of race, bloodlines and violence, even in the post–Voldemort magical community, deconstructs the reading of Harry's sacrifice only in terms of Christian narrative of redemption. His sacrifice, though it saves the community from immediate destruction, does not solve the problems in the long run. Historical grounding of the narrative prevents it from being an absolute allegory of Christ's story: unlike Christ's sacrifice, which succeeds in redeeming man, Harry's sacrifice merely succeeds in showing the way. In *Harry Potter and the Half Blood Prince*, when Harry finally understands the significance, or rather the insignificance, of the prophecy, it can be seen as a comment on the adherence of the narrative to the pattern of the religious metanarrative:

It was, he thought, the difference between being dragged into the arena to face a battle to the death and walking into the arena with your head held high. Some people, perhaps, would say that there was little to choose between the two ways, but Dumbledore knew — and so do I, thought Harry, with a rush of fierce pride, and so did my parents — that there was all the difference in the world [*HBP* 271].

The course is chosen and the choices are made in context of the twentieth century, in absence of securities provided by faith, religion and God. Fantasies like that of Rowling's or Pullman's reveal the hope of a divine intermediary coming to redeem man to be a myth. God himself is silent and absent. How can the principles embodied by religion like Christianity uphold without the central binding figure of God? Rather than arousing despair, it transfigures into an opportunity for man to follow the example set by the savior. Therefore, unlike the progress of the Christian pilgrim to the transcendent Kingdom of Heaven, the growth of the adolescent protagonist is grounded in an intensely political arena of a failed utopia. Fredric Jameson comments that "at best Utopia can serve the negative purpose of making us more aware of our mental and ideological imprisonment; and that therefore the best Utopias are those that fail the most comprehensively" (*Archaeologies* xiii).

A part of this failure are the narratives of the unredeemed — those for whom the defeat of Voldemort matters little because their condition in the wizard world even without the rising powers of darkness is miserable. Unlike the adolescent hero who finds his place and power in the community, there is no option but subordination available to the lower orders of magical world — the monsters of the magical world whose problematic presence undoes the closure of the narrative. Their concerns persist beyond the end of the series. Hence the co-existence of their stories at the peripheries of the story of adolescent wizard undoes its coherence and closure.

4

The Monsters

"When I looked around I saw and heard of none like me. Was I then a monster, a blot upon the earth from which all men fled and whom all men disowned?" — Shelley 105

In Mary Shelley's *Frankenstein*, the monstrous creature of Victor Frankenstein gives a moving account of its encounters with the humankind. Its physical deformities obscure its gentleness and generosity; it meets disgust and hatred from the creator himself. Its kind advances are repeatedly spurned and paid back with acts of violence. This unfounded distrust of humankind, the monster argues, led it to evil and revenge. Abandoned by the "parent" who was disgusted at the sight of his creation, the monster is given no option but to follow the path ordained for the monster — of being violent, murderous and evil — as if the physical deformity *ought* to signal moral and spiritual deformity, as if the very existence of the one who does not fit into the human categories of normality is a threat. The story of the monster lays bare the central paradox projected by this anomalous figure; is it the monster who is fearsome and threatening or does the threat emanate from the vulnerabilities in humankind's conceptions of self and the other?

Hence the monster's story is an important corollary to the story of the hero. It offsets the central trajectory of the hero's quest, his growth and his integration into the adult world. The monster is the other of the adolescent hero for whom the templates of growth, development, maturity and integration are denied at every level. In dealing with the monsters, I do not refer to the evil or dark characters like the dark wizards in Rowling's series. Rather, the concern is to explore the fantastic characters who dwell in the liminal zones, at the borders of humanity, those who defy the logic of normality — creatures like Frankenstein's monster, like the giants, goblins, dwarves, werewolves and other such creatures of fantasy — the creatures who are *imputed* with qualities of evil. Scholars like Mary Douglas have pointed out how social boundaries are set up gradually by maintaining the ideas of purity and danger. The elements that disturb the neat structural categories — whether in an individual body or in a social body — are held at bay by being labeled dangerous.

Thus labels like the monsters become means to preserve categorical boundaries. The abnormality of the monster becomes an essential feature against which the parameters of normality are instituted. This has direct repercussions on those who are eliminated from legitimate structures, since abnormality takes on further connotations of immorality and evil, hence cementing the boundaries between "us" and "them," those who are included in the legitimate structures of society and those excluded from them. According to Jeffrey Jerome Cohen's *Monster Theory*:

> The monster is the abjected fragment that enables the formation of all kinds of identities — personal, national, cultural, economic, sexual, psychological, universal, particular (even if that "particular" identity is an embrace of the power/status/knowledge of abjection itself); as such it reveals their partiality, their contiguity [20].

Hence, the amoral zone of abnormality, of monstrosity is the space of the others, "the abjected fragments" left behind in the narratives of growth and formation of identity; these are the creatures of stunted growth who refuse to satisfy the imperatives of categorization and hence challenge the boundaries. They also refuse the category of bestiality, the other of humankind, into which they are thrust due to their abnormalities. If fantasy comes to an end with the growth and integration of the adolescent boy hero, then the monsters are the ones left behind permanently in the liminal zone of fantasy. They are the fantastical creatures of the magical world — characters like Hagrid, the half-giant who is warm and generous despite the wider belief regarding violence of the giants; Dobby, the house-elf, intelligent and politically-active, challenging the accepted notion that house-elves like slavery; and Remus Lupin, gentle and kind though he is a werewolf — all of them situated at the lower hierarchical levels of the magical world; their presence places Harry's growth and victory in the larger arena of politics and society.

Most of the magical creatures in Rowling's story come from fairy tales and folklore. Goblins in the series, like their literary predecessors, are miserly; unicorns are traditional symbols of purity and innocence, and kind-hearted but oafish giants are stock fairy tale characters. Though Rowl-

ing retains the traditional elements in her characterization of magical creatures, none of them appears in the story as simple *deux ex machine*, as aides
or obstacles in the quest of the hero. They locate the hero's quest in a specific social and political context. Each race has its own story — their his-
tories are tied to the society and culture of the magical world. The
self-proclaimed superiority of the wizards and the power of the magical
wand is a source of resentment for groups like the centaurs and the goblins.
Elizabeth E. Heilman and Anne E. Gregory point out the racial hierarchy
that dominates the social organization of the magical world (241–260).
Hagrid, the half-giant, lives on the periphery of the wizard community,
while Fleur, part–Veela, is accepted readily within the wizard society.
House-elves have their place in the magical world; they are the slaves who
ought to do the chores but never be seen. On an even lower level are the
werewolves, Remus Lupin and Fenrir Greyback, the permanent outcasts
of the magical world.

The narrative of these monstrous characters told along with that of
the hero elucidates cultural and ideological investment in the narratives
of adolescence and growth, of cultural integration and marginalization.
Adolescence, as discussed earlier, is not so much an age category but a
state of being characterized by its exteriority to dominant networks, its
disadvantaged position in power relations, and as the embodiments of the
upheaval that disrupt the status quo. The monsters embody the threat of
perpetual adolescence which needs to end with the closure of fantasy. The
boy hero leaves behind the pathological abnormalities of adolescence to
enter into the adult community. As Trites argues, the characteristic features
defining adolescent fiction is its issue with power and repression, the negotiations with authority and the end that propels the protagonist out of
adolescence into an acceptance of the adult world. Hence, it becomes
important to consider how a young adult fantasy negotiates with the figure
of the deviant monster.

The following discussion concentrates on Hagrid, Dobby and Lupin
since their narratives are juxtaposed to that of Harry's, their encounters
serve as points to compare and contrast the trajectories of their growth.
They are central to the social issues like race, blood purity and labor.
Hagrid, Dobby and Lupin are monstrous not simply because they are fantastical. They are monstrous in their vexed relationship with normal, in
their inability to be human and at the same time in their refusal to fit into
the mold of a giant, a house-elf or a werewolf as their culture expects them
to. Hagrid as a half-giant is a product of miscegenation while Dobby as a

house-elf is as much a creature of the mundane realm of a household as of the exotic magical world. Lupin the werewolf, on the other hand, as part-human, part-animal monster, presents an even more complex case of humanity contaminated by its other, the beast. Their liminal existence echoes the liminality of adolescence. Like the adolescent hero, they are the creatures of the boundaries. They live on the peripheries of the magical world. Their story runs parallel to the story of the adolescent hero. All three of them are closely associated with Hogwarts, the school of magic where the young wizards and witches are trained to join the adult world. Yet though integral to the landscape of Hogwarts, growth and integration, which are the central functions of the school, are denied to them.

So their very existence interrogates and challenges what it means to be a monster, whether monstrosity is innate or another cultural construction, and to what extent does the narrative of selfhood depends on narrating the selfhood of other. Dobby is labeled "freak" since his demand for freedom is "unnatural" for a race that is defined by its voluntary submission to slavery. Remus Lupin, the werewolf, is mature, gentle and intelligent though plagued by a cruel and violent beast latent in his being. By refusing the wizard culture's stereotype of a brutal giant, an enslaved household elf and a bloodthirsty werewolf, Hagrid, Dobby and Lupin reveal the way the constructions of normality depend on equally rigorous constructions of abnormality and monstrosity. Their narrative underscores the way a culture deploys stereotypes, underscores and maintains social hierarchies, and thus constructs the images of the outsiders. Hence, their presence at the margins offers a base to critique the grand narratives of the boy savior.

The story of the monstrous characters defamiliarizes the narrative of the boy hero and his growth, revealing the fantasy, or strangeness, that lies behind the ideas of normality. Unlike the story of the boy hero which is endorsed by the culture and emulated by the young readers, the story of a monster is about prohibitions and taboos, about how *not to be*. The etymology of the word *monstrum* encapsulates its political force. In the double sense of *monere* "that which warns" and *demonstrare* "that which reveals," the monster's narrative is meant to serve as a warning by its revelations. While the story of the hero reveals the process of integration, the story of the monster illustrates the process and the necessity to exclude or marginalize. In case of Dobby and Hagrid, monstrosity is magnified by physical signifiers common in folklore and fairy tales — in the dwarfishness of the former and the giant stature of the latter. They are associated with the world of child and childhood at various levels. They lack the skills and ability to grow up to become adult members of the community, especially in terms of basic skills like language acquisition, mental cognition or their response to tense situations. Hagrid is unable to understand the wider implications of his love of dangerous creatures, his attempts to domesticate them, and has to be repeatedly saved by Harry and his friends right from their first year. Similar techniques are at work in characterization of Dobby. Hence, house-elves as well as giants are portrayed not only as child-like but as creatures on the lower rung of the evolutionary scale, echoing the link between ontogeny and phylogeny and its relation to adolescent growth discussed in the introduction. The boy hero stands at the apex of evolution, the peak that the racial others can never scale.

Hence the hero and the monster, the two extremities, structure, define and invade each other. While Harry Potter, the hero, journeys from isolation to integration, towards formulating a self-concept that is stable and at one with the social role envisaged for him, the monsters traverse the path in the opposite direction. The story of Remus is of conflict and struggle to belong to the "civilized" wizard world; Hagrid, even after the war, continues to shepherd children to Hogwarts and lives on the peripheries of the magical world. While Dobby dies, we do not know the fate of SPEW — Society for Promotion of Elfish Welfare — or any change in the conditions of the house-elves. Their story undoes the hero myth which has been studied in context of individual ego formation and collective wish fulfillment. While the hero moves from the position of a marginalized orphan to an important member of his community, the monster's story is that of progressive isolation. While the hero grows and matures, the monster remains fixed.

Contrary to the story of the hero that iterates the values and aspirations of the community, the monster embodies all that lies beyond this neatly structured legitimized narrative of growth. These monster narratives are crucial to the dynamics of subversion and containment that drives the series.

The image of a monster therefore becomes an integral part of a young adult fantasy which seeks to destablize structures and hierarchies, at the individual as well as the social level. Their presence delineates the politics of inclusion and exclusion. Cohen argues that "the monster is a problem for cultural studies, a code or a pattern or a presence or an absence that unsettles what has been constructed to be received as natural, as human" (ix). Their narratives are crucial to the political dialogue that the series engages in.

So the *Potter* series borrows the stock creatures from folklore and fairy tale traditions, and revises and modifies them in a way that these fantastic monsters become a medium to reflect on the central theme of integration and marginalization. The fantastic creatures and hybrids become points of rupture in the narrative of "human-ity," of human community. Subsequently the portrayal of monstrous outcasts becomes a means to reflect and reveal the politics of power, gender, nationhood and a variety of other discourses that underlie the process of identity formation. Beginning with the story of Hagrid and the giants, the following sections examine how normality and abnormality, humanity and monstrosity are conflated with the themes of nationalism, gender, sexuality and so on.

Giants: The Trace of Pre-history

But ... Harry, they're just vicious, giants. It's like Hagrid said, it's in their natures, they're like trolls ... they just like killing, everyone knows that. There aren't any left in Britain now, though [*GoF* 374].

Ron's response to the discovery of Hagrid's parentage is complex; it brings together the notions of monstrosity and viciousness; being giant means being vicious and cruel; it also refers to the idea of a nation as an imagined community formed by firmly establishing boundaries between the self and others. Hence a set of creatures have been eliminated on account of their "monstrous" nature. With their brutal strength and troll-like intelligence, the giants are sub-human creatures in the magical world. They are dangerous and vicious. Hence, the wizard community feels safe once they have been pushed away to the mountains and other less habitable places of earth. The revelation of Hagrid's parentage makes him susceptible to all the stereotypes of violence and brutality that have traditionally been associated with the giants in the magical world. As it becomes evident in the following discussion, the portrayal of the giants, especially Hagrid, lies at the intersection of various discourses of folklore and fairy tales, of British history and nationhood, and also the narratives of Christian conquest and colonialism during the Middle Ages. In the peripheral narrative of the giants, the series explores and re-enacts the mythic and historical narrative of Britain, the time when the giants were sent to their "hideout in the mountains."

Hagrid is the half-giant offspring of a wizard father and a giantess named Fridwulfa. He enters Hogwarts as a student. However, after his expulsion in his third year, he continues as gamekeeper and later as a teacher at Hogwarts School of Magic. His hut, on the boundary between the school and the Forbidden Forest, symbolizes his peripheral position in the magical world. As mentioned earlier, he is "the Keeper of the Keys," the guardian at the threshold of the magical world. He brings the children to the magical school, ferrying the first years across the *giant* lake. To Harry, Hagrid is the first friend in the magical world — repeatedly bringing him back from death to life. After the attack on the Potters at the beginning of the series, Hagrid brings Harry to Dumbledore at Privet Drive. At the beginning of the seventh year, following the Order's plans to move Harry from Privet Drive to the Burrow, Hagrid is once again entrusted with the charge of escorting the real Harry Potter to the magical world. At the end of the series, after Voldemort's attempt to kill Harry, Hagrid, once again, carries him back from the Forbidden Forest to Hogwarts.

As a half-giant, Hagrid is clearly a borderland being — loved and detested simultaneously, partly belonging to the fearsome world of the Forbidden Forest and partly fitting in with the teachers at Hogwarts. Though he entered the school as a student, a peer of the Tom Riddle, he was expelled in his third year on the charges of breeding a dangerous creature in the school which led to the death of a student. His fascination with the dangerous fantastic creatures and his half-blood status work in favor of Tom Riddle:

> It was my word against Hagrid's, Harry. Well, you can imagine how it looked to old Armando Dippet. On the one hand, Tom Riddle, poor but brilliant, parentless but so brave, school prefect, model student ... on the other hand, big, blundering Hagrid, in trouble every other week, trying to raise werewolf cubs under his bed, sneaking off to the Forbidden Forest to wrestle trolls [*CS* 267].

As a punishment, Hagrid is forbidden to do magic (though his pink umbrella is suspiciously magical). Yet Dumbledore believes in his innocence and retains him at the school. Though ousted from the structures of the school and the magical world, he is continues to live at the threshold. His gamekeeper's hut at the periphery of the school becomes a place where he can continue his disorderly existence and yet his knowledge and wisdom can be harnessed for the school.

At the same time, he is a security threat, as much for his size as his naiveté and child-like nature. His unreasonable fascination with the monsters and slow thinking often makes his own friends doubt him. In *Harry Potter and the Deathly Hallows*, as everyone sits thinking about the person responsible for revealing the plans of transporting Harry from the Privet Drive to the Burrow to the outsiders, Harry's eyes fall on Hagrid immediately. Despite the headmaster's insistence and his years of service, Hagrid is constantly subject of suspicion, fear and prejudice. He is the first to be suspected for opening the Chamber of Secrets and letting out the monster of Slytherin in his own third year at Hogwarts and later in Harry's second year. As a student, he was expelled; as a teacher he is sent to Azkaban. In the fifth year, targeted maliciously by Dolores Umbridge, the representative of the Ministry of Magic at the school, he is again forced to flee.

Yet Hagrid seems to accept his position at the peripheries of the magical world. The injustice and distrust are endured without any questions or self-consciousness. Unlike Dobby's political activism or Lupin's troubled self-awareness, Hagrid's presence is strangely unproblematic. Despite being the target of prejudice and false charges, there is no self-conscious agonizing over the injustices of the wizard world like Lupin's. Even when he is expelled in his third year on false charges and prohibited to do magic, he exhibits no anger, no sense of betrayal. Indeed he remains grateful to Dumbledore for letting him continue in the school as a gamekeeper. The maliciousness of the Slytherin students and constant targeting by the Ministry of Magic even when he is a teacher do not lead Hagrid to question the political ideologies of the world he lives in.

Hagrid's knowledge, his ability of train and tame the magical creatures, his fascination with dangerous creatures — all becomes a part of his portrayal as a giant half-breed. The suspicion and distrust that mark his position at the peripheries also reflect the situation of the giants in the magical world at large. In Harry's third year, Hagrid joins the staff of Hogwarts as a teacher for Care of Magical Creatures. His success as a teacher is dismal. At different points, other characters like Parvati, Lavender, Luna and even Hermione voice their preference for Professor Grubbly Planks over Hagrid. Draco and the Slytherins think of him as an uncouth, oafish and incompetent teacher. His lessons often go out of control. Students often get injured; though forbidden to breed new hybrids by the Ministry of Magic, he experiments with creatures like the Blast-ended Skrewts that cause injuries to the students. Skeeter's article exposing his parentage cites these lessons: "An alarmingly large and ferocious-looking man, Hagrid has been using his newfound authority to terrify students in his care with a succession of horrific creatures. While Dumbledore turns a blind eye, Hagrid has maimed several pupils during a series of lessons which many admit to be 'very frightening'" (*GoF* 381). Skeeter's article draws a telling link between his fascination with dangerous creatures and his giant blood. Citing his lessons, the article states: "If his [Hagrid's] antics during Care of Magical Creatures lessons are any guide, however, Fridwulfa's son appears to have inherited her brutal nature" (*GoF* 382).

Through characters like Ron and Hagrid, the series provides a sketchy history of giants, their nature and community and their defeat by the wizards. Giants inhabited Britain before they were eliminated by the wizards. Their violent nature made their elimination imperative in order to establish a safe and "civilized" community. These sketchy details of the history of giants are filled in, on a closer look, by British historiography and mythic traditions on which the series builds. The portrayal of the giants in the Potter series, their cruelty, the threat they pose to the "civilization" and their exclusion echoes the nation-founding legends of Britain that repeatedly feature combats between Anglo-Saxon heroes and the giants. These mythic encounters frequently end with the killing of the giant. The legends and myths which embellish layers of history also link it to the narratives of nationalism and warrior heroes. These legends were over determined by other historical events like the spread of Christianity. Hence, placed in this historical context, Hagrid, the half-giant of Rowling's story, emerges as a trace of forgotten history of the British Isles, the history of the colonization of the land known as Albion.

Geoffrey of Monmouth's twelfth-century *Historia Regum Britanniae* (or *The History of the Kings of Britain*) compiles the historical information along with the existing legends and folk narratives to provide a coherent, linear and a heroic history of Britain. It narrates the founding myth of Britain — the conquest of Albion by Brutus, a descendant of the Trojan hero, Aeneas. Prior to Brutus' arrival, the island was populated by the giants, the offspring of Greek princesses, Albina and her sisters. Exiled to this faraway land for plotting against their husbands, the sisters attempt to found a matronymic community in this far-off land by calling it Albion. However, their intercourse with the devil creates a nation of giants whom Brutus and his Trojan warriors come and slay. The giants, slain in nation's founding myth, frequently return to haunt its legends and literature: as Gogmagog, thrown off a cliff by Corineus, Brutus' companion; as Grendel, killed by Beowulf; or as the giant of Mont Saint Michel, slain by Arthur — the giants, as the vanquished aboriginal inhabitants of the land, have been a part of the nation-building myths of Britain. The legends have their root in the conquest of Britain by the Germanic tribes. Cohen cites the arrival of the Germanic tribes on the coast of England and their first encounters with towering structures like Stonehenge or the temples of Bath. For them, Cohen remarks, these alien structures were *enta geweorc*, "the work of giants" (*Of Giants*, 28). The "monsters" already inhabiting the land, then, had to be defeated and vanquished to make space for the new arrivals. Cohen mentions the Germanic folktale of a giant child who picks up a human to play with it as a toy. The child is rebuked by the parents who warn him that the creature he thinks to be a plaything was going to vanquish the giants in the future. Hence the defeat of the giants by mankind is preordained.

The giant folklore therefore emerges as a complex blend of history, ideologies and myths of the England. According to Cohen,

> Anglo-Saxon England was relentlessly pondering what it means to be a warrior, a Christian, a hero, a saint, an outlaw, a king, a sexed and gendered being.... The limits of identity were under ceaseless interrogation because they were confronted by almost constant challenge. It is not surprising, then, that the monster became a kind of cultural shorthand for the problems of identity construction, for the irreducible difference that lurks deep within the culture-bound self [*Of Giants* 5].

Studying the role of giants like Gog and Magog (often fused together as Gogmagog) in various narratives, Victor Scherb cites how such monsters "performed a kind of cultural work by creating a context within which a community could define itself. These two monstrous names situate the geographical and temporal horizons of medieval and, in their manifestations, English culture" (60). Hence the giants on the periphery — the monstrous others who are constantly set up as the antithesis of the warrior hero — became integral to the myths of the culture; they illustrate the values that the culture upholds by constantly challenging those values and being punished for the transgressions.

Therefore, the giants appear at the originary moment, their slain body is the starting point of civilization. They seem to represent the prehistory of mankind. In most of the mythical narratives, the course of evolution moves from the giants to the gods or humans, thus relegating the giants to the lower rung of the scale, an equivalent of the Neanderthal man. Similarly, motif of displacement and hostility to the new established order recurs in various mythological traditions. In most of the narratives, including Rowling's, the giants, the original inhabitants of the land, are displaced by a more powerful race. In Greek mythology, the giants, the children of Gaea and Uranus, rise against the Olympians to restore the rule of the Titans. In Norse myth, the giants or the *Jotun* again appear as the antagonists of the gods. The giants predate the creation, which is itself fashioned out of the body of a giant named Ymir. They are a constant threat to Asgard, the abode of gods, which they enter during the final battle of Ragnarok along with other monsters. At the same time, there are sexual encounters between gods and the giants resulting in monstrous progenies like Fenriswolf. Similarly in Geoffrey's history, the giants of Albion are born out of the union between human princesses and the devil. In Rowling's story, Hagrid is a miscegenate, a product of a union between a giant and wizard. Since giants are a product of primal miscegenation, their eradication is necessary for the establishment of the laws that delineate exogamy and endogamy. The displacement of the older monstrous race can also be read in terms of Freudian analogies.

> These culture heroes are always *young* warriors (sons); they always vanquish *old* and ancestral ogres, giants, dragons, and the like, many of which are depicted, like parents, as remnants from some distant past when the earth was young, that is, during *infancy* of the human race [Gilmore 17].

Along with the pagan myths, the legends surrounding the giants also overlap with the stories of the Bible and the spread of Christianity. Christian history begins with a single family of Genesis and comprises of a series of events involving men whose ancestry is crucial. Stressing on one God and his chosen people excludes outsiders, the others and the aliens. The monstrous races are often connected to the transgressors and sinners like Cain, the progenitor of the giants, Ham, Noah's sinning son and Babel. Hence, situated in a Christian context, giants acquire a proximity to the devil. The motif of transgression suggests continuity between the biblical tradition and the pagan legends. Struck repeatedly by God's wrath, these narratives underscore giants' survival before and beyond the ordered "civilized" world.

This challenge to the ordered world of culture and civilization is embodied literally by the gigantic body that often merges with landscape in their wild and grotesque aspects. Hagrid's first encounter with the giants in the mountains illustrates this conflation of giants and nature.

> "Found 'em," said Hagrid baldly. "Went over a ridge one night an' there they was spread ou' underneath us. Little fires burnin' below an' huge shadows ... it was like watchin' bits o' the mountain movin'" [*OotP* 321].

Similarly Harry mistakes Grawp for a mound of earth when he first sees him. In the categorization of nature against the culture, which Claude Levi-Strauss re-designates as the "raw" against the "cooked," a giant represents an overabundance of the "raw" nature and hence an affront to cultural systems. The huge proportions are an embodiment of transgression against order at the level of physical existence. Usurping the limits of size and proportion, a giant represents monstrosity that reduces the normal and the human to a miniature. Its gigantic size threatens to surround, engulf and annihilate. The magnified proportions focus on the body that is strange and misshapen.

> Grawp knelt between two trees he had not yet uprooted. They looked up into his startlingly huge face that resembled a grey full moon swimming in the gloom of the clearing. It was as though the features had been hewn on to a great stone ball. The nose was stubby and shapeless, the mouth lopsided and full of misshapen yellow teeth the size of half-bricks; the eyes, small by giant standards, were muddy greenish-brown and just now were half gummed together with sleep. Grawp raised dirty knuckles, each as big as a cricket ball, to his eyes, rubbed vigorously, then without warning, pushed himself to his feet with surprising speed and agility [Ootp 624].

In the figure of wild, dim and unpredictable Grawp, Hagrid's otherness is magnified at the physical as well as the mental level. Just as the giants of mythology who are often fooled by the gods, Hagrid is often duped. In the first book itself, he reveals the whereabouts of the Philosopher's Stone in exchange of an egg of a baby dragon. He is punished wrongly for opening the Chamber of Secrets. The narratives of the giant and his foolishness, popularized by fairy tales like "Jack and the Beanstalk," merge with stories like Oscar Wilde's "The Selfish Giant" to portray a kind but a dim-witted monster. While Hagrid's speech is unrefined, Grawp does not know the language. As mentioned earlier, language is an important means of characterization in case of Dobby and Hagrid, underlining their difference. According to Farah Mandehlson's discussion of Hagrid, the "lack of intelligence and self control actually *fulfill* the stereotypes associated with his ethnicity, thus permitting Harry and his friends to demonstrate their 'tolerance' and to show that Harry is a 'good chap'" (166).

These stories surrounding the figure of a giant, including Rowling's series, are gendered narratives — the defeat of the giant by the warrior hero is a masculine narrative of heroism and nation building. Like the boy hero, the monsters and their narratives, are gendered — most of the giants that we meet in various legends and myths are male monsters. These masculine narratives assign a peculiar role to the feminine. The giant monster is an offspring of a monstrous mother who disappears once the son, a projection of her own monstrosity, appears on the scene. Hagrid is brought up by his wizard father. The mother, a giantess named Fridwulfa, disappears after giving birth to a half-giant. Similarly in the founding myth of Britain, the femininity of Albina and her sisters is synonymous with maternity; their ability to produce monsters against whom the Anglo Saxon heroes can produce their narratives of wars, conquest and nationhood — and hence their biological function of reproduction — is the only point of reference for their feminine identity. It is inscribed only at the moment of origin where the narrative of monstrous excess begins. The monster mothers beget sons who are extensions of their own monstrous nature. Introducing his brother Grawp to Harry and Hermione, Hagrid describes what is important for giant mothers: "See, with giantesses, what counts is producin' good big kids, and he's always been a bit on the runty side fer a giant — on'y sixteen foot" (*OotP* 621). Going by the criterion, Hagrid's mother fails in both her sons — one of her sons is a half-giant and other, a weak one. Like Albina and her sisters, Fridwulfa the giantess refuses her position as a docile wife. Hagrid refers to this "unnatural" nature of Fridwulfa: "Turns put me mother took up with another giant when she left me dad, an' went an' had Grawp here" (*OotP* 621). Hence, in a way, then, Hagrid and Grawp, the giants of Rowling's stories, are continuous with Fridwulfa, the giantess who begets them. Just like Harry Potter, the adolescent boy hero who carries within him the strain of his mother's sacrifice, Hagrid and Grawp, the giants, carry the unnaturalness of Fridwulfa, her bestiality, which makes it important to repudiate her; her rebellion against the norms of femininity, matrimony and motherhood, which makes it imperative to oust her from the "civilized" community.

Hagrid's parenthood has its palimpsest not only in the Albina myth but also in the Bible where giants are described as products of union between women and the fallen angels (Genesis 6:4). Just as the family of the devil, a lustful woman and a monster progeny parallel the holy family of God, Hagrid's parenthood — a giant mother and wizard father — parallels Harry's parenthood — a mudblood mother and a pure-blood father. After Rita Skeeter reveals his ancestry, Hagrid shuts himself off in his hut till Dumbledore, Harry, Hermione and Ron persuade him to return. Hagrid tells Harry how Harry reminded him of his own earlier self.

> "Yeh know tha', Harry?" he said, looking up from the photograph of his father, his eyes very bright. "When I fris'met you, you reminded me o' me a bit. Mum an' dad gone, an' you was feelin' like yeh wouldn' fit in at Hogwarts, remember? Not sure yeh really up to it ... an' now look at yeh, Harry! School Champion!" [*GoF* 396].

It is one of the rare moments in the series where Hagrid expresses a sense of alienation. Yet his identification with Harry is mistaken. While Harry moves from being a novice to the school champion, Hagrid's position remains precarious forever. In Hagrid's story, the repeated emphasis on his status as a borderland being serves to underscore the consequences of miscegenation and straying from the regulations of matrimony and family.

The confused equations of gender lead to a family unit that is faulty at every level. While the hero limits and encodes manhood, Cohen points out that the giant's exaggerated features represent everything that is in excess, the aspects of masculinity that cannot be integrated socially. Hence, in the form of a giant like Grawp, a culture repudiates brutality, aggressiveness and physicality. In Hagrid, the half-giant, instead of aggression and brutality, we find concern, caring and nurturing that the narrative repeatedly feminizes. The narrative itself seems to project this feminine aspect on Hagrid as he appears repeatedly tending to the injured creatures, doing the household chores, delivering the young wizards and witches to the magical world. Hagrid constantly and willingly takes on role of a mother, especially for his monstrous pets. For instance, when he adopts the Norbert, the baby dragon: "'I've decided to call him Norbert,' said Hagrid, looking at the dragon with misty eyes. 'He really knows me now, watch. Norbert! Norbert! Where's *Mummy?*'" (*PS* 172). When parting he promises, "Mummy will never forget you!" (*PS* 175). He scares the Dursleys by his stature and aggression at his first appearance: "a giant of a man was standing in the doorway. His face was almost completely hidden by a long, shaggy mane of hair and a wild tangled beard, but you could make out his eyes, glinting like black beetles under all the hair" (*PS* 39). Yet immediately after the appearance, he takes out the paraphernalia of domesticity, pans, matchboxes, sausages to serve food. This is not to say that these are "feminine" tasks and hence they feminize Hagrid. However, it is noteworthy that none of the other wizards are associated with such chores. The only parallel offered is by Molly Weasley and Petunia Dursley.

These anomalies are not limited to an individual; they characterize the entire community of giants. In *Harry Potter and the Order of the Phoenix*, Hagrid describes the tribal community of the giants he found in the mountains, the gifts that he gave to the leader of the community whetting his greed, the violent takeover by a younger leader overnight by beheading the older leader; their unreasonable and irrational thought process coupled with their gigantic strength makes them a threat to the "civilized" society. Rowling's portrayal of the giants echoes the description of the one-eyed Cyclops by Odysseus: "giants, louts, without a law to bless them.... Kyklopes have no muster and no meeting, no consultation or old tribal ways, but each one dwells in his own mountain cave dealing out rough justice to wife and child, indifferent to what the others do." The giants of Britain, as Ron and later Hagrid himself recounts, have been pushed away to the mountains. There are few left; though Ron and Hagrid acknowledge that some were killed by wizards, it is their own brutal and violent nature that is responsible for their constantly diminishing numbers. The violent and fratricidal giant community, eliminated from the civilized world of the wizards, lives in a state of precarious peace — slightest disagreements lead to bloody fights and killing. Their brains, says Hagrid, are not capable of processing too much information. It is proven true by the events. In the last battle, most of the giants join the Death Eaters, thereby confirming stories about their viciousness and cruelty and hence justifying their exclusion. Hagrid, the half-giant who accepts his peripheral position, is the only one allowed to continue in the magical world, albeit fixed on its peripheries. Though he tries to civilize his half-brother, it remains doubtful whether Grawp would ever overcome the prejudices and suspicion to be accepted in the wizard community. There seems to have been little change in Hagrid's position at Hogwarts after the defeat of the Dark Lord. Despite his interest in Madame Maxime and their journey to the mountains where they develop a sense of companionship, there is no mention of the future of the relationship. Unlike the marriage and fatherhood of the hero, which cements his position in the community, there is no happy ending for Hagrid the half-giant or the giant community at large.

Hence a variety of meanings accrue to the gigantic physical size of giants. Though the text situates Hagrid and the giants on the peripheries of the narrative and there seems to be no change in their positions even when the democratic order comes into being at the end, a close look reveals the moral, social and cultural ambiguity that persists beyond the closure challenging the neat end of the hero's story. Cohen points out that "the monster is intriguing beneath his repulsiveness because he challenges any easy attempt to stop or place him as he slides from one cultural meaning into the next" (*Of Giants* 38). The giants exist on the interstices of the discourses of gender, nationhood and civilization, not just in the magical world but in the legends and mythologies that have shaped England. They need to be repeatedly ousted in the grand narrative of the culture to make way for, to centralize, and to legitimize the story of the hero. While they reveal the crisis at the originary moment of the nation, the following section focuses on the house-elves, the domestic slaves of the magical world and the faultlines in the existing systems of social order and hierarchies.

House-elves: The Politics of Domesticity

The term "house-elves" signifies the peculiar position of the elves in Rowling's magical world. One the one hand, they are the elves — the creatures of fantasy, exotic and strange; at the same time, these fantastic creatures are associated with the most mundane sphere of the magical world — the household. The interlacing of the two realms leads to an extremely complex narrative strand. What happens when the creatures of fantasy are inserted into the realm of domesticity? How does this interruption by elements of fantasy impinge on the relationship between the domestic realm and with the larger concerns of authority and power? This interlinking of fantasy and the mundane is crucial since fantasy defamiliarizes the "naturalness" of domestic order; it exposes the strangeness of everyday life. And since household is seen the unit of civilization, a training ground for the larger cultural order, such portrayal has important implications. It provides a material grounding for fantasy; at the same time narratives like that of the house-elves illustrates the ambivalent aspects of domesticity and household labor.

Like the giants, Rowling's house-elves have important literary predecessors. Discussing the closure of Shakespeare's *Midsummer Night's Dream*, scholar Wendy Wall draws attention to the link that Puck's last chore establishes between the realm of fairies and the world of domesticity in Elizabethan England.

> I am sent with broom before,
> To sweep the dust behind the door [Act 5, Scene 1, 396–97].

While the unraveling of the plot draws together the discourses of matrimony and the body politic, the image of Puck sweeping away the dirt inserts the chaotic realm of fantasy into the mundane world of domesticity. According to Wall, the image at the end of the play links domesticity with political authority and,

> for the brief moment that it does so, allows a glimpse of an Englishness founded on principles that the play has not generally endorsed — the vernacular broadly defined. As Puck assumes the part of the very English

> Robin Goodfellow, the exotic mythological realm to which he is attached
> expands to include local and domestic association that reverberate oddly
> with the flexible civil monarchy that founds the social order in *Dream* [67].

Rowling's house-elves can be seen as heirs of Puck and Robin Goodfellow, the "very English" rustic creatures merging the realms of fantasy with political concerns and inserting them into the mundane world of domesticity.

The political debate surrounding Dobby and the house-elves in the series has been studied through the lens of slavery and racism (Carey 108, Mendlesohn 159). These issues are undoubtedly echoed by the textual descriptions. Dobby, the first house-elf to enter the narrative in *Harry Potter and the Chamber of Secrets*, also introduces Harry Potter and the reader to the netherworld of the magical society. Till then, for Harry Potter, as well as the reader negotiating the narrative along with Harry Potter, magical world is a place where the hero gets his due, where the injustices of the "normal" world are balanced. Dobby is the first character to bring to fore the issues like cruelty, slavery and racism that hold sway in the magical world. Used to indifference and violence, Dobby is surprised at Harry's politeness. Dobby punishing himself for speaking against his master is one of the most disturbing scenes of the series. Hence, the first encounter with Dobby sets the tone for the portrayal of the house-elves and also the issues that their presence brings to fore throughout the series. The value of a house-elf lies in its service to the domestic world of the household. They are bound to slavery by their very being as *house-elves*. At 12 Grimmauld Place, the family home of Sirius Black, the heads of house-elves grace the walls — the house-elves beheaded when they grew too old to carry tea trays. So the purpose of life for a house-elf is to serve the wizards. As Winky, Barty Crouch's house-elf, voices her disapproval of Dobby's freedom, she makes it clear: "House-elves is not supposed to have fun, Harry Potter. House-elves does what they is told" (*GoF* 34).

The portrayal closely linked with the identity politics that is central to the series: while the figure of a school boy and the boarding school fiction, discussed in the earlier section, centers on elitism that is central to the conceptualization of colonial English identity, the portrayal of the house-elves is permeated with strain of the vernacular, the rustic lower orders of English population. Hence the discourse of slavery that characterizes the portrayal of the house-elves in the *Potter* series is interlaced with the ideologies of domesticity and housewifery situated within the intensely secluded realm of the household.

Rowling's house-elves can be traced to the hobs or hobgoblins, folkloric figures of British and Scottish origin. In the folklore of northern Britain, the hob is a kindly spirit, helpful to local people when they needed healing or farmwork. Like the house-elves, it is important to remember never to reward the hob in any way, for that would scare him off. Discussing the typology of English fairies, Leigh Hunt, in a London journal dated October 1834, mentions "homestead fairies":

> the House or Homestead Fairy, our Puck, Robin Goodfellow, Hobgoblin, &c (the *Nis* of Denmark and Norway, the *Kebold* of Germany, the *Brownie* of Scotland and *Tomteygubbe or Old Man of the House* in Sweden). He is of a similar temper, but good upon the whole and fond of cleanliness, rewarding and helping the servants for being tidy, and punishing them for the reverse [232].

Hobs are frequently associated with household tasks and domesticity and hence, as the following description from Milton's *L'Allegro* reveals, they recur as an integral part of English pastoral landscape and culture.

> Then to the spicy nut-brown ale,
> With stories told of many a feat,
> How faery Mab the junkets eat;
> She was pinch'd and pull'd, she sed;
> And he, by friar's lantern led;
> Tells how the drudging Goblin swet,
> To earn his cream-bowl duly set,
> When in one night, ere glimpse of morn,
> His shadowy flail hath thresh'd the corn,
> That ten day-laborers could not end;
> Then lies him down the lubbar fiend,
> And, stretch'd out all the chimney's length,
> Basks at the fire his hairy strength:
> And crop-ful out of door he flings,
> Ere the first cock his matin rings.
> Thus done the tales to bed they creep,
> By whispering winds soon lull's asleep.

Associated with values of economy, hard work and industry, Hob, as a symbol of domesticity, appears repeatedly, especially as a part of the rural landscape. They regularly influence the creation of fantastical creatures in literature like Tolkien's Hobbits or Nesbit's Psammead, the sand-fairy. William Mayne, in a series of *Hob Stories for Children*, portrays a hob as a friendly spirit looking after a household, visible only to the children. Mayne's hob "gets reward by the fireside each night, and hopes he never is given clothes. He says, 'Never give him leather or thread, Or into the weather he will tread'" (1). Edward Thomas, in his poem "Lob," portrays

Lob as a fantastical hob-like creature that sums up the character of England
as it evolved through time. Hence a hob is a recurring figure borrowed
from the vernacular narratives that at times challenge and at times run
along with the elitist narratives like the school boy fiction or the hero's
quest.

Hence unlike Roald Dahl's Oompa Loompas, pygmies brought from
far off lands to work in Willie Wonka's chocolate factory, Rowling's house-
elves are not slaves who come from a far off exotic land. They embody the
English landscape and its people; they are also the outcasts of the community, wild, unconfined, yet steadily continuous with the spirit of rural
England. In the magical world of the series, the house-elves are the devoted
servant to a wizard family doing anything that a master commands. As
pointed out, Rowling's term for the hob-like figures, "house-elf," itself
illustrates their role in a household. Though often used for dangerous and
secretive tasks, the main task of a house-elf is looking after the domestic
chores. Winky, the house-elf of Barty Crouch, looks after the house and
the fugitive son of the master secretly after the death of the mother.
Kreacher is repeatedly seen serving and cleaning the House of Blacks. Similarly, in the memories of Hepzibah Smith in *Harry Potter and the Half
Blood Prince*, her house-elf Hokey is seen carrying the tea tray and serving
the mistress. Their clothes signify their labor. Winky wears a tea-towel
draped like a toga. Harry first sees Dobby wearing "what looked like an
old pillowcase, with rips for arm- and leg-holes" (6). Presenting them with
clothes means freeing them of the link with the family — a condition that
supposed to be "unnatural" and "abnormal" for a house-elf. Hence clothes
have an important symbolic import for the house-elves.

But the most efficient house-elves are the elves marked not by their
appearance but by their invisibility. At Hogwarts, the house-elves cook
and clean and keep the school running efficiently. Indeed, so efficient are
they that the tasks seem to be accomplished by magic. The food appears
magically on the tables. The dormitories are cleaned magically. So well are
the chores are managed that it is only in the fourth year that Harry and
his friends discover the existence of the house-elves in the school. This
invisibility of the "perfect" house-elves marks the way in which the domestic chores and labor, especially that within the household, are written off
in the larger political and cultural systems.

The house-elves literally embody the lower spheres of the domestic
world; they stand at the intersection of discourses of domesticity, class and
fantasy. Fantasy warrants a new look at "mind forg'd manacles" of con-

ventions, rules and order that govern this world of domesticity and hold it in its place. They hold sway not only over the house-elves but the entire magical world. Despite her pleas, Barty Crouch, the Minister of Magic "frees" Winky because he had "no use for a servant who forgets what is due to her master, and to her master's reputation" (*GoF* 47). Horace Slughorn, a professor at Hogwarts, has no qualms testing his drinks for poison by making a house-elf drink first. The indifference is deemed "natural" because, as Ron tells Harry and Hermione, the house-elves like slave labor. Indeed at Hogwarts, Winky tells Harry that she is properly ashamed of being free. Equation of freedom and shame makes Dobby, the free house-elf, a freak. He not only revels in his freedom but works for wages — something that other house-elves at Hogwarts frown at.

The conflation of fantasy with the volatile issue of slave labor set against the backdrop of English household and society serves multiple purposes. Fantasy throws a new light on the regular organization of a household. Indeed, Dobby's first appearance at the Dursleys puts Harry's plight in a new perspective. After hearing an account of Dobby's life with his masters, Harry first reacts with disbelief: "'And I thought I had it bad staying here for another four weeks,' he said. 'This makes the Dursleys sound almost human. Can't anyone help you? Can't I?'" (*CoS* 9). Harry is quick to understand the similarities between his position in the Dursley household and the position of the house-elves in the magical world. In fact, during his stay at the Dursleys, the kitchen is one of the foremost places that the reader associates with Harry, apart from the cupboard under the stairs. The first sight of eleven-year-old Harry Potter is being woken up by Aunt Petunia and sent from his room under the stairs to the kitchen.

> Well, get a move on, I want you to look after the bacon. And don't you dare let it burn, I want everything perfect on Duddy's birthday [*PoS* 15].

Later we see him frying eggs and serving breakfast. Thus the story of the young boy hero who grows up to save the world by vanquishing evil is closely linked to the banal world of the household. Harry's position in the Dursley household echoes that of a house-elf. To don the role of a masculine hero, it is important for Harry to leave behind the sphere of domesticity — a world loaded in terms of class as well as gender implications. A household usually organized on the principles of the division of labor, domestic space becomes culturally and socially a "feminine" space associated with either the woman of the house or the maid. In the world of magic, they are replaced by a house-elf in the wealthy wizard families. In the Crouch household, Winky replaces the dead mother. Kreacher continues to serve his mistress, Sirius' mother, even after her death. According to Wall, domesticity and the fairy lore associated with childhood, maids and lower orders of society are "positioned not only as the abject belief system jettisoned in the culture's march toward progress but also as the pastoral life endangered by the social ills of the present world. It is the world, good or bad, that people forgo as they supposedly mature, and as such, it remains the object of fascination and disgust" (Wall, "Why does Puck Sweep?" 73). Hence, a crucial stage in the growth of the boy hero is his departure from the domestic realm of the household.

Thus, while a house-elf is tied to the world of domesticity, the boy hero must and is able to leave behind this sphere of lower order, the feminine realm of domesticity and enter the school, a space of intellectual pursuits — the elite and closed "masculine" world. This elite order rests on the indispensable labor of the lower order that is embraced and shunned at the same time: Hogwarts employs house-elves, even those "disgraced" by being free, yet those house-elves remain invisible, confined to their space in the kitchen. Essential to prop the dominant order, the subordinate order is embraced within specified parameters.

Yet the house-elves wield a magic of their own. The magic that binds them to the master whom they serve also endows them with the power to subvert the dictates of loyalty. Despite punishing himself repeatedly, Dobby does invent ways to help Harry against the Malfoys. Kreacher's resentful submission to Sirius becomes ominous as he finds a way to escape Sirius' commands and pass on the useful information about Sirius and the rest of the Order to the Death Eaters. Kreacher's anger and insubordination narrates not only the suffering of the house-elves but also their resentment. He lures Harry and his friends, and later the members of the Order of the Phoenix to the Ministry of Magic. Sirius' death in the following encounter is a result not just of Kreacher's treachery but, as Dumbeldore tells Harry, of the indifference of the whole wizard-kind to the lower order of beings.

> "Sirius did not hate Kreacher," said Dumbeldore. "He regarded him as a servant unworthy of much interest or notice. Indifference and neglect often do much more damage than outright dislike ... the fountain we destroyed tonight told a lie. We wizards have mistreated and abused our fellows for too long, and we are now reaping our reward" [*OotP* 752].

By the end of the series, Kreacher becomes crucial to the search for the Horcruxes. In the last battle, he is seen leading the house-elves to fight against the Death-Eaters. Through the narratives of Dobby, Kreacher and

Winky, the series opens a space to critique the dominant power block of the wizard world from within.

With Dobby's death while saving Harry and his friends, the story of the house-elves and their suffering becomes linked with the larger fight of the wizard world. The peripheral narrative seems to be appropriated by the central narrative. Similarly Kreacher's battle cry indicates that he fights not for the house-elves but for his masters, the wizards: "Fight! Fight! Fight for my Master, defender of house-elves! Fight the Dark Lord, in the name of brave Regulus! Fight!" (*DH* 619). Yet this integration is not totally seamless. The preceding narrative reveals the faultlines in the dominant value systems and hierarchies that the closure is not able to resolve. Although we hardly know of its future course, Hermione's political project Society for Promotion of Elfish Welfare, or SPEW, opens a model for political engagement. In the series, as Carey points out, "young people are implicitly invited to follow Hermione's lead, unpopular though it might initially seem to be, and take political action against prejudice" (114).

Thus, the presence of the house-elves and their narratives establish a direct link between the mundane domesticity, state authority and the world of fantasy. Slavery of the house-elves emerges as a perversion of the relationship between these institutions. Their presence also signals an overarching interest in the realms of childhood, its links with the domestic life, and its lower orders, and links them to the story of boy hero's quest, knowledge and growth. In the series, it becomes the center of a powerful dialogue that emerges from the rural roots, feminine spaces and mythologies of a culture, grounding the magical world of fantasy into the material realities of the familiar world. While the house-elves and the giants portray the complexities of the social organization of a culture, presence of the blood-thirsty werewolf, the half-man, half-animal monster foregrounds the tensions within the subject's self.

Werewolves and the Narratives of Dis-ease

A detailed look at the house-elves and the giants reveals their links to the historical and socio-cultural systems of England. On the other hand, the werewolf monsters in the series are borrowed from a variety of literary traditions. Werewolves — the monsters that shift between man and animal — recur repeatedly in the Western narrative traditions ranging from classical mythology to folklore and fairy tale. They have been appropriated through time and epochs by a variety of discourses — of religion, morality, pathology, even medical sciences — signifying the changing perceptions of the monster figure from its position in early theology to later secular images. In the folk traditions, shape-shifting like that of a werewolf has been associated with the transgression and regeneration. Harry Senn describes the Roman festival of *Lupercalia* where "young men of the wolf fraternities run through the crowds of spectators in the streets spreading fear and disorder," "purifying the ground" of the evil influences and propitiating fertility (Senn 208). In *Lupercalia*, the playful transformation between man and animal is associated with themes of fertility, community welfare and resuscitation. At the same time, a werewolf's habitual transgression of the basic rules of humanity, its embodiment of the contaminated state of humanity, has led to its associations with uncontrollable violence, terror and excess. As a prime emblem of deviance and hybridity, a werewolf engenders psychological excess; it is an abject threatening the unity of a human subject from within; simultaneously, they also represent a social threat that has to be kept under rigorous control.

The werewolf monsters in the *Potter* series have been approached at various levels. Roslyn Weaver studies them as metaphors of disease and illness. Pugh and Wallace, in their study of the *Potter* series as a school story refer to the queer subtext that seems to underlie the portrayal of Remus Lupin. Hence, a werewolf foregrounds fragility at multiple levels — its bodily malady signals a psychological as well as social fragmentation. The self and the other, the human and the beast, the insider and the outsider, confront each other within the same body. Since body is considered to be the prime locus of selfhood, of identity, a werewolf's shapeshifting disturbs idea of embodied unity of a subject. The bite of a werewolf marks a break in the coherent identity of mankind; the contamination by the bite reveals the bestial abject who persists in disturbing the human self— from within and without. Like Kristeva's abject, periodically transforming body of a werewolf is a threat to the self— the bestial other within a human subject whose expulsion enables a subject a set up neat and clear boundaries of the self. A werewolf, therefore, represents twin motifs — an alien "other" threatening the self and at the same time, the other that has welled up from within the subject's psyche. According to Cohen, such category crisis is a constitutional characteristic of a monster (*Monster Culture* 6). The disturbance that a werewolf monster embodies at the individual level is extended on to a wider social level. A shape-shifting monster like a werewolf— who regularly moves between humanity and animality —

becomes a site where the psychological production of selfhood coincides with the sociological production of social reality.

In the *Harry Potter* series, the man-animal hybrid becomes a site that reveals the fragility behind the narratives of selfhood so central to the story of the boy hero. The portrayal of two werewolves in the series — Remus Lupin and Fenrir Greyback — though diametrically opposite, becomes a means to reflect and reveal the disturbing undercurrents that, along with the story of the hero, highlight the politics of inclusion and exclusion. Fenrir Greyback is a stereotypical werewolf — bloodthirsty, savage and fearsome. Greyback is one of the most fearsome of Rowling's villains. His violent nature, his relish for human blood and his "fondness" for children — all are repulsive. In the figure of Fenrir, the bestial aspect of the werewolf seems to have completely overcome the "human" impulses.

Remus Lupin, on the other hand, is gentle and friendly. He is one of Harry's loyal guardians, a competent and intelligent teacher. Bestiality surfaces in Lupin also — during the sole moment of werewolf transition that we witness in the series, Lupin attacks Harry in his transformed state. Clearly, a werewolf is too dangerous to be included in the human community. It connotes wildness, violence, unbridled instinct and cannibalism, and these traits well up from within an individual — traits which have to be repressed and sublimated to achieve and maintain a "civilized" society. Hence, despite his goodness, Lupin can only join the society around him on the sly — till his "true condition" is revealed. The element of threat, though latent, is ever present. It can be seen in his own frustration at not being comfortable in his own body, in his constant battle against the "bestiality" that is alien to his "true" "human" nature. In his figure, the incomplete process of abjection haunts the subject with fragility, a human identity which is under a perennial threat of dissolving into the bestial other.

A werewolf, hence, emerges as an ambiguous symbol — fearsome and at the same time fascinating. Bodily transgression and excess permeate the image of a werewolf in cultural imagination. Rowling links Lupin with his folkloric predecessors whose presence at the margins symbolized such disturbance. He is named after one of the legendary founders of Rome, Remus, who, along with his brother Romulus, was suckled by Luperca, a she-wolf. According to the legend, in their youth, Remus and Romulus led young boys on hunts and attacks on robbers. The school adventures of Lupin and his friends James Potter, Sirius Black and Peter Pettigrew — all shape-shifters accompanying Lupin on the full moon nights — remind of the mock terrorism of *Lupercalia*.

Yet, while wolf-lore refers to carnivalesque transgressions, when men don animal masks during annual festivities, Lupin and his friends literally transform into animals. Such literal transformations are deeply disturbing since corporeal materiality of the body is often seen as the locus of identity. But in the case of Lupin's friends, who are voluntary shape-shifters, the link between the man and the animal is carefully and firmly established. The animal form is dictated by the nature of the wizard. The "beast within" in the above cases is a metaphoric extension of an individual; it reinforces the personality and traits of the wizard, a literal embodiment of the nature and motivations of a particular individual. Such shape-shifting is common in the magical world of the series.

Thus, it is not shape-shifting itself that causes anxiety, but the shape-shifting of a werewolf which undoes the illusion of active control over one's own body. A werewolf monster complicates the elements of folkloric man-wolves. The transformation is involuntary, painful, dangerous and contrary to "human" nature.

The complexities of man and animal dualism, the mind-body dichotomy that such metamorphosis foregrounds, have been explored at various levels in werewolf literature. The literature of wolf metamorphosis can be traced back to classics like Ovid's Metamorphosis. In Ovid's story, Zeus turns Lycaon into a wolf for serving him human meat. The metamorphosis of Lycaon into wolf is a punishment for the disrespect shown to divinity. Like Lupin's friends, Lycaon's true nature is reflected in his bodily transformation. While in Lycaon's case the physical body comes to reflect his mental disposition, Marie de France's werewolf Bisclavret, in a 12th-century story by the same name, remains honest and noble, though he transforms into a wolf. His wife betrays him by stealing his clothes, thereby letting him languish in the beastly form till he gets his clothes back. In his wolfish form, Bisclavret becomes a part of the royal retinue. But getting back in his clothes is essential for returning to the human society. The emphasis on clothes underscores the inner and outer or the over- and under-dualism central to the werewolf narratives.

Lupin's lycanthropy, on the other hand, is an image of a divided self. Unlike Lycaon, whose bodily form becomes an extension of his mental state, or Bisclavret, where the mind-body dichotomy is preserved, Lupin's nature alters as he shifts from man to wolf. It is a terrifying experience of opposites as they fragment the unitary entity. The combination of opposites in the potent monstrous figure disrupts the images of subjectivity developed through the dichotomies, man and beast, mind and body, culture and nature. It develops even further as we see Lupin, the wizard constantly at odds with his bestial self. His wolfish state is clearly not an extension of his true nature; neither is he allowed to be a man in a wolf's skin.

Lupin's involuntary transformation marks the disruption of embodied identity of a man. In the form of a beast, a werewolf is an alien and its otherness is constructed as everything that goes against "normal" "human" identity. He bites and scratches himself, is dangerous to his friends, cannot be trusted and is therefore a threat to the entire community. In the human form, when the danger is potentially lurking within the figure of a human being, or during the transformation, the moment of hybridity, werewolf expresses the internal grotesqueness of the human subject, the terrifying experience of the universalized subject contaminated by its other.

Yet this fractured body is unequivocally gendered. In popular texts, a werewolf is depicted as undisputedly masculine, raw image of a mad warrior, associated with violence, physical strength and aggression, a part-man, part-animal carnivore in contrast to an effeminate vampire figure. At the same time, it also disrupts the rules of respectable masculinity — the virtues of self-mastery, restrain and discipline. Andrea Gutenberg has pointed out feminine dimension in this essentially male monster. "It is curious that wolf men under go metamorphoses in the full moon, smitten by a monthly mania for blood. In this sense, a werewolf is a man with monthlies, a wolf woman, in effect; and the myth of lycanthropy bespeaks the ineradicable ambiguities of gender." These ambiguities find space in the close knit group of Marauders — four friends who break rules to spend nights together roaming in the forest forbidden to them — intimate, close to each other, exploring the forbidden grounds in their liminal condition of animality. Though much later Remus Lupin enters into a "normal" albeit short-lived marriage and fatherhood, the most significant relationship for him, even after the school, is being a Marauder, a part of the adolescent part-animal, part-boy group.

The sexual deviance embodied in the figure of a werewolf is further monsterized in the stereotype of a fairy tale wolf— Fenrir Greyback. Rowling names him after the ferocious Fenris Wolf of Norse mythology, the son of trickster god Loki prophesied to swallow Odin during the mythic battle of Ragnarok. The stereotype has been visited and revisited in literature and cinema. In Rowling's story, Fenrir appears as loathsome and horrifying figure in *Harry Potter and the Half-Blood Prince* who would not miss a trip to Hogwarts: "Not when there are throats to be ripped out ... delicious, delicious..." (Rowling, *HBP* 554). The horror he engenders makes it easy and justifiable to condemn him. Lupin claims that Fenrir "specializes" in children. Sexual innuendos make him even more terrifying. When he claims Hermione as his victim, his glee is guised in language full of sexual threat. The sexually predatory werewolf has been common since Charles Perrault told the story of Little Red Riding Hood and the bite of a wolf acquired a new meaning altogether. Perrault's 17th-century tale established wolf as first and foremost a figure of lechery and pederasty, condensing the greatest fears of the society in a single deviant form.[1] The characterization of Fenrir Greyback, following the same stereotype, suggests that the contamination of man by the bestial is obscene, horrible and threatening, engendering deviance and disgust at every level. It becomes a justification for Fenrir's exile and, consequently, of all the werewolves.

Through Fenrir, pederasty, "unnatural" sexuality, and cruelty become an extension of the condition of being a werewolf. These are instituted as the norm for the werewolves and a justification for their complete social marginalization. Judith Halberstam in discussing the insistence on the sexual deviancy of a monster insists that "where sexuality becomes the identity, other 'others' become invisible and multiple features of monstrosity seem to degenerate back into primeval sexual time" (7). In other words, the issues of cultural prejudice, injustice and marginalization, so evident in Lupin's case, are all subsumed within the sexualized body of the monster like Fenrir. Though jaded and repetitive, the society's image of a monster consistently gains strength and potency through these very stereotypes which legitimize their exclusion.

Hence, the series uses lycanthropy to explore process and politics of othering, social abjection and political marginalization. Often lycanthropy is expressed in terms of a disease, a diseased form of the ideal bodily self. Harry insists Lupin is normal; he just has "a problem." James Potter, Lupin tells Harry, called it his "furry little problem" (Rowling, *HBP*, 314). The "problem" can be held at bay by the Wolfsbane potion which helps the werewolves to retain their "human-ness." Therefore, with care and alertness, a werewolf can be rehabilitated within the society. Yet, as Margrit Shildrick, in a detailed study of nonconformity, bodily deviance and monstrosity, highlights the fear of contagiousness and vulnerability surrounding the monsters exposes "the vulnerability at the heart of the ideal model of body/self" (54). The cultural narratives of sickness and unhealthiness that lycanthropy indicates elevate bodily abjection to a social level.

The marginalization and eventual elimination of the werewolves in Rowling's magical world seems to be a response to the vulnerability that is embedded at the heart of the coherent and civilized social self. Were-wolves in the wizard world are shunned, are unable to find paid work because of social prejudices and policies like "anti-werewolf legislation." Lupin's own attitude towards his transformation — his self-pity as well as his awareness of injustices of the magical community — reflects his society's dilemma when confronted with a monster that upsets the notions of "nor-mal" and "natural."

A werewolf thus reveals the faultlines in the closure of normativity — textual, organic, mythical and political. Its loyalty comes with an uneasy demand, demand for equality and rehabilitation — in other words, a refor-mist demand that Lupin articulates by his kindness, his "humanity." There-fore, the death of the werewolf forecloses an array of possibilities in the seemingly democratic order that comes into being in the end of the series. While Fenrir Greyback is "brought down" by young boy heroes like Ron and Neville, Lupin also dies in the battle. His wife Tonks, who defied her family and society to marry a werewolf, also dies. With the death of the two werewolves, the magical world is, in a way, a less dangerous place. At the same time, the death of Remus Lupin leaves a gap; it evades the questions raised by the figure of a gentle and friendly werewolf, the vulnerabilities that he brought to the fore. It challenges the new democratic order of the magical world that denies the demands of integration or rehabilitation. In the story of the hero which iterates the values and aspirations of the com-munity, the monster embodies all that is excluded from its neat structures. The narratives that formulate and enforce cultural categories also create the outsiders and the marginalized, the "harbingers of category crisis" (Cohen 6); as the end instates boy heroes as the saviors of the community, the fears concerning the monsters — the polluted, contaminated, illegiti-mate others — are put to rest. The central theme of the series, its preoc-cupation with the purity of blood, falters when it comes to the werewolves.

However, Lupin is survived by his son Teddy. The trace of the mon-ster lingers, arousing unease and demanding recognition. In his being, the series also gestures towards the modes of existence that accept and integrate the existence of the other. In the epilogue, Harry's son sees him with Vic-toire, daughter of Bill, who was bitten by Fenrir, and Fleur, who is a part–Veela, the beautiful non-human sirens of the series. Teddy, and to some extent Victoire, represents the trace of the monster that is never completely externalized, a threat that is embedded within the social fabric; it constantly breaches the fortifications of the normative standards. In this dual role — as a member of the wizard community as well as the son of a feared outcast — the offspring of a werewolf embodies a sense of openness and vulnerability that the social constructions of identity and selfhood insist on veiling. Writing about the theme of werewolf metamorphosis in the literature of entertainment, Caroline Bynum argues that, built on folklores as well as classical accounts, "such literature destabilizes reality, making boundaries fluid, categories and interpretations problematic. It lodges at the heart of the world (not just on its margins) events that seem to make all identity labile, threatening and threatened" ("Metamorphosis" 998). The revision of the werewolf motif in the *Potter* series destabilizes the narrative of organic wholeness and identity constitution that is central to fantasy stories. Therefore, despite its conventional end, the series succeeds to some extent by problematizing the basic categories of humanity and structures of human community by pitting it against a monster who is disturbing due to his gentleness and goodness.

Conclusion

While marginalized and ousted from the wizard world, these monster figures still play a crucial role in Harry's victory. The close alliance of the adolescent protagonist with the deviant monstrous characters provides a new perspective on adolescence and growth. Threat emanating from the monstrous creatures mirrors the perceived threat of adolescence: "Pathologized as deviant, ascribed with endless maladies that capitalize on social anxieties and intolerances, and diagnosed as irrational, dependent, and non-conforming, young adults are viewed as dangerous and unpredictable aberrations that must be cured of their reckless nature. In a word, they are transgressors, who blatantly resist their assignment to 'normal' cultural boxes" (O'Quinn 54). The non-human associations emphasize the fluidity of the state of adolescence and childhood and hence its queerness. If the non-normative inter-personal relationships reflect the nature of adolescence — its position on the peripheries of the magical community, then Harry's victory and his coming of age that signifies the end of adolescence also brings about the conventionalization of these relationships. Therefore, it is important to oust the monsters: Lupin and Dobby, the marginalized who engage in the political discourses of racism and actively resist the ideological fictions of wizard world, are no longer present. The ones who survive are Hagrid and Kreacher, who accept the place for them ordained by the wizard world.

At the same time, the monster and the series' preoccupation with its narrative reveals the fact that the tidy closure rests on ideologies as unnatural and strange. These narratives at the margins decentralize and question the legitimacy of the central plot. The monsters speak from a zone that Judith Butler calls "a domain of unlivability and unintelligibility that bounds the domain of intelligible effects" (*Bodies That Matter* 22); Butler points out that even when discursively closed off, this narrative offers a base for critique, a margin from which to reread dominant paradigms. Fantasy, especially Young Adult fantasy, which has been accused of reproducing the dominant ideologies and value systems, with these multiple narratives of arrested growth and stunted development serves as a discursive field that could be read in diverse ways. It is not just the story of the hero but also that of the monsters who have no space to grow up. These monstrous characters become means to question the "naturalized" orders of growth. Monsters thus probe the normative discourses of growth undoing the naturalized logic of development revealing the culturally constructed investments.

Conclusion

The study has been an attempt to explore cultural conceptualizations of growth and boyhood and their literary expressions, especially in popular fantasy. Through the story of Rowling's boy wizard and his monstrous allies, the book explored the role models disseminated by children's and young adult literature for its young readers. Within the practices of cultural containment, of acculturation and socialization, emerged moments of subversion and resistance, moments that slip out of the linear pattern of a *Bildungsroman*. A detailed textual analysis of the series revealed the ambiguities within the stereotypical cultural patterns of growth, foregrounding the queerness of adolescence and the resistance it puts up against being fixed, analyzed and summed up.

Reading through the prism of popular fiction opened several interesting possibilities. The reading revealed the space of possibilities, of alterity and difference within the structural constraints of *marvelous* literature that is opened up by the conflation of fantasy and adolescence. Fantasy and adolescence are linked in their insistence on the interstices — while fantasy emerges from the interstices of reality, adolescence lies on the cusp between childhood and adulthood. Fantasy therefore becomes a means to express fluidity and otherness that characterizes the state of adolescence, especially in face of the drive for fixity and determinacy. In fantasy, adolescence emerges as a zone of play. It plays with, critiques and subverts the narratives of containment. Thus, though the movement of fantasy is traditionally meant to propel the protagonist, and thereby the reader, out of adolescence and into the role ordained for them in the adult world, adolescence itself opens up as a time for non-linear and deviant modes of being that lie outside the mapped and graded models of growth. Fantastic tools of defamiliarization and difference become effective means to explore the non-normative and uncustomary ways of being. An essential part of an adolescent's journey towards personal maturation therefore lies in the moments that spill beyond the formulas of normalization and conventionalization. Therefore a *marvelous* text like the *Potter* series enacts the struggle between the two conceptions of childhood outlined by David Rudd — one, the "constructed" child, a child posited as a *tabula rasa*, like Rousseau's Emile whose malleability underlines the project of containment and guidance, and its "other," the "constructive" child, the child who frequently disrupts our notion of an amenable, obedient angel and also the pattern of growth that is envisaged for him or her. Focusing solely on the generic pattern, the narrative of young adult fantasy like Rowling's can be read as return to the humanist theories of growth and development through which we seek to understand and guide the process of childhood and adolescence. On the contrary, the point of this study has been to deconstruct these linear narratives of socialization and growth by locating the points of discord and queerness within the iconic role models of boyhood.

One of the central arguments of this study has been against collapsing popular literature and culture into the conditions of ideology and market. In the *Potter* series, the eclectic mix of popular genres — fantasy and adventure, the hero myth, schoolboy fiction and the story of a savior presents the formulaic patterns of boy-to-man transition. At the same time, these generic traditions undercut each other and also the ideology that underpins each genre. They are further undercut by the peripheral narratives that underpin the narrative of the hero. Rather than presenting the formula in an uncritical manner, a close look at these narratives of growth in the Potter series reveals the contradictions inherent in the popular myths surrounding an adolescent and growth.

The preceding chapters are concerned with the grand narratives of boyhood — the hero, the schoolboy and the savior and their deconstruction through the narrative of the monsters. Each chapter locates the Potter series in the tradition of these grand narratives of boyhood that have been revised and repeatedly retold in varied guises throughout Western history. In *Retelling Stories, Framing Culture*, Robyn McCallum and John Stephen suggest that the main function of the repeated and retold stories is to maintain "conformity to socially determined and approved patterns of behaviour, which they do by offering positive role models, proscribing undesirable behaviour and affirming the culture's ideologies, systems and institutions" (3–4). Therefore, these fictions of boyhood outline the expected trajectories of growth and cultural expectations and also prescribe gender and sexual roles. Boys are meant to ensure cultural continuity, firstly, by saving the world or rather the existing world order from external and internal threats and secondly, by passing on the same task to their children. Therefore, the "masculine" narratives of war, exploration and adventure as well as marriage and fatherhood all find an important place in the fictions of boyhood.

At the same time, a close look at the Potter series reveals the way in which these formulations of boyhood are undercut or queered in popular literature of adolescent fantasy. Wizard heroes, with their "unnatural" magical talents, accentuate and displace the fictions of masculinity, drawing attention to their constructed-ness. Fantasy underlines the gaps and the points of suture in the cultural constructions of adolescence, growth and boy-to-man transition. The traditional "performance" of masculine heroism is unhinged by the ambiguous or, as Annette Wannamaker calls them, the "witchy masculinities" of the wizard heroes. Therefore, by studying the narratives of heroic growth separately, the study explores and deconstructs the grand narratives of boyhood and growth.

The hero monomyth is outlined in the *Potter* series as a narrative of ego formation. The monomyth outlines the structure of psychic growth, resolution and repression of various crises, a movement away from Oedipal attachments, perverse sexualities and peer group attachments to heterosexual marriage and fatherhood. However, the *Potter* series uses the ideas of an orphan hero, of mirror-images, of doppelgängers, of mentors and fellowship to problematize the seemingly simple story of the hero killing the evil wizard and marrying the princess in waiting. Though structured by the generic paradigm of the hero myth, fantasy fiction explores the themes and motifs that have the potential to undercut the linear movement towards the dominant cultural positions. Adolescence in the Potter series emerged as an area of playful fantasy, of engagement with difference exemplified by underground student groups, like the Marauders and the Weasley twins. In the Dumbledore's Army, led by Harry Potter, the playful disobedience of adolescence became a serious assertion of difference and defiance against the dominant establishments of the magical world.

The hero myth also emerged as a fertile ground for exploring the adolescent concerns with sexuality and death. The chapter explored the insistent subtext of sexuality that resurfaces repeatedly in Harry's relationships, especially in his friendship with Ron. Despite a kind of sexual sanitization, the subtext insistently impinges on the narrative in the form of love triangles, peer group attachments and fellowships. The presence of sexual concerns, especially in the narrative concerned with childhood and growth, underlined the queerness of adolescence. The theme seemed to echo across the subgenre of adolescent fantasy, in narratives like Philip Pullman's series *His Dark Materials* and Tamora Pierce's The Song of the Lioness. Most of these narratives subvert the normative assumptions regarding the "a-sexuality" and "innocence" of a child by highlighting the perverse sexual pre-occupations of an adolescent. In the Potter series, these "perversities" are underscored by Harry's shifting relations with his parents and surrogate parents, his relationship with his friends and teachers. The course of development in the hero monomyth approaches conditions of heterosexuality, marriage and fatherhood as the final goal. Yet the journey traverses the region of perverse sexualities and queer attachments.

The resolution of heroic growth in marriage and fatherhood is tied up with the wider concerns of family, citizenship and nationalism. These themes recur in other images of boyhood in literature like the schoolboy. The narratives of schooling link pedagogy, concerns of education, discipline and punishment with the conceptualization of the "correct" patterns of growth. The "correct" pattern of growth is implicated with the issues of identity, race, and nationalism — issues that have been crucial since they ensure continuity and preservation of a culture. Therefore, school fiction, especially boarding school fiction (since a boarding school takes over play, leisure hours and the concerns that lie beyond technical education in a more effective manner) rose and flourished during the British colonial enterprise. As a boarding school story, Rowling's series situates the theme of growth in a wider social context. The chapter examines Rowling's text in the context of the ideological history that has driven British boarding school literature. The revival of the genre in the last decade of the twentieth century situates these themes in a postcolonial, postmodern context. Therefore, Hogwarts is depicted as a co-educational and multicultural institution. A school of magic, Hogwarts complicates the ideological assumptions that surround a regular school. The discussion centers on the figure of a schoolboy and his magical counterpart — the apprentice wizard. An apprentice wizard adds another dimension to the figure of a schoolboy. Young wizards and witches who enter the school magic already possess a certain skill — skills that make them outsiders in the "normal" world. This conception of the "otherness" and difference of the wizards and witches emerged as a site for contesting the hegemony of the dominant ideologies. It underlies the conception of magic in the Potter series and also in young adult fantasy fiction. Hogwarts differs from other fictional schools in terms of its engagement with magic as a form of power that is wielded from the peripheries, from the interstices and gaps of a system, a "bottom-up" kind of force that is unique to the outsiders including the adolescent protagonists. The element of magic, therefore, disturbs the conventional trajectory of growth. As the narrative progresses, Hogwarts emerges as a space of counter-ideology where the temporary non-conformity of adolescence progresses from playful pranks on Argus Filch, the caretaker, to the resistance put up against the diktats of Dolores Umbridge and the officialdom of the magical world and finally culminating in the war against the Dark Lord and his Death-Eaters.

The series also problematizes other traditional norms of the school stories. The traditional stereotypes of gender and race are simultaneously reinforced and undercut. The issue of house-elf slavery, injustice and resentment of centaurs and werewolves, the central issue of blood purity — all these are important to the textual politics of the series. Complicating the traditional positions on race and gender is the portrayal of characters like Hermione Granger, a "mudblood" who can see through and raise her voice against the prejudices of the magical world; Remus Lupin, an outcast werewolf who, though self-pitying, is also conscious of the unjust treatment meted out by the magical community to its "others"; and Dobby, the house-elf who is traditionally meant to slave for the wizards, but insists on his wages and his rights. These cultural "outsiders" are politically vocal characters whose presence exposes the weaknesses and prejudices inherent in the social order of the magical world. In their existence outside the social order and hierarchies, in their resistance and challenge to the cultural stereotypes, they mirror the position of an adolescent and therefore are the "natural" allies of the adolescent protagonists of the series. They enunciate the social and political context of the story. Along with the adolescent protagonists, these characters emerged as crucial part of the series as they highlighted the issues of otherness and difference and constantly shaped and re-shaped the quest of the hero giving it a wider social and political significance.

While the hero monomyth and the school story place the narrative of identity constitution in the social and political context, the image of the savior places the series in the Christian tradition. The idea of growth is linked to the idea of Christian pilgrimage. The image of the savior is especially relevant in the view of the debates accusing the Potter series of luring children away from Christian teachings towards witchcraft and occult. Readers like John Granger have done a detailed study of the religious analogies in the series. With the focus on love, sacrifice and death underlining the Christian worldview of the series, Rowling's story follows the fantastic tradition of C.S Lewis and George MacDonald. Yet the course of study revealed important differences. The adolescent protagonists of the Potter series came across as disobedient, manipulative, powerful and active children. While the adult establishment is riddled with prejudices, the adolescent heroes can see through the problems of the magical world. In its conception of childhood, therefore, the series differed from the Christian concept of the child as sinful and weak, the lowest on the rungs of humanity and, therefore, closest to the kingdom of God. These findings were reflected in other contemporary texts like Phillip Pullman's series, *His Dark Materials*. Lyra Belacqua completely disrupts the stereotype of angelic, innocent little girl; she is portrayed as lying, willful and disobedient. She is repeatedly called the "second Eve." In a narrative that parallels the biblical story of the Genesis, the awakening of sexuality in the two teenaged protagonists, Lyra and Will, leads to the "second" Fall that reworks the biblical story. The end of Harry's story, on the other hand, parallels Christ's passion and resurrection. Yet we saw how Harry's sacrifice is placed in the context of his secular relationships, his concern for his friends and family. We also saw how it is also marked with the heightened awareness of his oneness with humanity — the conscious choice to sacrifice himself, the insistent reminder of the body and the earthly life that is being sacrificed — all portray sacrifice as an act of human agency.

The idea of death itself emerged as one of the most problematic concerns in fantastic literature. Death and mortality, as critics like Trites have pointed out, recur as frequently in adolescent fiction as sexuality. The final stage of coming of age is the acceptance of mortality. Yet we saw the way the series complicated the idea of death at several levels. In context of the Christian narrative, in this study of young adult fantasy, sacrificial death emerged as the final act of belonging. Rather than a punishment for transgression of mankind, death itself becomes the moment of grace. The study also underlines the ambiguity surrounding the idea of death as an end to growth and development. In fact, this is the conception of death that Voldemort is scared of, the death that he tries to evade by searching for eternity. In fantasy literature like Rowling's and also Pullman's series, death emerged as an important moment in the cycle of life. In the hero myth, the hero's return from the land of the dead is an important structural device; Harry submits to death to emerge as the Master of Death. The structural device is used to establish continuity into the future. By subverting the authority of death as an "end" of growth, the narrative ensures that death becomes a stage in regeneration of life. Accepting mortality is linked with accepting "human-ity" and oneness with humanity at large — a theme that resonates with the theme of sacrifice and the narrative of the savior.

Another key Christian reference dealt with is the magical power of love. Love holds a central position in the Christian framework. It is the source of grace and redemption for mankind. In the Potter series, love emerged as a combative power rather than as divine bestowal. It emanates from interpersonal relationships. Individual choices and acts are the keys to the receptivity of graces. Harry is saved repeatedly not by divine intervention but by friends and aides who are ready to sacrifice themselves for the cause and for him, personally. Griphook, the Centaurs, even his friends like Neville and Luna first become committed to Harry before joining the cause. Dobby remains personally committed to Harry. The sacrifice of Lily Potter re-surfaces again and again, every act and choice is put in context of this sacrificial act till Harry himself submits to death to end the reign of terror and save the magical world. There is no God-like figure or a divine representative in the series; the magic of love emanates from interpersonal relationships. Singer sums this up as the conception of love in the postmodern world: "We perceive that love is a choice of one's being by means of judgments and decisions that influence emotional response" (*Nature*, vol. 3, 439). Christian concepts of love and sacrifice therefore emerge as active forces especially when placed in the context of textual politics of the magical world and also the global political context of the series itself.

These templates of growth — the hero, the schoolboy and the savior — are then juxtaposed to the narratives of the monsters — the deviant and abnormal characters of fantasy to whom these trajectories are denied. The monsters are the borderland characters existing between the fantastic and the real world. While the adolescent hero achieves growth and maturity and hence leaves behind the space of fantasy, these characters are continuous with the liminal world of fantasy. A deep analysis of the portrayal of the giants, the house-elves and the werewolves reveals the cultural investment in the politics of exclusion, marginalization and monsterization and the way it is shaped by discourses of normativity, nationhood, gender and sexuality. The process of construction of selfhood (one of the primary functions of young adult fiction) emerges to be a process that is closely linked to the constructions of otherness.

Therefore, the study reveals the way the Potter series subverts the cultural narratives that seek to appropriate and contain the dangerous figure of an adolescent. The closely structured pattern of fantasy exists in a dialectical position — upholding as well as subverting the grand discourses of growth and boyhood. On the surface, Rowling's magical world is a fairy-tale world filled with binaries like good and evil manifested in the form of the "two sides" of the war in the magical world. The moral framework of good and evil invokes a dualism around which the narrative turns — the victory of good over evil is central to most fantasy narratives. But as Harry and his friends age, they discover subtleties, minute differences and uncertainties. The series situates the child at the center of the complexities and ambiguities of the contemporary (adult) world. The children negotiate through a world of moral relativism, challenging and deconstructing the efforts to guide and instruct. Deborah Thacker and Jean Webb insist that in postmodern children's literature "the child, removed from the 'norms' of the nuclear family and the certainties of organized religion, consumed by materialism and the proliferation of sexualized, 'adulterated' images of the body, has become a threatening, uncontrollable force" (140). Rather than fear and anxiety, fantasy envisions this state as a state of possibility — possibility of questioning the absolutes and deconstructing traditional expectations.

The adolescent characters of the Potter series are placed amid the political and cultural debates of their contemporary world. The persistence of these debates reveals the way the series problematizes the structural device of closure. The closure is an important device in the *fantastic-marvelous*. The closure of the story calls for the termination of the fantastic adventure along with the completion of the process of adolescence. It is a closure in order with the Anglo-Western tradition of fairy tales.

> Following the protagonist's development towards happiness is what lies at the heart of the Anglo-Western fairy tale, and it is for this reason that once this state of happiness has been attained, that tale has come to an end. The classic closing formula "and they lived happily every after" seals off the tale once it has attained such narrative closure, warding off any further questions of the type *what happened next?* [Klapproth 360].

Therefore, on the surface, the domestic image in the epilogue can be summed up as a "happily ever after." After saving the world, the story of the adolescent boy hero ends in marital bliss and fatherhood symbolized by the new Potter family. Fantasy, therefore, ends with the end of adolescence. Critics like Maria Nikolajeva have pointed out how fantasy in children's literature begins with an escape into a "neverland" and ends with a return to the familiar and the "real." For instance, Max's adventures with the wild things, which begin when he dons his wolf suit and threatens to eat his mother, end with his return to home, mother and hot food. This circular end in children's fantasy signals a return to safety and security provided by home and parents. Fantasy, or the adventures with the wild things, are therefore a kind of "detour" in a schematic *bildung*. The time and space of fantasy is tightly bound by the closure or the end which circumscribes the time of childhood and adolescence.

So the Potter series ends with the death of the Dark Lord, seemingly the source of all evil and ills in the magical world, and instates a sense of peace and security. Yet Voldemort is clearly not the first and most probably not the last wizard who has gone over to the side of the evil. He is the successor of Grindelwald, even though in the last book Grindelwald is seen repenting in his last days. In the course of narrative, Voldemort, his obsession with the purity of blood, and his attitude to other creatures emerge as reflections of the unjust attitudes of the wizard world.

Therefore, the image of domesticity in the epilogue at the King's Cross Station is a deceptively simple moment; social and cultural issues persist beyond the mist that surrounds the station nineteen years after the death of Voldemort as the next generation of Potters and Weasleys leave for Hogwarts.[1] The traditional animosity between Gryffindor and Slytherin resurfaces in the banter between Harry's children, James and Albus, and also in Ron's continuing hostility to Draco. The preoccupation with blood purity and racial imagery persists as Ron warns his daughter that "Grandad Weasley would never forgive you if you married a pure blood" (*DH* 605). Victoire, daughter of Fleur, a part-human, and Bill, a man "contaminated" by a werewolf bite, is reported to be with Teddy Lupin, son of a werewolf. Hagrid remains a part-giant teacher living on the peripheries of the school. The issue of the house-elf slavery is evaded and silenced. So, the problems of race and prejudice still plague the magical world of Rowling. The fantastic remedy to extirpate the root of all evil by killing off Voldemort, is rendered problematic by the course of the narrative. As problematic as the death of Voldemort is the death of the truly monstrous allies of Harry, Lupin and Dobby, the marginalized figures who engaged in the political discourse of racism and actively resisted the ideological fictions of wizard world, do not survive.[2] Neither does Nymphadora Tonks, a social outcast who, despite being human, chooses to marry a werewolf. Though the series culminates in an overt reassertion of dominant positions vis-à-vis race, gender and sexuality, it is easy to see the ruptures that render the closure fragile and unstable. Rather than a fairy-tale ending into an "ever after," the end of the series follows the nineteenth-century narratives where the imposed resolution actually fails to resolve the contradictions raised during the course of the narrative. It creates tensions that live beyond the conventional plot of the victory of good over evil.

Hence, looking from the vantage point of the end, the closure of the Potter series seems to be an end of Harry's individual story of revenge rather than of the troubles plaguing the wizard world that become central to the narrative during the course of the series. Sarah Gilead notes that at times "instead of restoring or inverting conventional orders of significance, the return (to the 'reality,' that is, the closure of fantasy) may function as the point at which the text most dramatically turns on itself to reveal its duplicities and discords" (Gilead 288). The unresolved issues followed by a conventional closure leaves behind a strong sense of dissatisfaction; it undoes the reading of fantasy as a *bildung*. Eternal bliss summed up by "happily ever after" remains doubtful. Though the end frames cultural expectations of unidirectional growth and development of adolescence suggesting a successful maturation of the child protagonist and the readers, it also casts an ironic shadow on the "unreal" and partial nature of such interpretations. Rather than yielding narrative consolation and comforting the reader with the "happily every after," the closure can be seen as an ironic comment on the generic convention itself.

Thus the narrative of adolescent growth, the journey of an outsider from the peripheries to the center, emerges as a critique of the norms of growth as well as of the structural fantasy. Alice Mills, in her analysis of Jungian archetypes in Rowling's and Diana Wynne Jones' fantasy, argues that "the patterns of Harry Potter books render them as 'trickster texts'; they are far from simplistic in their treatment of (generally) formulaic material" ("Archetypes" 8). Like a trickster, an adolescent exists as an "other" vis-à-vis the dominant adult position. To become a part of the system, a trickster has to reform and conform. At the same time, a trickster's trickery calls into question fundamental assumptions about the way the world is organized and reveals the possibility of transforming it. Irreverence, secrecy, defiance — we see how these elements of a trickster characterize the subversive subtext of the *Potter* series. The adolescent protagonists, who exist on the peripheries of the society, embrace the position of an outsider and the active potential of intervention it offers. Towards the end of the series, Hermione sides with the concerns of the "others" of the magical world raised by goblin Griphook: "Mudblood and proud of it!" (*DH* 418). The clichéd solution of love as a solution to all the ills of the hence is transformed into love that can combat and fight prejudice and injustice.

The narratives that this study focuses on are essentially masculine. An important part of the project has been to look at gender politics by decoding the male coming of age fantasy. Rather than ignoring the complicated aspects of female adolescence and coming of age, the study concentrates on studying the forceful way in which masculinity impinges on femininity. It is especially relevant for popular texts like the *Potter* series that have been read and re-read by children of either gender as they dealt with the similar "crisis" of growing up. What does this imply for the female characters and the readers of the genre? If heroic fantasy is supposed to encourage the young readers to mature with a particular set of values and morals, are female readers' subjectivities stifled with female characters typically cast as dependent, intelligent aides or helpless maidens waiting to be rescued? Writers like Tamora Pierce and Garth Nix situate a female protagonist at the center of the heroic fantasy. Pierce's *The Song of Lioness* tells the story of a female knight and in Nix's *Sabriel*, an adolescent girl inherits the mantle of her father, who is a necromancer. By situating girls at the center of an essentially boy's narrative, these texts destabilize the notions of gender roles. These texts illustrate the sophistication of themes and concerns of young adult fantasy literature.

Rowling's text, on the other hand, brings together the popular images of boyhood. As several critics have pointed out, Rowling does not seem to overtly challenge the norms of gender, sexuality or race. Hence, the conventional discourses that surround the figure of an adolescent boy and his growth seem to retain control and contain the narrative. At the same time, the main concern of this study has been the way the series is able to deliberate on these cultural containments and the "natural" assumptions that surround the figure of a boy. The coming of age of an adolescent male wizard is revealed to be an intensely gendered and racialized performance. The hero monomyth is the central myth of a patriarchal culture. It is an essentially androcentric story. Similarly, the nature and role of education for boys and girls envisioned by the school story emerged as being highly gender specific. Above all these is the Christian story of the savior that shifts the women to the periphery as the male savior imbibes "feminine" virtues of love, sacrifice and caring as well as the "masculine" task of saving the world. Conscious and unconscious forces impinge on the author's attempt to tailor these role models to the "politically correct" contexts of the twentieth- and twenty-first century, hence, the presence of strong female characters like Hermione Granger, Minerva McGonagall, Mrs. Weasley, Lily Potter and Bellatrix Lestrange. Yet these characters remain subordinate to the male characters.[3] The central figure of the hero remains reserved for an adolescent boy. Similarly, though Rowling tries to engage with racial politics in the magical world in the manner of a liberal, certain prejudices emerge in her depiction of multiculturalism in the school itself, especially in reference to actual races and ethnicities. The narrative itself remains troubled by these gendered and racialized equations — consciousness of the contemporary understanding of gender, race and sexuality exists at odds with the traditional stances that impinge unconsciously but powerfully on the narrative. Though the growth through the medium of generic fantasy seems to lend a sense of coherence and security, on a closer look, the narrative itself seems to be aware of the tenuousness of such assurances, pointing out the need for an engagement with the issues beyond the generic closure. The later books, especially those published after 9/11, show an increasing awareness of the changing cultural and political climate, the implications of the multicultural order and the paranoia generated by the threat of terrorism. The books use the liminality and fluidity of adolescence in conjunction with fantasy to reflect upon the material foundations of society and the formalized social institutions.

Therefore, rather than pure escapism, the series emerged as a dialogue with contemporary issues and politics. The study looks the charges of escapism and irresponsibility leveled at the text and also at the genre of the *fantastic-marvelous* through the theoretical framework provided by psychoanalysis and the cultural study of adolescence. The study becomes an attempt to trace the cultural unconscious through fantasy and adolescence. It also becomes a means to understand cultural perceptions and anxieties regarding adolescence through its representations by the codes of fantasy. The framework offered by queer theory gives an interesting and provocative approach to adolescence and magic, especially in understanding the fluidity, liminality and disruptive potential. The tension between normativity and queerness underwrites the generic formula of fantasy and also the state of adolescence. It becomes difficult to overlook the paradigm, especially its implications on boyhood and heteronormativity in narratives like that of a hero, a school boy or a savior which come together in Rowling's story. While gender studies reveal the cultural stakes and investments in the figure of a boy, queer analysis performs the additional task of understanding difference and otherness — within and without. Even as the narrative underlines the gradual immersion into normative masculinities, the queer subtext highlighted the non-normativity or disturbance inherent in the state of adolescence and in the subcultures of boyhood.

Queer analysis therefore deconstructs the cultural privilege assigned to the figure of a boy and, at the same time, highlights the performative aspect of boy-to-man growth. Queer theory and its insistence on performative aspects of identity also provided an interesting way to understand magic and wizardry as a performance of "difference." The grand narratives of growth emerged as performative acts that sought to construct and contain boyhood. Presence of magic and wizardry queered the normative performance, highlighting moments of subversion and defiance inherent in these cultural templates of containment.

Therefore, while Harry's coming of age reflects the investment in the symbolic signifiers by reinstating the male white savior, fantasy exposed the historically and culturally specific nature of these signifiers. Carrie Hintz notes that "young adults novels honor dissent and agitation, and action based on a prolonged and combative questioning of the society in which the protagonists find themselves" (255). The dissent, the rebellion and heroism become an argument for an active integration of adolescent into political life of the community. The clichéd answer of love, especially sacrificial love, that will save mankind, is here exemplified as a politically active force, a combative force. It is especially significant in adolescent literature where the sense of selfhood is inevitably based on the sense of the "other."

The study therefore unravels the dynamics of containment and subversion inherent to the cultural role models of adolescence in the *Potter* series. The focus on the single series makes an in-depth analysis of this voluminous text possible. Rowling's text is a suitable text for a generic approach to young adult literature as well as popular fantasy and also the representations of adolescence and its concerns. There are other important texts and authors, notably Philip Pullman, Tamora Pierce, Diana Wynne Jones, Jane Yolen and others. Their texts are equally complex and interesting and have yielded important insights to the Potter series.

Noting the trajectory of the growth of an adolescent, Spacks insists that "like women, adolescents constitute, in their own perception, an oppressed class; like women, they possess hidden weapons. Unlike women, they inevitably win in the long run, if only by growing up and succeeding their parents" (5). Though an adolescent is finally "put in place" in the adult world, the foremost concern of the present study has been the narratives of adolescent fantasy — narratives that deal with the experiments of a borderland individual, an adolescent's negotiations with power and autonomy within the socio-political structures. The tension between overt text and the subversive subtext embodies the tension between the way adults would like to see the teenagers and the way teenagers would like to see themselves. The purpose of the study is not to prove the truth of either. Both narratives co-exist in a dialogical relation in fantasy; while neither can be taken as completely "truthful" pictures (presence of fantasy debunks the concept of truth itself), both are equally valid as fantasies of adolescence. John Morris insists that "the enchantment of the story is not just engrossment or absorption — beyond that — even beyond giving us an insight about us and self awareness — it is the potential to participate in creation and creating" (83). It is the potential of active intervention in the narrative of redemption and salvation by human that underlies Rowling's narrative; rather than escape and irresponsibility, then, the conflation of adolescence and fantasy emerges as a zone of possibility. Therefore, despite being a part of the cultural discourse that seeks to reassure that adolescence, a temporary pathological stage of rebellion and hormonal mayhem, will pass, Rowling's series portrays its adolescent protagonists as fantastic and postmodern. The story of Harry Potter is not just about a boy hero but about the ideals of boyhood and their performance in contemporary cultural and historical contexts. The critical task of this study has been to note how the text participates in the norms that constitute identity and also locates the possibilities of contesting them. In narratives like those of adolescence, such queerness becomes an ideal; the formulaic closure of fantasy does not do away with the awareness that there are things in the world that are unknowable or queer.

Chapter Notes

Preface

1. S. E. Hinton's *The Outsiders* (1967) is commonly assumed to be the beginning of YA fiction (Herez and Gallo 10, Anderson 113).

Introduction

1. Of the important features of YA fiction cited by Herez and Gallo, the most noteworthy is that the main character is a teenager who is perceptive, intelligent, and independent and whose actions and decisions are the major factors in the outcome of the conflict (8–9).

2. The series undoes the over-humanist narrative with subversive and unsettling stories. While the readings of heroic fantasy or school story suggest that pleasure is derived from the genre's humanist messages, the central point of this study is the unsettling premise of alterity, of disturbance arising by play of the indeterminate fantastic.

3. Peter Humm, Paul Stignant, and Peter Widdowson in *Popular Fictions* argue that "most fiction is of course a product in the sense that it is written and made to be sold and marketed, but one characteristic of 'popular' fiction must be its relationship to the market; its place in the socio-economic relations of production, is different from that of 'non-popular' fiction" (8).

4. Defining "popular" in *Keywords*, Raymond Williams notes that while the term referred to a "system constituted by the whole people," it simultaneously contained a "strong element of setting out to gain favour with a sense of calculation," an element evident in the phrase "deliberately popular" (235).

5. While literary critics insist that the popularity of the series is the result of aggressive promotion, analysts looking at market trends in book publishing assert that "it is impossible to sell books by advertising" (Berreman 235). Advertising in book publishing serves to "boost the sales of a book that is already selling, serving rather to reinforce than to create or initiate sales popularity" (Berreman 234–235). The marketing blitzkrieg of ten years can hardly disguise the fact that the *Potter* series has sustained this phenomenal interest and sold for over a decade and beyond.

6. With growing numbers, greater amount of pocket money and more choices of entertainment, the books for adolescents, like most other commodities of youth culture are inescapably linked to the market forces (Maugham). Perry Bacon Jr., pointing

out the close association between YA fiction and market, insists, "Teenagers are the demographic that almost everyone in the book industry — librarians, publishers, booksellers — wants. As the number of teenagers in the population has risen, so has teen buying power for all kinds of items, including books." Tapping the teen market, publishers have instituted separate imprints for children's and YA fiction — for instance, PUSH by Scholastic and Pulse by Simon and Schuster.

7. The seven books of the *Potter* series were published over a span of ten years with the first book appearing in 1997 and the last, *Harry Potter and the Deathly Hallows*, in 2007.

8. Critics like Toni Bennett have argued that social relations that constitute a particular society invariably support its generic dominants. As we shall see, the moments of rise, ruptures and changes in the popular fantasy, its anxieties and nodes of tension as well as its interaction with other generic conventions can be traced along with the changing socio-historical dominants. The present study is concerned with locating generic dominants of fantasy in the context of the Western, specifically British history. It would also trace the changes in fantasy diachronically and locate it in context of the twentieth century.

9. Zipes (*Fairy Tales* 174–175) and Jackson point out the complexities that accrue to Freud's *das unheimlich*, the term he uses for the Uncanny. The term can be read at two semantic levels. *Das unheimlich* is that which is in the condition of estrangement and alienation. It is also the discovery or the revelation of that which had been hidden. Uncanny, therefore, could be the strain of magic that is hated and suppressed and yet it makes an appearance in the bloodline of Petunia Dursley's family. It could be the estranged and alienated part of the self that returns with the Uncanny through the projections of the unconscious desires on the environment.

The element of desire underlying fantasy already hints at an absence, a lack. Lack and fantasy produce each other. Everything present in a fantastic scenario incites desire that it is supposed to satisfy. Lacan, therefore, takes on Freud's concept, further pointing out that the narrative of fantasy itself stages desire; it brings about the lack that makes fantasy desirable. Jackson claims that the "fantastic, then, pushes towards an area of non-signification. It does this either by attempting to articulate 'the unnameable,' 'the nameless things' of horror fiction, attempting to visualize the unseen, or by establishing a disjunction of word and meaning through the play upon 'thing-less names'" (Jackson, 41).

10. Though later scholars like Linda Pollock (*Forgotten Children: Parent-Child Relations from 1500–1900*), Hugh Cunningham (*Children and Childhood in Western Society since 1500*), Colin Heywood (*A History of Childhood*), and many others find the arguments of Philippe Aries's *Centuries of Childhood* untenable, the overall work remains an important starting point for the study of childhood and its cultural constructions. Aries's study offers constructivist arguments linking cultural and institutional changes and its effects on the "idea" of childhood. Hence, he places childhood amid the socio-cultural shifts in Europe from the medieval times onwards.

11. A puzzling text like *The Curious Case of Benjamin Button* works by overturning this conception of the order of growth and development through the means of literary fantastic. Fitzgerald's text leaves the reader without explanation and hence in the fantastic zone of hesitation with no movement outside the fantastic.

12. Allison James and Alan Prout in *Construction and Reconstruction of Childhood* explain the scientific concerns behind the construction of childhood: "The scientific

construction of the 'irrationality,' 'naturalness,' and 'universality' of childhood through psychological discourses was translated directly into sociological accounts of childhood in the form of theories of socialization during the 1950s" (12). They also point out the link between childhood and Western philosophical tradition: "As heirs to a Western intellectual tradition centered on scientific rationality, 'the child' represented a laboratory specimen for the study of primitive forms of cognition and indeed children were brought into the laboratory to be studied" (12).

James Hersey's novel *The Child Buyer* indicts such conceptualization of child and childhood. The novel takes the form of a court hearing against a company attempting to buy exceptionally gifted children and upgrade their brains at the cost of bodily normality to serve as ultimate resources for mankind. The testimony, comprised of teachers, social workers, company officials, scientists, psychologists, parents, and the potential brain slave, ten-year-old Barry, critiques various discourses that surround and construct the figure of a child.

13. Kenneth Kidd borrows the term "boyology" from Henry William Gibson's *Boyology or Boy Analysis*, published in 1916. *Boyology*, according to Kidd, is a "practical handbook for parents, teachers, and character builders, devoid of 'technical or scientific terms,' written for lay readers 'short in psychology, physiology, pedagogy, and sociology, but who are long in common sense and "heartology"'" (48). Though Kidd's concern is American boyhood, preoccupation with boyhood can be traced in other cultures. English literary enterprises like the school stories or the adventure fictions reflect the discourses of boyology.

14. YWCA came into being in 1855, eleven years after YMCA. The central aim of both the organizations has been to put Christian principles and faith into practice. In case of YMCA, the thrust has been on the spiritual development of an individual through a healthy body (hence the focus of athleticism and physical exercise) and a healthy mind (leading to the integration of the movement with educational institutions) and a healthy spirit (through the cultivation of body and mind and integrating them with Christian principles). The focus of YWCA, on the other hand, has been on issues like peace, justice, human rights, and social change.

Subtle disparity dictates the distinction between Boy Scouts and Girl Guides that came into being in 1910. The Boy Scouts, founded by Robert Baden Powell, a lieutenant general in the British Army, focused on outdoor activities that Baden Powell found indispensable during his stint in the army in South Africa during the Boer War. The organization drew its principles from his books on military scouting, training boys for a future in the army.

15. For anthropologists like Margaret Mead, culture holds the key to the so called "storm-and-stress" of adolescence. In *Coming of Age in Samoa*, Mead studied the process of adolescence in tribal communities of Samoa, coming to the conclusion that the "problems" that trouble contemporary adolescents are intricately linked with their milieu, in this case the Christian, patriarchal, late-capitalist Western world.

16. Hutcheon cites Roland Barthes's usage of the term "doxa" to signify the public opinion, "the voice of nature" and consensus, insisting that postmodernism works to "'de-doxify' our cultural representations and their undeniable political import" (*The Politics* 3). To de-doxify this representation is to denaturalize the contrived reality that is assumed to be the truth. Fantasy in a Bildungsroman works towards a deconstruction of the "naturalized" pattern of growth.

17. Heroic fantasy has traditionally been a male-dominated genre. In *Watership*

Down, though Richard Adams's protagonists are rabbits, they are still male rabbits and the goal of the search is first a safe rabbit warren and then does to populate the warren.

18. Harry's preoccupation with the father figures and their gradual distancing, as a detailed discussion chapter 1 insists, is crucial to the culmination of his growth into a heteronormative adult.

19. The word is used 62 times in Frances Hodgson Burnett's *The Secret Garden*.

20. The Stonewall riots were a series of spontaneous, violent protests retaliating against police raids in June 1969, at Stonewall Inn near New York City. It was the first instance in America when gays and lesbians acted against the state system that persecuted homosexuals. The riots became the defining event in gay rights movement in the US.

21. Rather than fall into the binary distinction between good and evil, magic emerges as an amoral concept (much like adolescence and fantasy) which is appropriated by different narratives for a variety of ideological purposes, hence good magic and dark magic. Rowling also points out this neutrality of magic and the politics of appropriation. In the introduction to the *The Tales of Beedle the Bard*, a collection of fairy tales from the magical world, Rowling points out that in Muggle fairy tales, magic tends to lie at the root of the hero or heroine's troubles — the wicked witch has poisoned the apple, or put the princess into a hundred years' sleep, or turned the prince into a hideous beast. In *The Tales of Beedle the Bard*, on the other hand, we meet heroes and heroines who can perform magic themselves, and yet find it just as hard to solve their problems as we do. Beedle's stories have helped generations of wizarding parents to explain this painful fact of life to their young children: that magic causes as much trouble as it cures [xi-xii].

22. Spacks points out this as a common and "successful" course of adolescent growth: "Like women, adolescents constitute, in their own perception, an oppressed class; like women, they possess hidden weapons. Unlike women, they inevitably win in the long run, if only by growing up and succeeding their parents" (5).

Chapter 1

1. For Eliot, the term "tradition" represents a "simultaneous order," by which he means a kind of historical timelessness, a sense of present temporality. A poet embodies "the whole literature of Europe from Homer" at the same time expressing his contemporary environment. This "historical sense" is not only a resemblance but also an awareness and understanding of the historical tradition to a work.

2. In Rick Riordian's *Percy Jackson* series, half-blood offspring of the Olympian gods like Percy, the son of Poseidon the sea god, are marked out by features like dyslexia and myopia. Therefore, what are seen as disorders in the normal human world become distinguishing features of the demi-gods.

3. Hagrid can also be seen as a literary descendent of Charon, a Greco-Roman mythological figure who appears in Dante's *Inferno*, ferrying dead spirits to Hades. The analogy is especially relevant since, as we shall see, Hogwarts emerges as a place of danger and strife instead of a safe and secure educational institution. Death is a constant presence at Hogwarts, which is full of ghosts, photographs of dead teachers watching over the school, and ghostly professors like Mr. Binn, who teaches History of Magic. Hagrid himself repeatedly visits or is made to visit the places of the dead

like the Forbidden Forest, which is full of dangerous beasts and spirits, or Azkaban, guarded by the Dementors.

4. Since the hero monomyth as well as the Oedipal drama are predominantly male narratives, the protagonist has been referred to as the male subject. The *Potter* series as well as the most of the other heroic fantasy that the study refers to are masculine coming-of-age narratives.

5. The element of choice is central to fantasy since it manifests the power to act and choose and therefore manifests a sense of control over oneself and one's life. The power differential that choice sets up, especially in adolescent fiction, is explored in the next chapter, against the background of the social, cultural, and ideological institution of a school.

6. Since fairy tales, quest romance, and myths are the prime genres from which heroic fantasy emerges, I find the critical readings analyzing of these genres suitable in approaching coming-of-age fantasy.

7. Despite these words of wisdom, Dumbledore too is caught in the web of desire and wish fulfillment. He also seeks unification with his long-dead family — a latent desire that he does not confess till the end. He also finds a stone to bring them back. In terms of stages of mourning and melancholia in growth, unlike Harry, who has mourned, grieved, and reconciled, Dumbledore continues to feel a sense of failure and guilt, which he admits to Harry at the end at King's Cross Station, thus "developing a melancholic stance of trying to sustain a connection with that which is always already lost" (Coats, *Looking Glass* 37).

8. Freud, in "Family Romances," expresses the wider context that frames a child's narrative. In the essay, Freud argues that one of the greatest fantasies of a child is that of royal parentage; a child imagines that he is not really the child of his own father but comes from a couple of much higher status. This double identity, Anthony Easthope points out, in fiction bears further meanings: it stands for the split between the sense of a "better" self and an ordinary, everyday self (*What a Man's* 28). It points out not only the dissatisfaction with the parents but also the desire for the "better" (signified by the royal parentage of the princes and princesses in the fairy tales), which can be defined only in social, economic, or cultural terms. Thus, the individual relations of the protagonist, especially those with the parents, can be located in the broader framework of constantly changing relations between the self and the other. These negotiations between the self and the other are basic to the fantastic mode of narrative as well as adolescent fiction.

9. Apart from the rivalry between the self and other, the founder's myth and the Gryffindor and Slytherin can also be explored (as it has been done in the following chapters) as an aspect of the house system central to boarding-school fiction and also in terms of Christian metanarrative. The good/evil axis of the Rowling's narrative therefore seems to be constructed at multiple intertextual levels.

10. Anthony Burgess, in his preface to *Clockwork Orange*, another young adult novel, though diametrically different from Rowling's, underscores similar conception of choice and destiny: "by definition, a human being is endowed with free will. He can use this to choose between good and evil.... It is as inhuman to be totally good as it is to be totally evil. The important thing is moral choice. Evil has to exist along with good, in order that moral choice may operate" (IX).

11. Prophecies and omens, according to Frye, suggest "an existential projection, a conception of ineluctable fate or hidden omnipotent will. Actually it is a piece of

pure literary design, giving the beginning some symmetrical relationship with the end, and the only ineluctable will involved is that of the author" (*Anatomy* 139). However, as we shall see in the later chapter, in the Potter series, the prophecy itself becomes a point of classically Miltonic debate over theology, which involves operations of free will.

12. In the third book, he needs Sirius to sign the form to visit Hogsmeade and Lupin to learn the defensive magic. Therefore, in the early books, he is clearly subject to the limited authority Lupin and Sirius have by the virtue of being adults. Later in the book, when he rescues himself and Sirius from the Dementors, he initially believes that James saved them. However, it turns out that in going back through time, Harry "becomes" James and assumes his father's role.

13. Alice Mills, in analysis of the Jungian archetypes of the series, identifies the polarized *puer/senex* distinction in the single child archetype. *Puer* is the force of beginning while *senex* is the maintainer of the order. Mills maintains that "Rowling's novels are unusual among quest fantasies in their frequent and explicit shifts of archetypal imagery between characters: the *puer* between the weakened Voldemort and the innocent Harry; the *senex* between Voldemort as Dark Lord and Harry as hero; the trickster between the Weasley twins and the plotting Dark Lord and his followers; the scapegoat between Harry and the scapepig Dudley" ("Archetype" 8).

14. Hagrid is repeatedly identified as a mother figure. He often takes on the role willingly and with great pleasure; for instance, when he shows the baby dragon Norbert to Harry, Ron, and Hermione, he says, "I've decided to call him Norbert," said Hagrid, looking at the dragon with misty eyes. "He really knows me now, watch. Norbert! Norbert! Where's *Mummy?*" (*PS* 172). On parting, he promises, "Mummy will never forget you!" (*PS* 175). Later, he takes on the task of nurturing and "civilizing" his half brother Grawp, who had been abandoned by their mother and is too small for a giant.

15. A sword features frequently in fantasy literature. Its greatest significance can be understood from its importance as a phallic symbol and its links to the cultural traits of masculinity. The sword, usually wielded by the hero, is powerful and unique; some, like the Excalibur, become metaphors for a particular type of heroism. Swords therefore are persistent symbols in heroic fantasy. In Terry Goodkind's *Sword of Truth*, the sword functions almost like a wand of a wizard sharing his magic, thereby integrating magic and martial prowess of the male hero. Similarly, the subtle knife of Will Parry (Pullman, *Subtle Knife*) has to be wrested from its previous owner. Gryffindor's sword passes through various hands. It is bequeathed by Dumbledore to Harry. Later, Neville uses it to kill Nagini, Voldemort's pet snake. Therefore, masculinity, power, and heroism become conflated in the symbol of the sword of a hero.

16. Roger Caillois in *Man, Play and Games* suggests the two opposite poles between which the activity of play is placed: "uncontrolled fantasy" or *paidia*, where "an indivisible principle, common to diversion, turbulence, free improvisation ad carefree gaiety is dominant. At the opposite extreme, this frolicsome and impulsive exuberance is almost entirely absorbed or disciplined by a complementary, and in some respects inverse, tendency to its anarchic and capricious nature: there is a growing tendency to bind it with arbitrary, imperative and purposely tedious conventions" (13). This he calls *ludus*. *Ludus* and *paidia* co-exist in the play of fantasy.

17. Kreacher, the house-elf at Grimauld Place, keeps calling the twins "unnatural little beasts" (*OotP* 101).

18. Neville Longbottom, until the final battle, remains what Judy Norton calls a kind of a "transchild." Not only is he timid, but he is the only one from Harry's year in Gryffindor who has no close male friends. Most of his close friendships are with girls — Hermione, Luna, and Ginny. However, at the end, when he takes on the leadership of the Dumbledore's Army, Luna and Ginny are removed from the immediate plot. The stories he tells about the students' resistance to Harry, Ron, and Hermione are about mostly about boys — for instance, about Seamus Finnegan and Michael Corner. The narrative therefore places him at the center of a male peer group, but there is little given by way of explanation for this sudden transformation.

19. The quest and the battle are quintessentially male arenas where the presence of women, however competent, can be problematic and distracting. Hence, the girls serve the role of "princesses-in-waiting," a kind of reward that comes after fulfilling the quest, or they are de-sexualized until the end like Hermione.

20. Death, however, also provides a thematic link with the essential theological core in adolescent fantasy. The theme of death and sacrifice in the religious context is explored in the third chapter.

21. According to Catherine Belsey, "death is alien to the subject of Western culture, constituted as it is in the symbolic and divided in the process from the organism that we also are. Our languages, with their continuous present and future tenses, enable us to imagine eternal life but, while culture survives (always subject, of course, to the effective control of weapons of mass destruction), the real withholds the possibility of immortality in this world for the individual human being" (*Culture* 79).

Chapter 2

1. The year of publication itself hints a strong association between genres of children's fiction and British colonial venture. The publication of the *Tom Brown's Schooldays* in 1857 coincides with the establishment of first modern university in India and also the year of mutiny.

2. Sherry Truffin, therefore, studies the school fiction under the rubric of "Schoolhouse Gothic," where tradition manifests itself as the self-replicating hierarchies and power inequalities resulting in disintegration of an individual in terms of loss of sanity, loss of control or life, and, finally, loss of humanity or monstrosity. This is the price of deviance that a schoolboy who refuses to conform has to pay.

3. Roderick McGillis points out the link between the queer connotations of the word "fairy" and the fairy tale itself, which sets out to vex the conventions of gender and sexuality ("Is Fairytale" 87). Hence, the presence of the aspects of a fairy tale or fantasy in Harry's school story itself problematizes the norms favored and upheld by the school story.

4. George M. O'Har, in "Magic in Machine Age," points out that the conflict between magic and technology is evolutionary in nature in which magic always loses. In terms of teleology of growth, this "marginalized" or "lower" knowledge of magic becomes the power of the adolescent, which "loses," since an adolescent inevitably grows up.

5. As an impregnable castle, Hogwarts literally embodies, in its architectural layout, the hegemonic position that a school occupies in a society. Easthope, in his study of representations of masculinity in popular culture, draws parallels between

the male ego and the architectural plan of a castle. The power that it stands for, the impregnable defenses, and the rigid lines that define its boundaries — all make a castle an apt metaphor for masculinity; the chief function of the castle, says Easthope, is to "*master* every threat, and here the male term is particularly appropriate. The castle of the ego is defined by its perimeter and the line drawn between what is inside and what outside. To maintain its identity it must not only repel external attack but also suppress treason within" (*What a Man's* 40). Therefore, Hogwarts Castle as a school stands for the authority of adulthood, of patriarchy, and of the official establishment of the magical community.

6. Another alchemist mentioned briefly is Agrippa. According to the Chocolate Frog card featuring Agrippa, he was imprisoned for his writings because Muggles thought they were evil. Agrippa, a German alchemist, belongs to a time when science, magic, and philosophy were not mutually exclusive disciplines, the time before James Frazer segregated them permanently and imposed a hierarchy by calling magic pseudo-science. In *Frankenstein*, Mary Shelley mentions Agrippa as a scholar whose works were read and admired by Victor Frankenstein. In the series, Flamel and Agrippa find a place of honor in the magical world. Their achievements are the points where Harry's world overlaps ours.

7. McGonagall resembles the severe, authoritative, but kind English mistresses who appeared regularly in Blyton's school stories. Similarly Snape, as a bullying teacher who is repeatedly confounded by Harry and his friends, takes after schoolmasters like Mr. King, the antagonistic bullying master in Kipling's *Stalky and Co.* Apart from Dumbledore, the eccentric headmaster, Harry's main allies in the school are teachers like Lupin and Hagrid, the misfits in the official establishments of the magical world.

8. Though girls also play Quidditch, in the narrative, as we shall see in the later discussion, the game of Quidditch seems to remain a male arena — a place where male rivalries ad solidarity hold sway.

9. Gender in the theatre of a sports field is repeatedly revealed to be a performance. In the World Cup final, the two male seekers — Lynch and Krum — perform acts of heroism, playing despite injuries. The spectacle they present upstages the match-winning performance by the Irish Chasers, who are all witches. Thus, the gender roles in the sports arena are often presupposed. Cho Chang also plays as the Seeker for the Ravenclaw team, but she is never able to beat Harry. She often ends up crying and sulking after a game. Ginny, on the other hand, can fill in for Harry as a Seeker when he is not playing, but she is never as good as Harry.

10. In Hughes' *Tom Brown's Schooldays*, when Tom Brown and Harry East get badly hurt while playing football, the narrator tells about the satisfaction and adulation waiting for them.

> Meet them like Englishmen, you School-house boys, and charge them now. Now is the time to show what mettle is in you — and there shall be a warm seat by the hall fire, and honor and lots of bottled beer to-night, for him who does his duty in the next half-hour.... This is worth living for; the whole sum of school-boy existence gathered up into one straining, struggling half-hour, a half-hour worth a year of common life [100–101].

11. There are teams in the Quidditch league with names like the Stonewall Stormers and Holyhead Harpies.

12. The Harry Potter movies portray him as a black boy.

13. In a supplementary book to the series, *Fantastic Beasts and Where to Find*

Them, Rowling describes the way the wizard community established the distinction between the "beings" and the "beasts" describing a "being" as "any creature that has sufficient intelligence to understand the laws of the magical community and to bear part of the responsibility in shaping those laws." Thus the magical community itself becomes the parameter of defining a "being" and a "beast." And even then, though centaurs, goblins, and even the house-elves display "sufficient" intelligence, they are subservient to the wizards. The description inevitably reminds one of the modern-day dialectics of racial politics in Robert Young's hypothesis in *Colonial Desire* that "modern racism is an academic creation."

14. Northrope Frye points out the presence of characters that embody the "spirits of nature" in fantasy and romance. He cites figures like Ariel in *The Tempest* and Gollux in *The Thirteen Clocks*, defining them in terms of their amorality and inscrutability of origin and intention. "The paradox that many of these children of nature are 'supernatural' beings is not distressing in romance as in logic. The helpful fairy, the grateful dead man, the wonderful servant who has just the abilities the hero needs in a crisis, are all folktale commonplaces. They are romantic intensifications of the comic tricky slave, the author's *architectus*" (*Anatomy* 197). However, Rowling's Dobby and Kreacher are not like Gollux. The house-elves, the giants, the goblins, and the centaurs all have a socio-cultural history in the magical world that is linked to the wizard history in complicated ways. The fantastic creatures and the aid they provide is highly politicized.

Chapter 3

1. Writers like Tolkien and MacDonald have argued against the common association between fairy stories and children. Tolkien notes that "children as a class — except in common lack of experience — they are not one — neither like fairie stories more, or understand them better than adults do; and no more than they like many other things" (*Tree and Leaf* 34).

2. St. Augustine describes adolescence not in terms of rebellion, angst, or sexual puberty, but in terms of lawlessness and indiscipline (Stortz). Inbuilt in the description is incontinence, recklessness, and the savagery of adolescent boys, which have been explored in books like *Lord of the Flies*.

3. Jean-Luc Nancy, in *The Inoperative Community*, cites the idea of community that comes from Christian communion, a connection that was to be organic, life-giving which is lost. The quests for community are always nostalgic attempts to return to some fantasized moment of union and purity.

4. At the same time, it is worth mentioning that language plays a more complex role in magic than just reflecting the logocentric act of creation. Books by Diana Duane, LeGuin's Earthsea series, Funke's Inkheart series, and many others deal with the complex association between language and magic. In the Potter series, language of magic, or spell casting itself is a performative activity — performed in a specific way and in a specific setting. Most importantly, it is an act that brings about what it describes. For instance, *Locomotor* literally makes the inanimate object start moving. Therefore, the magic of a wizard lies in this power to use language in a performative way. And this use of language makes a wizard. Hence, there is an elliptical relationship between language and magic. Language (as spell casting) constitutes magic and magic gives language its performative power.

It also opens the possibility of wizard's magical word failing or rebounding on him (unlike God's creative word). The series is full of instances of failed magical words. In fact, as the last spells of Harry and Voldemort show, the failure or success of a spell lies beyond the words of a spell — magic, in fact, lies in the things beyond language. A spell always carries in it the trace of the other spells and other moments of magic. This complex association of magic and language that deconstructs logocentrism has been the concern of the present study.

5. The emphasis on love as a secular intersubjective relationship rests on the theme of otherness. McCallum notes that "since we can never see ourselves directly, we construct a sense of ourselves by appropriating the position of the other, outside of the self" (72). Therefore, a hero can be seen as a narcissistic reflection of self. Yet, as the hero grows, the intersubjective relations move beyond the mirror image paradigms. But the other does not passively reflect our self-love but is an active participant in the relationship. Lily chooses to die for her son. Similarly, Hermione, Lupin, Dobby, and Hagrid choose to stand by Harry.

6. Some recent thinkers have pointed out the ambiguities that characterize Christian *agape* and also an integral element of sexuality in Christian love (Elizabeth Stuart, "Christianity Is a Queer Thing"). Traditionally, sex in Christianity is unitive — one embraces the other by surrendering the boundaries of body in the body of Christ. One can glimpse the queer subtext in the conception of Christian sexuality in the surrender that is a part of discipleship. It is evident in the *Song of Solomon*. On the one hand, it gives way to marriage and monasticism regardless of sexual orientation, modeled on the relationship of Christ and Church, since the body of Jesus from the moment of its incarnation is gendered male, while the church itself is conceived of as female. Yet Christ is a male body coming from purely female matter. It is unstable, transfigureable through the rituals like Eucharist, through resurrection and ascension. Therefore, Stuart argues that there is queerness inherent in the Christian model that deconstructs complicates the notions of love, gender, and power.

7. Thacker and Webb point out the tradition of dominance of feminine in the imaginative realms, which provided the challenge to the growing masculine world of nineteenth-century England and America. Writers like MacDonald emphasized the spiritual powers of his female characters. Similarly in Kingsley's *The Water Babies*, Tom is redeemed by female guides — Mrs.Doasyouwouldbedoneby and Mrs. Bedonebyasyoudid. Therefore, the texts propose that the female characters "allow the male children they encounter to find redemption. At times, it is as though attaining a feminised sensibility is a return to a prior and superior state of being" (46). In the case of Harry, Lily Potter and her sacrifice, rather than being a return to a pre-symbolic past, present an alternative and a more sensitive state of being.

8. The idea echoes Pullman's conception of the "Republic of Heaven" in his series *His Dark Materials*.

9. Sports, as discussed in the last chapter, have been central to the stories of boyhood, especially when placed in a school. However, in these crucial moments, especially towards the end of the series, Quidditch loses importance as Harry and his friends become involved in issues that go beyond on-field rivalries.

10. Irving Singer traces the roots of the concept of *eros* and *philia* to Plato and Aristotle's conception of the godhead respectively. According to Singer, of the four forms of Christian love, while *eros* and *philia* can be traced to Greek thought, the other two — *nomos* and *agape* — can be linked to the Judeo Christian origins.

11. Stag, as a symbol for Christ, worked itself into Christian mythology through its Celtic roots noted in the earlier chapter.

12. The following chapter explores the affinity between the category of monsters and adolescents not only in their deviance and pathology but also in the politics of utopic possibilities and future they engage in.

13. In *Fantastic Beasts and Where to Find Them*, Rowling tells that the song of the phoenix is "reputed to increase the courage of the pure in heart and to strike fear into the hearts of the impure" (32).

14. Granger points out the Christian symbolism of the act. With the *twelve* cups of the poisonous potion, Dumbledore takes on himself the totality of sins and evil. Like Christ in the Garden of Gethsemane, he suffers horribly and dies in his voluntary acceptance of the bitter cup. He rises with warmth and light to save Harry from the Inferi, the dead bodies animated by dark magic.

15. The pagan myths refer to the unicorn or the beast with one horn that can be tamed only by a virgin. In Catholic writings, the myths became an allegory of the relationship between Virgin Mary and Christ. In Catholic tradition, therefore, the unicorn and its death came to be identified with the Passion of Christ. Hence, the pagan symbolism finds its way into the Christian symbolization of a unicorn.

Chapter 4

1. Jack Zipes, in the introduction to *The Trials and Tribulations of Little Red Riding Hood*, traces the origin of the story in the social and historical context of the European witch-hunts in the sixteenth century. Zipes claims that the story's villain was originally a werewolf who later changed into a natural wolf when werewolves lost their significance after the decline of the witch-hunts.

Conclusion

1. Despite its efforts at distancing itself from its generic predecessors, the return of the series to its generic predecessors is frequent. The next generation of Potters and Weasleys leaving for Hogwarts reminds one of the traditional British boarding school and boarding-school fiction, where respectable and worthy schools like the Malory Towers or St. Clare's or even rugby are patronized by a family generation after generation. However, in the magical world, Hogwarts is the only school of magic in England and therefore admits all the witches and wizards of England.

2. According to Franco Morreti, the most daemonic aspect of the figure of the monster is the fear it arouses by its demand of citizenship, of equal consideration is the real source of anxiety that a monster figure arouses.

3. The roles that Rowling assigns to her major women characters, though strong, remain subordinate and continue to embody the classic binary of good and evil. Therefore, in terms of gender, the story seems to be reverting back to the patriarchal status quo. However, some minor characters seem to go beyond the stereotypes. Narcissa Malfoy, for instance, is characterized as much as a caring mother as a Death-Eater, ready to defy the Dark Lord to save her son. In the forest, she even goes to the extent of helping Harry. Fleur Delacour too is as much a snob as a dedicated and loyal friend and wife.

In *Harry Potter and the Chamber of Secrets*, Ginny Weasley too seems to be an ambiguous character. In fact, Ginny and Moaning Myrtle seem to mirror each other in their aggressive pursuit of Harry (Cummins). By writing in Tom Riddle's diary, she also "opens her heart" to the Dark Lord: "No one's ever understood me like you, Tom.... I'm so glad I've got this diary to confide in.... It's like a friend I can carry around in my pocket" (*CoS* 228). Ginny not only vandalizes the school corridors by painting threats on the walls, but also releases the deadly Basilisk in the Chamber of Secrets. Though she is excused as an innocent dupe, she seems to be aware of the evil in the diary and yet is unable to resist it. After throwing the diary away, she steals it back from Harry, and again follows its dictum to write about her own capture and death in the Chamber of Secrets, helping the Dark Lord to lure Harry to the Chamber.

Bibliography

Primary Sources

Harry Potter Novels

Rowling, J. K. *Harry Potter and the Chamber of Secrets*. London: Bloomsbury, 1998.
_____. *Harry Potter and the Deathly Hallows*. London: Bloomsbury, 2007.
_____. *Harry Potter and the Goblet of Fire*. London: Bloomsbury, 2000.
_____. *Harry Potter and the Half Blood Prince*. London: Bloomsbury, 2005.
_____. *Harry Potter and the Order of Phoenix*. London: Bloomsbury, 2003.
_____. *Harry Potter and the Philosopher's Stone*. London: Bloomsbury, 1997.
_____. *Harry Potter and the Prisoner of Azkaban*. London: Bloomsbury, 1999.

Other Works

Adams, Richard. *Watership Down*. New York: Avon, 1972.
Alcott, Louisa May. *Little Men: Life at Plumfield with Jo's Boys*. Toronto: Dover Juvenile Classics, 2001 [1871].
_____. *Little Women*. London: Scholastic, 1868.
Anderson, Douglas A., ed. *Tales Before Tolkien: The Roots of Modern Fantasy*. New York: Ballantine Books, 2005.
Barrie, J. M. *Peter Pan*. Delhi: Rupa, 2003 [1911].
Blyton, Enid. *Malory Towers—Terms 1 and 2 and 3*. London: Egmont, 2006 [1946].
_____. *St. Clare's Again: Final Three Years of Boarding School*. London: Egmont, 2006 [1941].
_____. *St. Clare's: First Three Years of Boarding School*. London: Egmont, 2006 [1942].
Blume, Judy. *Forever*. London: Picador, 2005 [1975].
Burgess, Anthony. *A Clockwork Orange*. New York: Courier, 1986 [1962].
Burnett, Frances Hodgson. *A Little Princess*. London: Penguin, 1996 [1903].
Canavan, Trudi. *Magician's Guild*. London: Atom, 2001.
Carroll, Lewis. *Alice in Wonderland and Through the Looking Glass*. London: Wordsworth, 1993 [1865].
Colfer, Eoin. *Artemis Fowl*. London: Puffin, 2002.
Cooper, Susan. *The Dark Is Rising Sequence*. New York: Aladdin Paperbacks, 1999 [1965].
Cormier, Robert. *The Chocolate War*. New York: Knopf, 1974.
Dahl, Roald. *Charlie and the Chocolate Factory*. London: Puffin, 2005 [1964].

_____. *James and the Giant Peach*. London: Puffin, 1996 [1961].

Dickens, Charles. *Hard Times*. Harmondsworth: Penguin, 1994 [1854].

_____. *Oliver Twist*. Harmondsworth: Penguin, 1982 [1837–1839].

Duane, Diane. *So You Want to Be a Wizard?* New York: Delacorte Press, 1983.

Farrar, Fredrick W. *Eric, or Little by Little: A Tale of Roslyn School*. London: Adam and Charles Black, 1858. Project Gutenberg (accessed October 2007, 8 January 2009).

Fielding, Sarah. *The Governess or, The Little Female Academy*. London, 1749. Project Gutenberg. (Accessed 26 March 2006).

Garner, Alan. *The Weirdstone of Birsingamen*. London: William Collins, 1960.

Golding, William. *Lord of the Flies*. London: Faber and Faber, 1999 [1954].

Goodkind, Terry. *Stone of Tears*. The Sword of Truth Series. New York: Tor Fantasy, 1995.

_____. *Wizard's First Rule*. The Sword of Truth Series. New York: Tor Fantasy, 1994.

Hersey, James. *Child Buyer*. Middlesex: Penguin, 1964 [1960].

Hinton, S. E. *The Outsiders*. New York: Puffin, 1995 [1967].

Hoban, Russell. *Turtle Diary*. London: Avon, 1978.

Horowitz, Anthony. *Groosham Grange*. London: Walker, 2003.

Hughes, Thomas. *Tom Brown's Schooldays*. London: Penguin, 1997 [1857].

Jones, Diana Wynne. *The Charmed Life*. Chrestomanci Series. London: Harper-Collins, 1977.

_____. *Howl's Moving Castle*. New York: Greenwillow, 1986.

_____. *The Lives of Christopher Chant*. Chrestomanci Series. London: HarperCollins, 1988.

Jordan, Robert. *The Eye of the World*. New York: Tor Fantasy, 1990.

Kingsley, Charles. *The Water Babies*. Bridlington: Priory Classics, 1980 [1863].

Kipling, Rudyard. *Stalky and Co*. London: Wordsworth, 1994 [1899].

Le Guin, Ursula. *The Earthsea Quartet*. London: Penguin, 1992 [1968].

L'Engle, Madeleine. *A Wrinkle in Time*. New York: Farrar, Strauss & Giroux, 1962.

Lewis, C. S. *The Chronicles of Narnia*. London: HarperCollins, 2004 [1949–1954].

Lowry, Lois. *The Giver*. New York: Laurel-leaf, 1993.

_____. *The Messenger*. New York: Laurel-leaf, 2004.

MacDonald, George. *The Princess and the Goblin*. Mahwah, NJ: Watermill Press, 1985 [1872].

Maupassant, Guy de. "Horla." *The Horla and the Other Stories*. Whitefish, MT: Kessinger, 2005 [1911].

Nesbit, Edith. *The Story of the Amulet*. London: T. Fisher Unwin, 1906. Classic Reader. www.classicreader.combook/409 (accessed May 2007).

Nix, Garth. *Lirael*. London: HarperCollins, 2001.

_____. *Sabriel*. London: HarperCollins, 1995.

Paolini, Christopher. *Eragon*. New York: Alfred A. Knopf, 2003.

Paterson, Katherine. *Bridge to Terabithia*. New York: Crowell, 1977.

Pierce, Tamora. *Alana: The First Adventure*. The Song of the Lioness Series. New York: Atheneum, 1983.

_____. *In the Hand of the Goddess*. The Song of the Lioness Series. New York: Atheneum, 1984.

_____. *Lioness Rampant*. The Song of the Lioness Series. New York: Atheneum, 1988.

_____. *The Woman Who Rides Like a Man*. The Song of the Lioness Series. New York: Atheneum, 1986.

Pullman, Phillip. *The Amber Spyglass*. Dark Materials Series. New York: Scholastic Point, 2000.
_____. *The Golden Compass*. Dark Materials Series. New York: Scholastic Point, 1995.
_____. *The Subtle Knife*. Dark Materials Series. New York: Scholastic Point, 1997.
Riordan, Rick. *Percy Jackson and the Last Olympian*. London: Puffin, 2009.
Rousseau, Jean Jacques. *Emile: or, On Education*. 1762. Institute of Learning Technologies. (Accessed 12 December 2006).
Rowling, J. K. "The Harry Potter Prequel." Waterstonewys.com. June 2008.
_____. *The Tales of Beedle the Bard*. London: Bloomsbury, 2008.
Sachar, Louis. *Holes*. New York: Laurel-leaf, 1998.
_____. *There's a Boy in the Girls' Bathroom*. New York: Random House, 1987.
Salinger, J D. *Catcher in the Rye*. Boston: Little, Brown, 1951.
Scamander, Newt [J. K. Rowling]. *Fantastic Beasts and Where to Find Them*. London: Turtleback, 2001.
Sendak, Maurice. *Where the Wild Things Are*. Harmondsworth: Penguin, 1970 [1963].
Shelley, Mary. *Frankenstein*. Delhi: Rohan, 2003 [1818].
Snicket, Lemony. *The Austere Academy: Book the Fifth*. A Series of Unfortunate Events. New York: HarperCollins, 2000.
Tales of Grimms and Anderson. New York: Modern Library, 1952.
Thurber, James. *The Thirteen Clocks*. New York: Simon & Schuster, 1950.
Tolkien, J.R.R. *The Hobbit*. London: HarperCollins, 1999 [1937].
_____. *The Lord of the Rings*. London: HarperCollins, 1995 [1968].
Townsend, Sue. *The Secret Diary of Adrian Mole, Age 13½*. New York: Avon, 1982.
White, T. H. *The Once and Future King: Camelot*. London: Collins, 1962 [1958].
Wisp, Kennilworth [J. K. Rowling]. *Quidditch Through the Ages*. London: Bloomsbury, 2001.
Yep, Laurence. *Dragon's Gate*. New York: HarperCollins, 1993.

Secondary Sources

Books

Aichele, George, and Tina Pippin, eds. *Violence, Utopia, and the Kingdom of God: Fantasy and Ideology in the Bible*. London: Routledge, 1998.
Anatol, Giselle Liza, ed. *Reading Harry Potter*. London: Praeger, 2003.
Anderson, Sheila B. *Serving Older Teens*. Westport, CT: Libraries Unlimited, 2004.
Aries, Phillipe. *Centuries of Childhood: A Social History of Family Life*. Trans. Robert Baldick. New York: Vintage, 1962.
Armitt, Lucie. *Fantasy Fiction: An Introduction*. New York: Continuum, 2005.
Arnold, Mathew. *Culture and Anarchy and Other Writings*. Cambridge: Cambridge University Press, 1993 [1882].
Ashcroft, Bill, Gareth Griffiths, and Helen Tiffin. *The Empire Writes Back: Theory and Practice in Post-Colonial Literature*. London: Routledge, 1989.
Balibar, Etienne, and Ian Wallerstein. *Race, Gender, Class: Ambiguous Identities*. London: Verso, 1991 [1988].
Barthes, Roland. *Mythologies*. Trans. Annette Levers. London: Vintage, 1993 [1972].
Battis, Jes. "Queer Spellings: Magic and Melancholy in Fantasy Fiction." Diss. Simon Fraser University, 2007.
Belsey, Catherine. *Critical Practice*. London: Routledge, 2001 [1980].

_____. *Culture and the Real: Theorizing Cultural Criticism*. London: Routledge, 2005.

Bennett, Toni. *Outside Literature*. London: Routledge, 1990.

Bettleheim, Bruno. *The Uses of Enchantment: The Meaning and Importance of Fairy Tales*. New York: Alfred A. Knopf, 1976.

Blake, Andrew. *The Irresistible Rise of Harry Potter*. London: Verso, 2002.

Bourdieu, Pierre, and Jean Claude Passerson. *Reproduction in Education, Society and Culture*. Trans. Richard Nice. London: Sage, 1977.

Bruhm, Steven, and Natasha Hurley, ed. *Curiouser: on the Queerness of Children*. Minneapolis: University of Minnesota Press, 2004.

Buckley, Jerome H. *Seasons of Youth: The Bildungsroman from Dickens to Golding*. Cambridge: Harvard University Press, 1974.

Bunge, Marcia JoAnne. *The Child in Christian Thought*. Grand Rapids, MI: Edermans, 2001.

Butler, Judith. *Bodies That Matter: On the Discursive Limits of "Sex."* New York: Routledge, 1993.

_____. *Gender Trouble: Feminism and Subversion*. New York: Routledge, 1999.

_____. *Psychic Life of Power*. New York: Stanford, 1997.

Caillois, Roger. *Man, Play, and Games*. Trans. Meyer Barash. Urbana: University of Illinois Press, 2001 [1958].

Campbell, Joseph. *The Hero with a Thousand Faces*. Princeton: Princeton University Press, 1949.

_____. *The Masks of God: Creative Mythology*. London: Secker and Warburg, 1968.

Clarke, Beverly Lyon, ed. *Regendering the School Story: Sassy Sissies and Tattling Tomboys*. New York: Garland, 1996.

Coats, Karen. *Looking Glasses and Neverlands: Lacan, Desire and Subjectivity in Children's Literature*. Iowa City: University of Iowa Press, 2004.

Cohen, Jeffrey Jerome. *Monster Theory: Reading Culture*. Minneapolis: University of Minnesota Press, 1996.

_____. *Of Giant: Sex, Monsters, and the Middle Ages*. Minneapolis: University of Minnesota Press, 1996.

Colbert, David. The *Magical Worlds of Harry Potter*. London: Puffin, 2003 [2001].

Douglas, Mary. *Purity and Danger: An Analysis of Concepts of Pollution and Taboo*. Hammondsworth: Penguin, 1966.

Du Coudray, Chantal Bourgault. *The Curse of the Werewolf: Fantasy, Horror and the Beast Within*. New York: I. B. Tauris, 2006.

Durkheim, Emile. *The Elementary Forms of Religious Life*. Trans. Joseph Ward Swain. London: George Allen and Unwin, 1915.

Easthope, Anthony. *The Unconscious*. London: Routledge, 1999.

_____. *What a Man's Gotta Do? The Masculine Myth in Popular Culture*. London: Routledge, 1992 [1986].

Eliade, Mircea. *Myth and Reality*. London: George Allen and Unwin, 1964 [1963].

_____. *The Sacred and the Profane: The Nature of Religion*. Trans. Willard Trask. New York: Mariner, 1987 [1957].

Erikson, Erik H. *Identity: Youth and Crisis*. London: Faber and Faber, 1971 [1968].

Filmer, Kath. *Skepticism and Hope in Twentieth Century Literature*. Bowling Green: BGSU Popular Press, 1992.

Fiske, John. *Understanding Popular Culture*. Sydney: Unwin Hyman, 1989.
Foucault, Michel. *Discipline and Punish: The Birth of the Prison*. Trans. Alan Sheridan. New York: Vintage, 1979.
_____. *The History of Sexuality*. Volume 1. Trans. Robert Hurley. New York: Vintage, 1980.
Freud, Sigmund. *Civilization and Its Discontents*. Trans. James Strachey. New York: W. W. Norton, 1961.
_____. *The Interpretation of Dreams*. Trans. A. A. Brill. New York: Macmillan, 1913 [1900].
_____. *Three Essays in Sexuality*. Trans. James Strachey. New York: Basic Books, 2000 [1905].
_____. *Totem and Taboo: Resemblances Between Psychic Life of Savages and Neurotics*. Trans. James Strachey. London: Routledge and Kegan Paul, 1950 [1913].
Frye, Northrop. *The Anatomy of Criticism*. Princeton: Princeton University Press, 1973 [1957].
_____. *The Secular Scripture: A Study of the Structure of Romance*. Cambridge: Harvard University Press, 1976.
Gilmore, David D. *Monsters: Evil Beings, Mythical Beasts, and All Manner of Imaginary Terrors*. Philadelphia: University of Pennsylvania Press, 2003.
Girard, Rene. *Violence and the Sacred*. Trans. Patrick Gregory. London: The Athlone Press, 1995 [1972].
Goldberg, David Theo, ed. *Multiculturalism: A Critical Reader*. Oxford: Blackwell, 1994.
Granger, John. *How Harry Cast His Spell: The Meaning Behind the Mania for J. K. Rowling's Bestselling Books*. London: Tyndale, 2008.
Green, Martin. *Dreams of Adventure, Deeds of the Empire*. London: Routledge and Kegan Paul, 1980.
Grixiti, Joseph. *Terrors of Uncertainty: The Cultural Contexts of Horror Fiction*. London: Routledge, 1989.
Gupta, Suman. *Re-reading Harry Potter*. Basingstoke: Palgrave Macmillan, 2003.
Hall, Donald. *Queer Theories*. New York: Palgrave Macmillan, 2003.
Hall, G. Stanley. *Youth: Its Education, Regimen and Hygiene*. New York: D. Appleton and Co., 1906. Project Gutenberg, 2005 (Accessed 11 January 2007).
Hall, Stuart, and Tony Jefferson, eds. *Resistance through Rituals: Youth Subcultures in Post-War Britain*. London: HarperCollins, 1991 [1975].
Hebdige, Dick. *Subcultures: The Meanings of Style*. London: Routledge, 1981.
Heilman, Elizabeth A., ed. *Critical Perspectives on Harry Potter*. London: Routledge, 2003.
Herez, Sarah K., and Donald R. Gallo. *From Hinton to Hamlet: Building Bridges between Young Adult Literature*. Westport, CT: Greenwood, 1996.
Hourihan, Margery. *Deconstructing the Hero: Literary Theory and Children's Literature*. London: Routledge, 1997.
Huizinga, J. *Homo Ludens: A Study of Play-Element in Culture*. Boston: Beacon, 1955 [1938].
Hume, Katherine. *Fantasy and Mimesis: Responses to Reality in Western Literature*. New York: Methuen, 1984.
Humm, Peter, Paul Stignant, and Peter Widdowson, eds. *Popular Fictions: Essays in Literature and History*. New York: Methuen, 1986.
Hunt, Peter, ed. *Understanding Children's Literature*. New York: Routledge, 2005 [1999].

Hunt, Peter, and Millicent Lenz. *Alternative Worlds in Fantasy Fiction*. New York: Continuum, 2004.

Hutcheon, Linda. *The Politics of Postmodernism*. London, New York: Routledge, 1989.

Illich, Ivan. *Deschooling Society*. Hammondsworth: Penguin, 1971.

Jackson, Rosemary. *Fantasy: The Literature of Subversion*. London: Methuen, 1981.

James, Allison, and Alan Prout, eds. *Constructing and Reconstructing Childhood: Contemporary Issues in the Sociological Study of Childhood*. London: Routledge, 2002.

Jameson, Fredric. *Archaeologies of Future: The Desire called Utopia and Other Science Fictions*. London: Verso, 2005.

_____. *The Political Unconscious: Narrative as a Socially Symbolic Act*. Ithaca: Cornell University Press, 1981.

Jones, Dudley, and Tony Watkins. *The Necessary Fantasy: The Heroic Figure in Popular Culture*. New York: Garland, 2000.

Jung, C. G., ed. *Man and His Symbols*. London: Picador, 1978 [1964].

Klapproth, Daniele M. *Narrative as Social Practice: Anglo-Western and Australian Aboriginal Oral Traditions*. Berlin: Mouton, 1962.

Kristeva, Julia. *Powers of Horror: An Essay in Abjection*. New York: Columbia University Press, 1982.

Kutzer, M. Daphne. *Empire's Children: Empire and Imperialism in Classic British Children's Books*. New York: Garland, 2000.

Lacan, Jacques. *Ecrits: A Selection*. Trans. Alan Sheridan. London: Routledge, 2007 [1977].

_____. *The Seminar Book II: The Ego in Freud's Theory and in the Technique of Psychoanalysis*. Trans. Sylvana Tomaselli. Cambridge: Cambridge University Press, 1988 [1954–1955].

Leonard, Elisabeth Anne, ed. *Into Darkness Peering: Race and Color in the Fantastic*. London: Greenwood, 1997.

Lesko, Nancy. *Act Your Age: A Cultural Construction of Adolescence*. London: Routledge, 2001.

Levi-Strauss, Claude. *Myth and Meaning*. London: Routledge, 1978.

_____. *Totemism*. Trans. Rodney Needham. Boston: Beacon, 1964.

Lewis, C. S. *Experiments in Criticism*. Cambridge: Cambridge University Press, 1965 [1961].

_____. *The Four Loves*. New York: Harcourt, Brace, 1960.

Lurie, Alison. *Boys and Girls Forever: Reflections on Children's Classics*. London: Chatto and Windus, 2003.

_____. *Don't Tell the Grown-Ups: The Subversive Power of Children's Literature*. London, Boston, Toronto, New York: Little, Brown, 1990.

Luthi, Max. *European Folktale: Form and Nature*. Bloomington: Indiana University Press, 1986.

Lyotard, Jean-Francois. *The Postmodern Condition: A Report on Knowledge Theory and History of Literature*. Manchester: Manchester University Press, 1979.

Macherey, Pierre. *Theory of Literary Production*. Trans. Geoffrey Wall. London: Routledge and Kegan Paul, 1978.

Malinowski, Bronislaw. *Magic, Science and Religion and Other Essays*. London: Souvenir, 1974.

Manlove, Colin. *From Alice to Harry Potter: Children's Fantasy in England*. Christchurch: Cybereditions Corporation, 2003.

Mauss, Marcel. *A General Theory of Magic.* Trans. Robert Brain. London: Routledge, 1972.

McCallum, Robyn. *Ideologies of Identity in Adolescent Fiction: The Dialogic Construction of Subjectivity.* New York: Garland, 1999.

McHale, Brian. *Postmodernist Fiction.* London: Routledge, 1987.

Mead, Margaret. *Coming of Age in Samoa: A Psychological Study of Primitive Youth for Western Civilization.* New York: Morrow, 1961.

Musgrave, P. W. *From Brown to Bunter: Life and Death of English School Story.* London: Routledge and Kegan Paul, 1985.

Nancy, Jean-Luc. *The Inoperative Community.* Minneapolis: University of Minnesota Press, 1991.

Nash, Cristopher. *World Games: The Tradition of Anti-Realist Revolt.* New York: Methuen, 1987.

Nel, Philip. *J. K. Rowling's Harry Potter Novels: A Reader's Guide.* New York: Continuum, 2001.

O'Keefe, Dorothy. *Readers in Wonderland: The Liberating Worlds in Fantasy Fiction: From Dorothy to Harry Potter.* New York: Continuum, 2004.

Orwell, George. *Such, Such Were the Joys.* London: Partisan Review, 1947. Charles George Orwell Links, Essays and Journalism (accessed 23 November 2006).

Propp, Vladimir. *Morphology of a Folktale.* Trans. Laurence Scott. Austin: University of Texas Press, 1968 [1927].

_____. *Theory and History of Folklore.* Trans. Adriana Y. Martin and Richard P. Martin. Manchester: Manchester University Press, 1984.

Rank, Otto. *The Myth of the Birth of the Hero: A Psychological Exploration of Myth.* Trans. Gregory C. Richter and E. James Lieberman. Baltimore: Johns Hopkins University Press, 2004.

Reynolds, Kimberley. *Modern Children's Literature: An Introduction.* New York: Palgrave Macmillan, 2005.

Richards, Jefferey. *Happiest Days: The Public Schools in English Fiction.* Manchester: Manchester University Press, 1988.

_____, ed. *Imperialism and Juvenile Literature.* Manchester: Manchester University Press, 1988.

Rose, Jacqueline. *The Case of Peter Pan or, The Impossibility of Children's Fiction.* Philadelphia: University of Pennsylvania Press, 1984.

Ryan, Michael, and Julie Rivkin, eds. *Literary Theory: An Anthology.* New York: Blackwell, 2004.

Said, Edward. *Orientalism.* New York: Vintage, 1979.

Sale, Roger. *Fairy Tales and After.* Cambridge: Cambridge University Press, 1978.

Sandner, David. *Fantastic Literature: A Critical Reader.* Westport, CT: Praeger, 2004.

Shildrick, Margrit. *Embodying the Monster: Encounters with the Vulnerable Self.* London: Sage, 2002.

Silverman, Kaja. *Masculine Subjectivity at the Margins.* London: Routledge, 1992.

Singer, Irving. *The Nature of Love: Plato to Luther.* Cambridge: MIT, 1984.

_____. *The Nature of Love: The Modern World.* Cambridge: MIT Press, 2009.

Spacks, Patricia Meyer. *The Adolescent Idea: Myths of Youth and Adult Imagination.* New York: Basic Books, 1981.

Stallybrass, Peter, and Allon White. *The Politics and Poetics of Transgression.* London: Methuen, 1986.

Stephens, John, and Robyn McCallum. *Retelling Stories, Framing Culture: Traditional Story and Metanarratives in Children's Literature.* New York: Garland, 1998.

Swinfen, Ann. *In Defence of Fantasy: A Study of the Genre in English and American Literature Since 1945.* London: Routledge and Kegan Paul, 1984.

Thacker, Deborah Cogan, and Jean Webb. *Introducing Children's Literature: From Romanticism to Postmodernism.* London: Routledge, 2002.

Timmerman, John. *Other Worlds: The Fantasy Genre.* Bowling Green: Bowling Green University Popular Press, 1983.

Todorov, Tzvetan. *Fantastic: A Structural Approach to the Genre.* Trans. Richard Howard. Ithaca: Cornell University Press, 1975 [1970].

Tolkien, J. R. R. *Tree and Leaf.* London: Unwin, 1964.

Tripp, Anna, ed. *Gender: Reader in Cultural Criticism.* Basingstoke: Palgrave, 2000.

Trites, Roberta Seelinger. *Disturbing the Universe: Power and Repression in Adolescent Literature.* Iowa City: University of Iowa Press, 2000.

_____. *Twain, Alcott and the Birth of the Adolescent Reform Novel.* Iowa City: University of Iowa Press, 2007.

Trupe, Alice. *Thematic Guide to Young Adult Literature.* Westport, CT: Greenwood, 2006.

Turner, Victor. *The Ritual Process: Structure and Anti-Structure.* New York: Aldine de Gruyter, 1995 [1969].

Van Gennep, Arnold. *Rites of Passage.* Trans. Monika B. Vizedom and Gabrielle L. Caffee. Chicago: University of Chicago Press, 1960.

Waller, Alice. *Constructing Adolescence through Fantastic Realism.* London: Routledge, 2008.

Westwater, Martha. *Giant Despair Meets Hopeful: Kristevan Readings of Adolescent Fiction.* Edmonton: University of Alberta Press, 2000.

Whited, Lana, ed. *The Ivory Tower and Harry Potter.* Columbia: University of Missouri Press, 2002.

Wieviorka, Michel. *The Arena of Racism.* Trans. Chris Turner. Thousand Oaks, CA: Sage, 1995.

Williams, Raymond. *Keywords.* New York: Oxford University Press, 1983 [1976].

Young, Robert J. C. *Colonial Desire: Hybridity in Theory, Culture and Race.* London: Routledge, 1995

_____. *White Mythologies.* New York: Routledge, 2004 [1990].

Zipes, Jack. *Breaking the Magical Spell: Radical Theories of Folk and Fairy Tales.* Lexington: University of Kentucky Press, 2002 [1979].

_____. *Fairy Tales and the Art of Subversion.* London: Routledge, 1985.

_____. *Sticks and Stones: The Troublesome Success of Children's Literature from Slovenly Peter to Harry Potter.* London: Routledge, 2002.

_____. *The Trials and Tribulations of Little Red Riding Hood.* South Hadley, MA: Bergain & Garvey, 1984.

Zizek, Slavoj. *Looking Awry: Introduction to Jacques Lacan through Popular Culture.* Cambridge: MIT Press, 1992.

Articles

Aichele, George, Jr. "Literary Fantasy and Postmodern Theology." *Journal of the American Academy of Religion* 59.2 (Summer 1991): 323–337.

Althusser, Louis. "Ideology and Ideological State Apparatus." *Lenin and Philoso-*

phy and Other Essays. Trans. Ben Brewster. *Monthly Review Press* (1971): 127–186.

Anatol, Giselle Liza. "The Fallen Empire: Exploring Ethnic Otherness in the World of Harry Potter." *Reading Harry Potter: Critical Essays*, edited by Giselle Liza Anatol. 163–178. London: Praeger, 2003.

Aronson, Marc. "'YA Novel Is Dead' and Other Fairly Stupid Tales." *School Library Journal* (January 1995): 35–37.

Atwood, Thomas A., and Wade M. Lee. "The Price of Deviance: Schoolhouse Gothic in Prep School Literature." *Children's Literature* 35 (2007): 102–126.

Bakhtin, M. M. "The Bildungsroman and Its Significance in the History of Realism (Towards a Historical Typology of the Novel)." *Speech Genres and Other Late Essays*. Trans. Vern McGee, Caryl Emerson and Michael Holoquist. 10–59. Austin: University of Texas Press, 1986.

Battis, Jes. "Gazing Upon Sauron: Hobbits, Elves, and the Queering of the Postcolonial Optic." *Modern Fiction Studies* 50.4 (Winter 2004): 908–926.

_____. "Transgendered Magic: The Radical Performance of the Young Wizard in YA Literature." *The Looking Glass* 10.1 (2 January 2006).

Belsey, Catherine. "Constructing the Subject: Deconstructing the Text." *Feminisms: An Anthology of Literary Theory and Criticism*, edited by Robyn R. Warhol and Diana Price Herndl. 257–273. Houndsmill: Macmillan, 1997 [1985].

Berreman, Joel V. "Advertising and the Sale of Novels." *Journal of Marketing* 7.3 (January 1943): 234–240.

Bird, Sharon R. "Welcome to the Men's Club: Homosociality and the Maintenance of Hegemonic Masculinity." *Gender and Society* 10.2 (April 1996): 120–132.

Bonnett, Alastair. "From White to Western: Racial Decline and the Rise of the Idea of the West in Britain, 1890–1930." *Journal of Historical Sociology* 16.2 (July 2003): 320–348.

Bucher, Katherine T., and M. Lee Manning. "A Boy's Alternative to Bodice-Rippers." *The English Journal* (March 2000): 135–138.

Butler, Judith. "Agencies of Style for a Liminal Subject." *Without Guarantees: In Honour of Stuart Hall*, edited by Paul Gilroy, Lawrence Grossberg, Angela McRobbie. 30–37. London, New York: Verso, 2000.

_____. "Critically Queer." *Gender: Readers in Cultural Criticism*, edited by Anna Tripp. 15–28. New York: Palgrave Macmillan, 2000.

_____. "Performative Acts and Gender Constitution." *Literary Theory: An Anthology*, edited by Michael Ryan and Julie Rivkin. 900–911. Malden, MA: Blackwell, 2004.

Bynum, Caroline Walker. "Metamorphosis, or Gerald ad the Werewolf." *Speculum* 73 (1998): 987–1013.

_____. "Shape and Story: Metamorphosis in the Western Tradition." *Jefferson Lecture in the Humanities*. Washington, D.C. 22 Mar 1999. National Endowment for the Humanities, http://www.neh.gov/news/archive/19990322b.html.

Cadden, Mike. "The Irony of Narration in Young Adult Novel." *Children's Literature Association Quarterly* 25.3 (September 2000): 146–154.

_____. "Simultaneous Emotions: Entwining Modes in Children's Books." *Children's Literature in Education* 36.3 (September 2005): 285–298.

Carey, Brycchan. "Hermione and the House-Elves: The Literary and Historical Contexts of J. K. Rowling's Antislavery Campaign." *Reading Harry Potter: Critical Essays*, edited by Giselle Liza Anatol. 103–115. London: Praeger, 2003.

Cawelti, John G. "The Concept of Formula in the Study of Popular Literature." *The Bulletin of the Midwest Modern Language Association* 5.2 (1972): 115–123.

Chappell, Drew. "Sneaking out After Dark: Resistance, Agency, and the Postmodern Child in J K Rowling's *Harry Potter* series." *Children's Literature in Education* 39.4 (December 2007): 281–293.

Chevalier, Noah. "The Liberty Tree and the Whomping Willow: Political Justice, Magical Science, and Harry Potter." *The Lion and the Unicorn* 29.3 (September 2005): 397–415.

Childs, Peter. "Popular Novel: The Ethics of Harry Potter." *Texts: Contemporary Cultural Texts and Critical Approaches*, edited by Peter Childs. 118–127. Edinburgh: Edinburgh University Press, 2006.

Clark, Beverly Lyons. "Domesticating the School Story, Regendering the Genre." *New Literary History* 26.2 (1995): 323–342.

Coats, Karen. "Adolescence and Abjection." *Journal of Psychoanalysis of Culture and Society* 5.2 (Fall 1999): 291–301.

Cummins, June. "Hermione in the Bathroom: The Gothic, Menarche, and Female Development in the *Harry Potter* Series." *The Gothic in Children's Literature: Haunting the Borders*, edited by Karen Coats, Anna Jackson, and Rod McGillis. 177–193. New York: Routledge, 2008.

Deavel, Catherine Jack, and David Paul Deavel. "Character, Choice and Harry Potter." *Logos* 5.4 (Fall 2002): 49–64.

Deleuze, Giles. "What Children Say." *Essays Clinical and Critical*, trans. Daniel W. Smith and Michael A. Greco. 61–67. London/New York: Verso, 1998.

Derrida, Jacques. "Difference." *Literary Theory: An Anthology*, edited by Michael Ryan and Julie Rivkin. 279–299. Malden, MA: Blackwell, 2004.

Dixon, Bob. "The Nice, the Naughty and the Nasty: The Tiny World of Enid Blyton." *Children's Literature in Education* 5.3 (September 1974): 45–61.

Doty, Gene. "Blasphemy and the Recovery of the Sacred." *Violence, Utopia and the Kingdom of God: Fantasy and Ideology in the Bible*, edited by George Aichele and Tina Pippin. 92–120. London: Routledge, 1998.

Fish, Stanley. "Boutique Multiculturalism or Why Liberals are Incapable of Thinking About Hate Speech." *Critical Inquiry* 23.2 (Winter 1997): 378–395.

Fiske, John. "Culture, Ideology, Interpellation." *Literary Theory: An Anthology*, edited by Michael Ryan and Julie Rivkin. 1268–1273. Malden, MA: Blackwell, 2004.

Foucault, Michel. "Of Other Spaces." *Diacritics* 16.1 (Spring 1986): 22–27.

Fouss, Kirk. "A Portrait of the Adolescent as a Young Gay: The Politics of Male Homosexuality in Young Adult Fiction." *Queer Words, Queer Images*, edited by R. Jefferey Ringer. 159–174. New York: New York University Press, 1994.

Freud, Sigmund. "Family Romance." *The Standard Edition of the Complete Psychological Works of Sigmund Freud*, vol. IX. 235–242. London: Hogarth Press, 1971 [1909].

_____. "Mourning and Melacholia." *The Standard Edition of the Complete Psychological Works of Sigmund Freud*, vol. XIV. 237–258. London: Hogarth Press, 1971 [1917].

_____. "On Narcissism: An Introduction." *The Standard Edition of the Complete Psychological Works of Sigmund Freud*, vol. XIV. 73–104. London: Hogarth, 1971 [1914].

_____. "The Relation of Poet to Daydreaming." *The Standard Edition of the Complete Psychological Works of Sigmund Freud*, vol. IX. 141–154. London: Hogarth Press, 1971 [1925].

_____. "The Uncanny." *The Standard Edition of the Complete Psychological Works of Sigmund Freud*, vol. XVII. 217–252. London: Hogarth Press, 1971 [1919].

Gallardo C. Ximena, and Jason C. Smith. "Cinderfella: J. K. Rowling's Wily Web of Gender." *Reading Harry Potter: Critical Essays*, edited by Giselle Liza Anatol. 191–206. London: Praeger, 2003.

Gilead, Sara. "Magic Abjured: Closure in Children's Fantasy Fiction." *PMLA* 106.2 (March 1991): 277–293.

Green, Amy. "Revealing Discrimination: Social Hierarchy and the Exclusion/ Enslavement of the Other in the *Harry Potter* Novels." *The Looking Glass* 13.3 (September–October 2009). http://www.lib.latrobe.edu.au/ojs/index.php/tlg/art icle/view/162/161.

Gundry-Wolfe, Judith M. "The Least and the Greatest: Children in the New Testament." *The Child in Christian Thought*, edited by Marcia JoAnne Bunge. 29–60. Grand Rapids, MI: Edermans, 2001.

Gutenberg, Andrea. "Shape-shifters from the Wilderness: Werewolves Roaming the Twentieth Century." *The Abject of Desire: The Aestheticization of the Unaesthetic in Contemporary Literature and Culture*, edited by Konstance Kutzbach and Monica Mueller. 149–180. Amsterdam: Genius, 2007.

Halberstam, Judith. "Parasites and Perverts: An Introduction to Gothic Monstrosity." *Skin Shows: Gothic Horror and Technologies of Monsters*, edited by Judith Halberstam. 1–27. Durham: Duke University Press, 1995.

_____. "What's that Smell? Queer Temporalities and Subcultural Lives." *International Journal of Culture Studies* 6 (September 2003): 313–333.

Hall, Stuart, "Notes on Deconstructing the Popular Culture." *Popular Culture*, edited by Raiford Guins, Omayra Zaragoza Cruz, and Omayra Cruz. 64–71. London: Sage, 2005.

Harding, D. W. "Psychological Processes in the Reading of Fiction." *British Journal of Aesthetics* 2.2 (1962): 133–147.

Heilman, Elizabeth, and Anne E. Gregory. "Images of the Privileged Insiders and Outcast Outsiders." *Critical Perspectives on Harry Potter*, edited by Elizabeth H. Heilman. 241–259. New York: Routledge, 2008.

Hollindale, Peter. "The Adolescent Novel of Ideas." *Children's Literature in Education* 26 (1995): 83–95.

Hughes, Felicity. "Children's Literature: Theory and Practice." *ELH* 42.3 (Autumn 1978): 542–561.

Hunt, Caroline. "Young Adult Literature Evades the Theorists." *Children's Literature Association Quarterly* 21.1 (1996): 4–11.

Hunt, Leigh. "Fairies." *London Journal* 27 (October 1834): 209–212.

Hunt, Peter, and Karen Sands. "The View from the Center: British Empire and Post-Empire in Children's Literature." *Voices of the Other: Children's Literature and the Post-colonial Context*, edited by Roderick McGillis. 39–51. New York: Routledge, 1999.

Hutcheon, Linda. "Harry Potter and the Novice's Confession." *The Lion and the Unicorn* 32 (2008): 169–179.

Jung, C. G. "The Psychology of the Child Archetype." *Myth: Critical Concepts in*

Literary and Cultural Studies, edited by Robert A. Segal. 402–426. London: Routledge, 2007 [1997].

Kidd, Dustin. "Harry Potter and the Functions of Popular Culture." *Journal of Popular Culture* 40.1 (2007): 69–89.

Kidd, Kenneth. "Boyology in the Twentieth Century." *Children's Literature* 28: 44–72.

_____. "Psychoanalysis and Children's Literature: The Case for Complementarity." *The Lion and the Unicorn* 28 (2004): 109–130.

Kimball, Melanie A. "From Folktales to Fiction: Orphan Characters in Children's Fiction." *Library Trends* 47.1 (Winter 1999): 558–578.

Klein, Melanie. "The Role of School in Libidinal Development of a Child." *International Journal of Psychoanalysis* 5 (1924): 312–331.

Kristeva, Julia. "The Adolescent Novel." *Abjection, Melancholia and Love: The Work of Julia Kristeva*, edited by John Fletcher and Andrew Benjamin. 8–23. London: Routledge, 1990.

Lefebvre, Benjamin. "From Bad Boy to Dead Boy: Homophobia, Adolescent Problem Fiction, and Male Bodies that Matter." *Children's Literature Association* 30.3 (2005): 288–313.

Lestvik, Linda S. "Using Adolescent Fiction as a Guide to Inquiry." *Theory Into Practice* 20.3 (Summer 1981): 174–178.

MacDonald, George. "The Child in the Midst." *Unspoken Sermons*. 13–23. London: Bibliobazar (2006).

_____. "The Fantastic Imagination." *A Dish of Orts*. London: Sampson Low Marston & Co., 1883. Gaslight Files. January 2000 (accessed 11 May 2005).

McGillis, Roderick. "Is Fairytale Just a Fairytale: George Macdonald and the Queering of Fairy." *Marvels and Tales* 17.1 (2003): 86–99.

_____. "Self, Other and Other Self: Recognizing the Other in Children's Literature." *The Lion and the Unicorn* 21.2 (1997): 215–229.

Mendlesohn, Farah. "Crowning the King: Harry Potter and the Construction of Authority." *The Ivory Tower and Harry Potter*, edited by Lana A. Whited. 159–181. Columbia: University of Missouri Press, 2002.

Mills, Alice. "Archetypes and the Unconscious in *Harry Potter* and Diana Wynne Jones's *Fire and Hemlock* and *Dogsbody*." *Reading Harry Potter: Critical Essays*, edited by Giselle Liza Anatol. 3–14. London: Praeger, 2003.

_____. "Harry Potter and the Terrors of Toilet." *Children's Literature in Education* 37.1 (March 2006): 101–113.

Moretti, Franco. "Dialectics of Fear." *New Left Review* I.136 (November 1982): 67–85.

Morris, John S. "Fantasy in a Mythless Age." *Children's Literature* 2 (1973): 77–86.

Nandy, Ashis. "Reconstructing Childhood: A Critique of the Ideology of Adulthood." *Traditions, Tyranny and Utopias: Essays in the Political Awareness*, edited by Ashis Nandy. 56–76. Delhi: Oxford University Press, 1987.

Nel, Philip. "Is There a Text in This Advertising Campaign? Literature, Marketing and Harry Potter." *The Lion and the Unicorn* 29.2 (2005): 236–267.

Nelson, Claudia. "Drying the Orphan's Tear: Changing Representations of the Dependent Child in America, 1870–1930." *Children's Literature* 29 (2001): 53–70.

Nelson, Cole, and Brooke Nelson. "What Is So Magic About Harry? A Young Reader and His Mother Explain." *ALAN Review* 28.1 (Fall 2000): 20–21.

Neumann, Iver B. "Pop Goes Religion: Harry Potter Meets Clifford Geertz." *European Journal of Cultural Studies* 9 (2006): 81–100.

Nikolajeva, Maria. "Exit Children's Literature." *The Lion and the Unicorn* 22.2 (1998): 221–236.

_____. "Fairy Tale and Fantasy: From Archaic to Postmodern." *Marvels and Tales* 17.1 (2003): 135–156.

_____. "Harry Potter: A Return to the Romantic Hero." *Critical Perspectives on Harry Potter*, edited by Elizabeth H. Heilman. 125–140. New York: Routledge, 2003.

_____. "Theory, Post-Theory, and Aetonormative Theory." *Neohelicon* XXXVI (2009): 13–24.

Nodelman, Perry. "Making Boys Appear: The Masculinity of Children's Fiction." *Ways of Being Male: Representing Masculinities in Children's Literature and Films*, edited by John Stephens. 1–14. London: Routledge, 2002.

Norton, Judy. "Transchildren and the Discipline of Children's Literature." *The Lion and the Unicorn* 23 (1999): 415–436.

Oakes, Margaret J. "Flying Car, Floo-Powder and Flaming Torches: The Hi-Tech, Low-Tech World of Wizardry." *Reading Harry Potter: Critical Essays*, edited by Giselle Liza Anatol. 117–130. London: Praeger, 2003.

O'Har, George M. "Magic in the Machine Age." *Technology and Culture* 41.4 (2000): 862–864.

O'Quinn, Elaine J. "Vampires, Changelings, and Radical Mutants Teens." *ALAN Review* 31.3 (Summer 2004): 50–56.

Ostling, Michael. "Harry Potter and the Disenchantment of the World." *Journal of Contemporary Religion* 18.1 (2003): 3–23.

Pennington, John. "From Elfland to Hogwarts, or the Aesthetic Trouble with Harry Potter." *The Lion and the Unicorn* 26.1 (January 2002): 78–97.

Pugh, Tison, and David L. Wallace. "Heteronormative Heroism and Queering the School Story in J. K. Rowling's *Harry Potter* series." *Children's Literature Association Quarterly* 31.3 (2006): 260–281.

_____. "Teaching English in the World: Playing with Critical Theory in J. K Rowling's Harry Potter Series." *English Journal* 96.3 (January 2007): 97–100.

Radley, Gail. "Coping with Death in Young Adults Literature." *ALAN Review* (Fall 1999): 14–16.

Rank, Otto. "The Interpretation of Myths." *In Quest of the Hero*, edited by Otto Rank and Alan Dundes. 3–12. Princeton: Princeton University Press, 1990.

Rauhofer, Judith. "Defence Against the Dark Arts: How the British Response to the Terrorist Threat Is Parodied in J. K. Rowling's 'Harry Potter and the Half Blood Prince.'" *International Journal of Liability and Scientific Enquiry* 1.1–2 (2007): 94–113.

Robertson, Judith P. "What Happens to Our Wishes: Magical Thinking in *Harry Potter*." *Children's Literature Association Quarterly* 26.4 (2002): 198–211.

Rudd, David. "Theorising and Theories: How Does Children's Literature Exist?" *Children's Literature: Critical Concepts in Literary and Cultural Studies* 2, edited by Peter Hunt. 356–374. London: Routledge, 2006.

Sartre, Jean-Paul. "Aminadab or the Fantasy Considered as a Language." *Literary and Philosophical Essays*. 56–72. London: Hutchinson, 1968 [1955].

Schanoes, Veronica L. "Cruel Heroes and Treacherous Texts: Educating the Reader

in Moral Complexity and Critical Reading in J. K. Rowling's Harry Potter Books."
Reading Harry Potter, edited by Giselle Liza Anatol. 131–145. London: Praeger,
2003.

Scherb, Victor I. "Assimilating Giants: The Appropriation of Gog and Magogin
Medieval and Early Modern England." *Journal of Medieval and Early Modern
Studies* 32.1 (2002): 59–84.

Sedgwick, Eve Kosofsky. "Gender Asymmetry and Erotic Triangles." *Feminisms:
An Anthology of Literary Theory and Criticism*, edited by Robyn R. Warhol and
Diane Price Herndl. 507–531. New Brunswick, NJ: Rutgers University Press,
1997.

Segal, Elizabeth. "Beastly Boys: A Century of Mischief." *Children's Literature in Education* 18.1 (1987): 3–12.

Senn, Harry. "Romanian Werewolves: Seasons, Rituals, Cycles." *Folklore* 93.2 (1982):
206–215.

Smol, Anna. "'Oh ... Oh ... Frodo!': Readings of Male Intimacy in *The Lord of the
Rings*." *MFS: Modern Fiction Studies* 50.4 (2004): 949–979.

Steege, David K. "Harry Potter, Tom Brown, and the British School Story: Lost in
Transit?" *The Ivory Tower and Harry Potter*, edited by Lana H. Whited. 140–158.
Columbia: University of Missouri Press, 2002.

Stephens, John. "'A Page Just Waiting to be Written On': Masculinity Schemata ad
the Dynamics of Subjective Agency in Junior Fiction." *Ways of Being Male: Representing Masculinities in Children's Literature and Films*, edited by John Stephens.
38–54. London: Routledge, 2002.

Stortz, Martha Ellen. "'Where or When Was Your Servant Innocent?': Augustine on
Childhood." *The Child in Christian Thought*, edited by Marcia JoAnn Bunge.
78–102. Grand Rapids, MI: Eedermans, 2001.

Strimel, Courtney B. "The Politics of Terror: Rereading Harry Potter." *Children's
Literature in Education* 35.1 (2004): 35–52.

Stuart, Elizabeth. "Christianity Is a Queer Thing." *Gay and Lesbian Theologies: Rep-
etitions with Critical Difference*. Aldershot: Ashgate, 2003.

Trites, Roberta S. "The Harry Potter Novels as a Test Case for Adolescent Literature."
Style 35.3 (Fall 2001): 472–485.

Tucker, Nicholas. "The Rise and Rise of Harry Potter." *Children's Literature in Education* 30.4 (1999): 221–234.

Wall, Wendy. "'Household Stuff': The Sexual Politics of Domesticity and the Advent
of English Comedy." *ELH* 65.1 (Spring 1998): 1–45.

_____. "Why Does Puck Sweep?: Fairylore, Merry Wives, and the Social Struggle."
Shakespeare Quarterly 52.1 (Spring 2001): 67–106.

Walton, Kendall. "Pictures and Make-believe." *The Philosophical Review* 82.3 (July
1973): 283–319.

Wannamaker, Annette. "Men in Cloaks and High-heeled Boots, Men Wielding Pink
Umbrellas: Witchy Masculinities in The *Harry Potter* Novels." *The Looking Glass*
10:1 (2 January 2006). http://www.lib.latrobe.edu.au/ojs/index.php/tlg/article/
view/96/81.

Washick, James. "Oliver Twisted: The Origins of Lord Voldemort in the Dickensian
Orphan." *The Looking Glass: New Perspectives on Children's Literature* 13.3 (2009).
http://www.lib.latrobe.edu.au/ojs/index.php/tlg/article/view/165/164.

Weaver, Roslyn. "Metaphors of Monstrosity: The Werewolf as Disability and Illness in Harry Potter and Jatta." *Papers: Explorations into Children's Literature* 20.2 (2010): 70–82.

Weaver, William N. "'A School Boy's Story': Writing the Victorian Public Schoolboy Subject." *Victorian Studies* 46.3 (2004): 455–487.

Westkott, Marcia. "Dialectics of Fantasy." *Frontiers: A Journal of Women Studies* 2.3 (Autumn 1970): 1–7.

Westman, Karin E. "Perspective, Memory, and Moral Authority: The Legacy of Jane Austen in J. K. Rowling's *Harry Potter.*" *Children's Literature* 35 (2007): 145–165.

_____. "The Weapon That We Have Is Love." *Children's Literature Association Quarterly* 33.2 (Summer 2008): 195–198.

Whited, Lana. "1492, 1942, 1992: The Theme of Race in the *Harry Potter* Series." *The Looking Glass* 10.1 (January 2006). http://www.lib.latrobe.edu.au/ojs/index.php/tlg/article/view/97/82.

Wood, Naomi. "Introduction: Children's Literature and Religion." *Children's Literature Association Quarterly* 24 (1999): 1–3.

Wood, Susan Nelson, and Kim Quackenbush. "The Sorcerer's Stone: A Touchstone for Readers of All Ages." *English Journal* 90.3 (January 2001): 97–103.

Zipes, Jack. "The Spectacle and Sacred Nature of Everyday Fantasy and Everyday Violence." *Violence, Utopia and Kingdom of God*, edited by George Aichele and Tina Pippin. ix–xii. London: Routledge, 1998.

Zizek, Slavoj. "Multiculturism or the Cultural Logic of Multinational Capitalism?" *New Left Review* I.225 (September–October 1997). http://www.newleftreview.org/?view=1919.

Internet Resources

Bacon, Perry, Jr. "Libraries, Stores Face a Teenage Mystery: Changes Target Young Readers." *The Washington Post* 13 July 2002. www.washingtonpost.com (accessed 8 August 2008).

Bloom, Harold. "Can 35 Million Book Buyers be Wrong? Yes." *The Wall Street Journal* 11 July 2000. http://wrt-brooke.syr.edu/course/205.0/bloom.html (accessed 6 April 2006).

Bronski, Michael. "Queering Harry Potter." *Z Magazine* 16.9 (September 2003). http://www.zmag.org/zmagsite/sept2003/bronski0903.html (accessed 7 October 2008).

Bruno, Dave. "Harry Potter 7 is Matthew 6." *Christianity Today.* August 2007. http://www.christianitytoday.com/48545 (4 May 2009).

Byatt, A. S. "Harry Potter and the Childish Adult." *New York Times* 7 July 2003. http://www.nytimes.com/2003/07/07/opinion/harry-potter-and-the-childish-adult (accessed 6 April 2006).

Chambers, Joseph. "Harry Potter and the Antichrist." *Paw Creek Ministries* 27 October 2001. http://www.tagrygge.dk/show_article.php?num=46 (accessed 4 May 2009).

Donaghue, Deirdre. "Orphans in Literature Empower Children." *USA Today* 7 February 2003. http://www.usatoday.com/life/books/2003-07-02-bchat_x.htm (accessed 5 November 2008).

Granger, John. "Postmodern Themes: Ms. Rowling as the Writer of our Times." *Harry Potter Book Club* 21 February 2007. http://booksclub.barnesandnoble.com (accessed 4 May 2009).

Henderson, Jonathan. "Globalization, Consumerism and Cultural Change in Modern China." *Harry Potter in China.* http://harrypotterinchina/index.html (accessed 11 October 2007).

Hensher, Philip. "A Crowd-Pleaser but No Classic." *The Spectator* 12 July 2003. http://www.spectator.co.uk (accessed 6 April 2006).

Iyer, Pico. "The Playing Fields of Hogwarts." *The New York Times on the Web* 10 October 1999. http://www.nytimes.com/books (accessed 26 November 2007).

Jones, E. Michael. "Education as Magic: Harry Potter and the Culture of Narcissism." *Culture Wars.* January 2002. http://www.culturewars.com/2002/potter.html (accessed 18 May 2008).

King, Stephen. "J. K. Rowling's Ministry of Magic." *The Entertainment Weekly* 11 January 2003. http://www.ew.com/ew/article/0,,20044270_20044274_2005068 9,00.html (accessed 6 April 2008).

Kriglebotten, Kjetil. "Voldemort's Rebirth and the 'Black Mass.'" *Virtuous Wizardry* 11 November, 2007. http://virtueofpotter.wordpress.com/2007/11/11/voldemorts-rebirth-and-the-black-mass/ (accessed 4 May 2009).

Lipson, Eden Ross. "Books' Hero Wins Young Minds: An Apprentice Wizard Rules the World (at Least Its Bookstores)." *The New York Times* 19 July 1999. http://query.nytimes.com/ (accessed 27 September 2006).

Lurie, Alison. "Pottery." *The New York Review of Books* 54.14 (27 September 2007): http://www.nybooks.com/articles/20595 (accessed 31 October 2008).

Maugham, Shanon. "Making the Teen Scene." *Publisher's Weekly* 18 October 1999 (accessed 24 January 2009).

Mokoto Rich. "Record First-day Sales for Last 'Harry Potter' Book." *The New York Times* 22 July 2007. http://www.nytimes.com/2007/07/22/books/22cnd-potter.html (accessed 24 January 2009).

Mukherjee, Souvik. "And Alice Played a Video Game: Alice, Harry Potter and the Computer Game: A Study of the Relationship between Children's Fantasy Adventure Stories and Interactive Computer Games." *London School of Journalism.* June 2002. www.english-literature.org/essays/alice_video.html (accessed 11 May 2005).

Prinzi, Travis. "The Fountain Told a Lie: Deconstructing the Wizarding World." *The Hog's Head* 20 June 2006 (accessed 6 August 2006).

Rollason, Christopher. *"Harry Potter," the Last Spell Cast? Critical Reflections.* July 2007. yatrarollason.info/files/HarryPotter2007.pdf (accessed 3 May 2008).

Schoefer, Christine. "Harry Potter's Girl Trouble: The World of Everyone's Favorite Kid Wizard Is a Place Where Boys Come First." *Salon* 13 January 2000. http://dir.salon.com/books/feature/2000/01/13/potter/index.html (accessed 6 June 2006).

Scholes, Robert. "Harry Potter and Whose Stone?" *Op-ed: Brown University News Service.* May 2001 (accessed 7 April 2006).

Turner, Julia. "When Harry Met Osama: Terrorism comes to Hogwarts." *Slate Magazine* (July 2005). http://www. slate.com/id/2123105 (accessed 25 October 2006).

Index